Protestantism
in Suburban
Life

FREDERICK A. SHIPPEY

Protestantism
in Suburban
Life

ABINGDON PRESS • NEW YORK • NASHVILLE

PROTESTANTISM IN SUBURBAN LIFE

Library of Congress Catalog Card Number: 64-20521

SET UP, PRINTED, AND BOUND BY THE
PARTHENON PRESS, AT NASHVILLE,
TENNESSEE, UNITED STATES OF AMERICA

To *Melda*

A la très belle, à la très bonne, à la très chère . . .

Preface

This book, as its famous predecessor *The Suburban Trend* by H. Paul Douglass, emerges also from a period of great social change in twentieth-century America. During the 1920's a strong outward trend from the city into the suburbs was detected. Douglass chronicled unforgettably this population shift, delineating the new problems created for the churches. Eventually the work became a classic.

The present volume considers the larger suburban explosion which followed World War II and is still continuing. Between the two periods there are significant differences with respect to nature, magnitude, and religious consequences. A comparison reveals that the current suburban expansion truly eclipses the first and that it possesses more frightening revolutionary significance for Protestantism. Suburban life has turned a sharp corner in recent years. The new directions of its development renders obsolete many old ways of thinking. Indeed, if the denominations slump in the 1960's or 1970's it will be because Protestantism has misunderstood the new suburban situation which is the key to the faith's future in America.

For whom is the book written? A short list of prospective readers includes: (1) Suburbanites—residents who desire to gain new perspectives on the changed milieu; (2) College Students—fledgling scholars who are taking courses in social science or in religion; (3) Seminarians—young men who are preparing for the ministry; (4) Clergymen—pastors and priests who currently are serving suburban parishes; (5) Church Administrators—religious leaders who occupy posts in denominations or in ecumenical agencies;

7

and (6) Teachers—college and seminary professors who can use the book in classes, supplementing the text by assigned collateral reading from the extensive bibliography of 150 book titles and 100 selected periodical articles. Many literate urban residents will be interested in this strident account of trends, features, and tensions of 60,000,000 Americans. They can find stimulation in the issues raised and in the prescriptions for action proffered.

Revolutionary changes with respect to race, religion, and economics form a focus of the volume which embraces the period from 1945 to the present. For the first time, Jews, Roman Catholics, sects, Negroes, and blue-collar workers have taken up suburban residence in noteworthy numerical strength. Their presence yields both tension and opportunity among the old-line denominations. What a disturbing impact these changes already have had upon suburban Protestantism, traditional stronghold of the faith! Indeed, a vast metamorphosis has been set in motion. Evidently a racial and economic "melting pot" has shifted out from the inner city. In view of these drastic changes, one wonders how adequate are the popular theories promulgated by William H. Whyte, Jr., Gibson Winter, Peter Berger, and kindred writers. Such discussions fail to describe reliably the suburban milieu of the Protestant church.

The present volume analyzes and prescribes for *nine basic problems of suburban Protestantism.* What reliably are the features and challenges of suburban life? What major changes have emerged since World War II? How can suburbanites be classified? To what extent are the opposing concepts of neighbor and nigh dweller relevant to the city's periphery? What are Satan's activities in the suburbs? What is family life like behind the picture window? What significant tensions harass and challenge suburbanites? What new facts and perspectives should inform church extension efforts? Which is the true face of suburbia—Zion or Calvary? While this list of problems is not exhaustive, it does disclose the broad new range of Protestant thinking demanded by the altered suburban situation. As suburbia goes, so will America go during the next two decades. Indeed, by 1980 a third of the nation will reside under suburban conditions. *As suburban Protestantism goes, so will the denominations fare during the next twenty years.* Postponement of a critical re-examination of Protestant suburban institutional and religious efforts assuredly will yield a second-rate, dwindling faith.

Many years of residence in the suburbs cannot substitute for a systematic perusal and analysis of the books, monographs, dissertations, novels, and periodical articles touching suburban changes since the early 1940's. To the insights gathered from these sources were added the findings of several new field research studies designed specifically to close important gaps in existing knowledge about suburbia. Findings from these special surveys appear here for the first time. All of the materials considered together and summarized yield insights of great importance. These are recorded in the present volume.

Grateful acknowledgment is made to the following publishers for permission to quote from the copyrighted titles listed: Appleton-Century-Crofts (H. P. Douglass, *The Suburban Trend*), Sheed and Ward, Inc. (A. M. Greeley, *The Church and the Suburbs*), University of California Press (Bennett Berger, *Working-Class Suburb*), and Simon and Schuster, Inc. (W. H. Whyte, *The Organization Man*).

The writer is greatly indebted to the following persons who read the manuscript as a whole or in part: Robert B. Goodwin, Henry L. Lambdin, Fred W. Michel, Bonneau P. Murphy, Lawrence H. Richards, William F. B. Rodda, Joel W. Shippey, and Theodore and Jean Taylor. To my students and professional colleagues for constant interest, criticism and encouragement, I owe much. Moreover, a hearty thanks is tendered to the clergy and laymen who co-operated in field research studies. To provide me the opportunity for concentration and writing essential to complete the project, my wife and children generously gave up many hours of familial activity. Each of these people has contributed importantly to the shape and content of the present book. The author, however, alone must bear responsibility for whatever shortcomings may appear in its pages.

—FREDERICK A. SHIPPEY

Contents

Contents

I

Suburbia: New Prototype of American Life

During recent years a spectacular growth of suburban communities has occurred throughout the United States. Millions of people have moved out of the city into the adjacent countryside. Others have migrated from farms and villages. Today one American out of four resides under suburban circumstances. By 1975 this ratio is expected to climb to an unprecedented *one resident out of three*. Small wonder that some writers already refer to America as a "suburbanized society."

Along with this amazing development there has emerged a growing criticism of the suburban way of life. Andrew Greeley places suburbia in a discussional category with the weather or the labor movement; people are for it or against it. No one holds a mediating position. The situation raises questions: Why do laymen and scholars delight in caustic comment here? Why are their polemical darts launched with a vicious relish bordering upon the pathological? Despite all the rationalizations which defend suburbia, there can be no mistaking the powerful challenge which is hurled currently at the leafy utopia where "look-alike houses are occupied by act-alike people." Polemical writers have singled out suburbanites and branded them as a type of social criminal who deserves reproach. What provokes this modern witch-hunt? What will be the outcome? These questions deserve an answer.

Further, many people have begun to wonder what role, if any, religion plays in the turbulent situation. Does the local church or synagogue capitulate to the organization man? Or to the American motif of material success? Does the local congregation or parish encounter special difficulty in achieving an effective ministry here? Is the task tougher than in the city? Do suburbanites believe that they have outgrown faith and hence are emancipated from organized religion? Are they embarrassed by and ashamed of personal religious practices? Indeed, in what sense has suburbia now become the new prototype for American life? Are suburban values, attitudes, behavior, and achievements now pacesetting and normative for numerous other residents throughout the United States?

WHAT IS SUBURBIA?

Years ago H. Paul Douglass described suburbia as a compromise between the country and the city, one which preserves the best in each. It is a commingling of rural and urban characteristics. This yields an interesting type of specialization which he explicates.

The suburb is a natural process of sifting and of the more or less efficient disposal of the specific elements of urban life in separate places. It is a series of areas devoted to partial and limited segments of the broad interests and activities necessary to civilization. It is a set of specializations with a geographical basis.[1]

Here is an abbreviated rationale for the existence of suburbs which is difficult to improve upon. Yet other dynamic perspectives are needed to round out the picture. In a scholarly study of Levittown (New York), John Liell discovered a paternalistic, mass-produced community, lacking heterogeneity and democracy.[2] Albert I. Gordon sees in the process a mass revolt from an intolerable urban way of life.[3] In concurrence with H. Paul Douglass, William M. Dobriner contributes the idea of places which are "culturally and economically dependent upon the central city." [4] Surprisingly Robert C. Wood finds in suburbia the blossoming of modern civilization.[5] Suburbia fulfills logically the implications of technological advance.

But for the thousands of residents of the slum and of the crowded, non-

---

[1] *The Suburban Trend* (New York: The Century Company, 1925), p. 121-22.
[2] "Levittown: A Study of Community Planning and Development" (Ph.D dissertation, Yale University, 1952).
[3] *Jews in Suburbia* (Boston: Beacon Press, 1959).
[4] Dobriner, editor, *The Suburban Community* (New York: G. P. Putnam's Sons, 1958), p. xvii.
[5] *Suburbia: Its People and Their Politics* (Boston: Houghton Mifflin Company, 1959), pp. 3, 4.

descript city, suburbia betokens a heavenly mirage which knows no headaches, no heartaches, and no evils of contemporary civilization. It beckons as a shining land of beauty and of promise. Thus the caustic comments of the critics fall as wasted caveats upon many unheeding ears.

What then is suburbia? No single definition can suffice here. Rather, suburbia is probably all the things which all the experts claim for the term and perhaps even more.

Despite the seemingly endless array of definitions, it is possible to assess suburbia fruitfully in a fivefold way: A geographical territory, a dependent urban satellite, a technological fulfillment, a way of life, and the American prototype. In geographical terms suburbia appears as a visible cluster of communities distributed in space around the edges of a major city. Yet development is almost never symmetrical. Some suburbs are contiguous, some adjacent, and others widely scattered within commuting range. Scrutiny of an available metropolitan map on the part of the reader will disclose this phenomenon. The major city and its suburbs usually resemble a mother hen with her chicks. In the largest metropolitan areas, however, the geographical concept so simply stated above would need to be modified to include portions of the major city itself. Most people, however, have little difficulty in recognizing suburban geography.

From the functional viewpoint suburbia belongs to the mother city. It is bound by transportation lines, by economic activity, by cultural facilities, by sociological structures, by its segmental community, and by manifold other relationships. The main bank, the principal department store, et cetera, remain in the major city. Usually only branch economic and social institutions are dispersed across the adjacent metropolitan territory. An incomplete commercial and institutional activity is carried on here. Hence the appropriateness of the term—a dependent urban satellite. Suburbia needs the major city in order to complete its functions.

Moreover, suburbia usually has most of the latest technological improvements and conveniences for modern living. From the electronic garage door opener to the garbage disposal, one sees the ingenuity of man displayed. The homes are newer and are equipped with eye-catching and sale-producing gadgets. Devices abound for regulating heat and air conditioning automatically. The model house of modern civilization is a familiar sight in suburbia. It is the fulfillment of the homemaker's dream.

15

Christopher Tunnard and Henry H. Reed conclude that since the 1930's suburbia has outrivaled the city in its appeal as a way of life.[6] It possesses an endemic attractiveness. Such comments refer especially to the material "blessings" which are manifest on the city's periphery. Here are found allegedly the finest material and spiritual values. Most of the writers subscribe to this thesis. Bennett Berger, however, dissents from the viewpoint of making suburbia a way of life; he prefers simply to call it a place.

A growing consensus of opinion hails the suburb as a new norm or object of aspiration in the United States. To the organization man, in his ascent to power and affluence, suburbia affords what William H. Whyte, Jr., calls "an ideal way station." [7] *The Split-Level Trap* speaks of suburbia as home of the twentieth-century *pioneer*.[8] Robert Wood contends that to discover modern man described with fidelity one must turn to the suburbs. Contemporary man's way of life, his institutions and beliefs, his family and associations, are reliably portrayed here. This "looking-glass" concept has the effect of establishing the suburbanite as the average American. Several decades ago, H. Paul Douglass spoke of the "more select quality of the elements entering into the suburb." [9] Today Andrew Greeley, among others, points out that "the positive elements in popular culture are stronger in suburbia than elsewhere." [10] Moreover, in *The Exploding Metropolis* attention is focused upon the "norm of American aspiration" which is said to be located in suburbia.[11] Publicity stressing a strong middle-class identification for some communities reinforces the purpose to make the suburb America's latest norm of aspiration. For better or worse suburbia is now accorded a significance which possibly yields a normative prototype for living. For countless American people this place and its way of life have become an object of aspiration.

Substantiating ascriptions by Greeley, Malcolm Boyd, Douglass, and Richard and Katherine Gordon are seen in the following quotations. Note that Douglass sees the suburbs as *the hope of the city*. Today this viewpoint is shared enthusiastically by numerous writers—Gordon, Seeley, and others.

[6] *American Skyline* (Boston: Houghton Mifflin Company, 1955).
[7] *The Organization Man* (New York: Doubleday & Company, Inc., 1957), p. 310.
[8] Richard E. Gordon, *et al.* (New York: Bernard Geis Associates, 1961).
[9] *Op. cit.,* p. 122.
[10] *The Church and the Suburbs* (New York: Sheed and Ward, Inc., 1959), p. 157.
[11] The Editors of *Fortune* (New York: Doubleday & Company, Inc.), pp. 9-10.

The suburb represents certain values to which most Americans feel they have some sort of right. It represents the culmination of the Good Life for which we all have the privilege of striving. Suburban bliss is one of the ends of the American success story.[12]

Our age, like every age, has its own standards of success. Its terms of measurement are material possessions, prestige, and facility in "living the good life." When the society of which he is a part is measuring success in these terms, it is incredibly difficult for the Christian to apply the specific Christian terms in which *he* must measure success.[13]

Because they constitute an unscrambling of an over-complex situation, because they are largely composed of like-minded people to whom cooperation should not be difficult, and because of the environmental advantages of roominess, the suburbs, in spite of their limitations, are the most promising aspect of urban civilization. By the very experience of revulsion by which they have taken themselves out of the central congestion of city life they are committed to finding or creating a solution of the city's problems as well as of their own. Formed out of the dust of cities, they wait to have breathed into them the breath of community sentiment, of neighborly fraternity and peace. They reflect the unspoiled and youthful aspect of urban civilization, the adolescent and not yet disillusioned part of the city, where, if at all, happiness and worthy living may be achieved, as well as material well-being.[14]

This country was built by tough, industrious people. Like the pioneers who settled the West, the men and women who have poured into the suburbs during the past twenty years have been predominantly people of strong fiber. They have not been afraid to strive for the things they have wanted. Hardship has not stopped them. They have made mistakes; they have gone about certain things in the wrong ways, as Harley did. But primarily their wish has been to earn—not to be given—their place in the sun.[15]

Who can dispute the sociologists, economists, journalists, educators, novelists, or religious leaders? Such diverse views arise from data selection and from differences in interpretation. Indeed, the situation recalls the classical dilemma of the six blind men inspecting the proverbial elephant. Each author cited in the foregoing discussion sees only part of the data necessary

---

[12] Greeley, *op. cit., pp.* 9-10.
[13] Boyd, *Christ and Celebrity Gods* (Greenwich, Conn.: The Seabury Press, 1958), p. 115.
[14] Douglass, *op. cit.,* pp. 36-37.
[15] Gordon, *et al., op. cit.,* p. 211.

to a total understanding of suburbia. Each man, according to his light, describes a segment of the phenomenon. Thus, while one man's views rarely coincide with another's, it is not necessary to deduce that one observer is right and another is mistaken. Each describes an authentic part of the total reality. But it remains just a part.

DYNAMIC SUBURBAN TRENDS

Although the emergence of suburbs can be traced back to 1819 or even earlier, actually the major population thrusts of this type in the United States are a twentieth-century phenomenon. Earlier development around the edges of American cities was limited because few families really could afford suburban residence. Indeed most people could not reside beyond the end of the trolley line.

The influence of the Garden City movement began to be felt soon after 1905. According to Tunnard and Reed by 1930 the suburb had come to rival the city as a way of life:

Despite Harriet Beecher Stowe's expository on the virtues of the suburban cottage in the 1870's, the suburb remained the rich man's paradise until after 1933. What good were the railroad and the early highway if the American employee had to put in an average of sixty hours a week in 1910? Not until the 1930's did the forty-hour week become standard.[16]

By this time the vastly improved and available automobile combined with other factors to draw out the potential of the suburb. The emergence of the superhighway eventually weaned residential development away from streetcar lines and railroads. People soon discovered that the automobile could be used advantageously for commutation. Moreover, government guaranteed mortgages introduced during the New Deal administration stimulated the residence construction industry.

A consideration of suburban development in the United States since 1900 inevitably focuses attention upon two epochs of extraordinary growth: First, the decade following World War I, and second, the period since World War II. The first period began about 1920 and closed with the advent of the depression of the 1930's. The latter period commenced while World

[16] *Op. cit.,* p. 240.

War II was in progress and has continued to the present time. Only highlights can be selected in the ensuing brief exposition.

Moreover, let the reader keep in mind the fact of steady growth which generally underlies American suburban trends. Despite the two great population thrusts alluded to here, flight from the city has been a continuous and expanding phenomenon since the turn of the century. Steady expansion is disclosed in the following statistics which reveal a pace of growth which jumped the suburbanite from one out of *twelve* in 1910 to one person in *four* today. Population totals leaped from 8,000,000 to 60,000,000. It is an amazing gain. This is the trend context for two spectacular thrusts, one in the 1920's and the other following World War II.

1910	8,000,000	1950	25,000,000
1920	11,000,000	1958	40,000,000
1930	16,000,000	1960	45,000,000
1940	18,000,000	1975	75,000,000

Growth in the 1920's. Chief reporter of the first great epoch is H. Paul Douglass. This distinguished churchman's classic treatment of the period, *The Suburban Trend,* is a work which has become a benchmark in the analysis of the suburban life. Its continuing importance is widely acknowledged.

In 1910 approximately 8,000,000 persons resided under what can be called suburban conditions. Many of these people were immensely wealthy and hence were housed in great country estates and lavish semirural residences. Only the rich and the upper-middle class could afford suburban life in those early days. Thus, by 1920, ten years later, suburban residents had increased by only 3,000,000.

Following World War I, however, a number of significant technical changes occurred in the United States which profoundly influenced population growth on the edge of cities. While the rise of a bewildering network of rapid transit systems should not be overlooked, one should recall especially the technical improvements of the automobile and the quick-spreading rash of installment buying of the horseless carriage. People could live anywhere accessible by a good road if they possessed adequate private transportation.

In 1910 there were only 15,000 automobiles in the United States. By 1920, however, the number of vehicles had increased nearly a thousandfold, or to 14,000,000, and by the end of the first great suburban epoch 20,000,000 cars were on the highways of America. Even residents of remote hamlets and villages now found themselves within easy driving distance from places of employment. The discovery accelerated the suburbanization of the country-side.

Douglass speaks of the genesis of suburbs. He points out that these com-munities usually develop from the mere overflow of cities and the engulf-ment of old towns and villages by the new hosts of commuters. The decen-tralization of residential population and of industry contributed importantly here. Thus before the 1920's were half over more than 15,000,000 persons were residing in the suburbs. Economically speaking, many of them were from the middle income bracket. The breakup of estates and extensive acreages into smaller home sites was inevitable and ubiquitous.

Growth Since World War II. Prior to 1945 the economic depression of the 1930's and the shortages of building materials during the early 1940's caused suburban development to grind to a halt. Indeed by 1940 the number of suburbanites had reached but 18,000,000, only 2,000,000 more than in 1930. In 1943 or 1944 city after city built no new homes. Then the second great suburban push began during World War II and is continuing currently. Today according to a recent study conducted by the Editors of *Fortune* Magazine, approximately 1,200,000 Americans move to the suburbs an-nually.[17] This is hailed as a colossal migration. To accommodate these incoming hordes many technical problems had to be solved. One outcome is the drastic changes in the design, erection, and sale of homes. Out of a maelstrom of efforts a streamlining procedure emerged. The mass produc-tion, erection, and sale of homes did for suburbia since World War II what the automobile accomplished in the 1920's. It yielded a sensational develop-ment. The second suburban wave has eclipsed the first.

Today estimates indicate that approximately 60,000,000 people reside under suburban circumstances. Such phenomenal increase would not have been possible without good housing, good roads, the automobile, increased in-come, and a strong bent toward middle classness. Without exaggeration, however, new housing plays a leading role in the exploding metropolis.

It costs money to build new homes. Therefore some spectacular change in wages and salaries had to take place. According to the Editors of *Fortune* 1,000,000 families per year now rise across the 4,000 dollar income line. This helps to account for the housing boom. Further, it is expected that in the

[17] *The Changing American Market* (New York: Garden City Books, 1955), p. 73.

foreseeable future a million families a year will rise across the 5,000 dollar income line. Thus, numerous people now can afford to purchase a new home in the suburbs, and probably many more will be able to do the same in the near future. This is the formula for an expanding metropolitan territory.

Geographically speaking, suburban development is found nearly everywhere in the United States, with the highest percentage of such population appearing in the Northeast, the far West, and around the Great Lakes. It has been noted that in the nation as a whole one person out of four today is a suburbanite, and that by 1975 the figure will rise to one out of three. John C. Keats predicts that 85 per cent of city growth during the 1960's and the 1970's will be suburban.[18]

Organized religion has a larger stake in the city's outskirts than often is surmised. Tomorrow's strong denominations will be those which have prominent numerical strength in suburbia. Denominational fortunes are likely to be reshuffled during the next two decades. Today suburbia is the greatest American spiritual frontier for all faiths. It beckons to alert religious leaders. Protestantism, especially, has an opportunity to extend its work both institutionally and spiritually.

FEATURES OF SUBURBAN LIFE

H. Paul Douglass observed that suburbs range from the "tin can" colonies of hoboes to the "mink and cadillac" arcadias. Some communities are settled predominantly by industrial workers, other places populated by middle-class residents, and still others domiciled the wealthy. There are suburbs of the poor and suburbs of the rich, plus the expected intermediate variations distributed along the economic gradient. Because the central city is regarded as a confusion of people, processes, and things, suburbia emerges from the Douglass analysis as an approved locale of homogeneity, rationality, and a simplification of modern life. This trinity of commendable features yields a kind of reverse urbanization process. In the discussion which follows two matters will receive consideration: Types of suburbs and features of suburban life.

Types of Suburbs. In 1926 *The Suburban Trend* provided a classification of suburbs based upon "the basic distinction between the decentralization of

[18] *The Crack in the Picture Window* (Boston: Houghton Mifflin Company, 1957), p. 173.

consumption and of production." [19] This typology rests upon the idea of *the geographical separation of residence from place of employment,* and in addition, upon the selective withdrawal from the city of both persons and the means of production. While the decentralization of industry has accelerated greatly since World War II, some exclusive suburbs have managed to keep industry out. Today, however, light industry is widely distributed around the edges of cities. The industrial park is a familiar sight.

Douglass, after citing in detail the difficulties which accompany the task of classification, proceeded cautiously with his own analysis. In brief, he divided suburban communities into two general groupings—principle types and minor types. The *principle* types are residential, industrial, and mixed, yielding a range from radically exclusive residential areas to industrially dominated mill villages and towns. The mixed suburb exhibits industrial and residential functions combined in an awkward truce. The *minor* types encompass various kinds of specialization—educational, political, medical, and recreational. These two primary categories were deemed essential in 1925.

Tunnard and Reed, in *American Skyline,* make significant use of the major classifications denoted above in a valuable history (1608-1960) of American suburban development. Moreover, Gordon, Greeley, and Wood accept the Douglass scheme in its general outline. Other scholars do the same. Recently, Edmund de S. Brunner, while acknowledging the "dated" character of *The Suburban Trend,* pointed out that Douglass had contributed importantly to the field.[20]

Nevertheless, we should note that the Douglass book reached print approximately forty years ago. Hence one should not espouse too eagerly any pre-World War II analysis as being fully adequate and valid for the 1960's. Because of the numerous intervening revolutionary changes in the world, some noteworthy modifications have overtaken present-day suburbia and have given it a new look. Consider the revolution in methods prevalent in the residential construction industry. Consider the universal availability of mortgage money, which encourages young married couples to purchase a new home as painlessly as paying rent. Consider the revolutionary changes in highway engineering and in mass automobile production. Consider the rise and canonization of the organization man since 1935. Consider the rise

[19] *Op. cit.,* p. 121.
[20] Brunner, *Review of Religious Research* (Summer, 1959), p. 8.

of the household-gadget industry and the "do-it-yourself" craze both of which currently regard suburbia as their number-one market. When the import of these and kindred developments are properly assessed there remains little doubt about how much the world has changed since *The Suburban Trend* was written. A vast revolution has taken place.

As important as has been the Douglass analysis, it is now essential to bring one's thinking up to date. Recent writers on suburbia emphasize the economic, along with the social class and status factors, as differentiating elements among suburbs. This constitutes a shift in emphasis away from the Douglass typology. Moreover, Wood stresses the revolutionary shift of "grass roots" democracy from the small town to the suburban community, yielding a new mood locally. John Keats, John Leill, William Whyte, and numerous others lament the debilitating homogeneity which prevails in suburbia today. Blizzard, Walter Martin, Shirley Greene, and others expound the virtues and problems of the rural fringe in relation to suburbia. Auguste Spectorsky describes the remarkable phenomenon of exurbia. Furthermore the rise and development of metropolitan planning agencies relegate suburbia to an unwelcome subordinate role in larger urban areas.[21] Thus the disturbing present-day situation demands an up-to-date and more adequate typological approach to suburbia. This calls for a thorough examination of the manifold features and dynamic processes which characterize American life in this sphere.

Aspects of Life in Suburbia. Exhaustive consideration of the manifold aspects of contemporary suburban life would fill volumes and hence the total task will not be attempted here. Discussions of the phenomena range in form and content from slick journalism to dispassionate scholarly analyses, from harsh polemics to sentimental apologia, from ivory tower dilettantism to pragmatic appraisals. How, then, shall the topic be approached in an adequate fashion? Possibly a brief survey of significant highlights can arouse interest in discovering the authentic nature of suburban life. Space permits the treatment of at least six aspects.

For many people suburbia affords *an escape from industrialism.* It is as simple as that. The noise, smoke, odors, vibration, truck traffic, blight, and other nuisances prevalent in industrial areas actually downgrade residential

---

[21] In 1963 Regional Plan Association conducted seminar-type discussion groups comprising 10,000 persons who considered plans for the New York Metropolitan territory projected to 1980 respecting housing, jobs, highways and mass transportation. Here many suburban leaders discovered their dependency upon the central city.

values. Hence a home in the suburbs, away from industry, makes a strong appeal. Its attractiveness possesses a convincing inner logic which is difficult to resist. Automobile, bus, or train enable the breadwinner to commute to the distant place of employment. He does not need to reside within view of smoke stacks in order to earn a living. He can separate his place of residence from proximity to the means of production. Moreover, what is possible for the blue-collar worker is feasible also for the organization man. The latter need not reside amidst the congestion of the city. He need not lodge his family in an apartment alongside the large office building. Modern means of commutation makes a house in the suburbs a viable alternative. Andrew Greeley speaks of this mass retreat from the city as "an artificial revolt against industrialism." Obviously, neither the white-collar nor the blue-collar employee is opposed to receiving a livelihood from industry or business. Rather *the individual simply objects to residence in close proximity to factory or office.* The escape from industrialism is really a flight from the ugliness and confusion of urban industrial and business operations. To millions of Americans the out-movement is an act demanded by common sense.

Further, suburbia is alleged to afford *a refuge from minority groups.* In urban areas of transition, some residents feel threatened when persons of a different ethnic group begin to settle in the neighborhood. Whether the newcomers are Negro, Puerto Rican, Mexican, Oriental, or any foreign-born groups, an uneasiness begins to pervade the neighborhood. Some long-term residents feel it more keenly than others, recalling nostalgically the old community before it changed. As a result, some people retreat to the suburbs, hoping to escape contact with in-migrants whose appearance, or customs, or ways of life seem strange. Sometimes strong prejudice motivates the flight to suburbia. In such cases the erstwhile city dweller relocates to that portion of suburbia where protective residential restrictions obtain. This general propensity to withdraw from polyglot areas whenever it is economically possible to do so has furnished grounds for accusing the suburbs of intentional homogeneity. Suburbia is supposed to afford at least a temporary escape from residential proximity to minority ethnic groups. Some Americans insist upon the "privilege" of selecting their next-door neighbors. Obviously this expectation can be but partly fulfilled.

Next, suburbia is *a guarantor of homogeneity.* H. Paul Douglass speaks of the sorting out process which occurs in the move to suburbia, yielding suburban communities for persons of various economic levels. The city is a kind of gigantic sorting machine by which people purchase or rent homes according to economic ability. There is a suburb for every pocketbook. Hence exclusive residential suburbs are actually inaccessible to persons of modest income. Initial cost of a house plus high taxes and other monetary considerations combine to eliminate families who cannot afford the price tag. This situation, combined with the strong desire for upward mobility, yields a second important point. After a few years persons who can afford to move up into a more expensive neighborhood usually do so. Eventually each suburbanite moves up as far as he can in the economic hierarchy of neighborhoods. Inevitably, however, income limitations prevent him from going any higher. There he remains, along with many other residents in kindred economic circumstances. In the nature of things suburbia is a guarantor of homogeneity on one's own level of financial achievement. While this homogeneity is essentially economic, it usually has concommitants in the sociopsychological realm. Attitudes, value systems, ways of doing things, habits of consumption, yield a high degree of conformity which has been described in shocking detail by John Keats, Auguste Spectorsky, and William Whyte.

Suburbia is *the abode of modern man.* Here is where he makes his home, raises a family, participates in social life, articulates his values, and establishes institutional relationships. He invests heavily in family life in the suburbs. From this investment of time, energy, and money he expects to derive a measure of happiness; to procure an attractive home, a contented family, personal recognition; to experience the values of high living; and to express his own philosophy of life. He is interested in self-determination in a thoroughgoing fashion. He looks nowhere else for ideas and norms. The individual who achieves residence in the suburbs is often convinced that he has "arrived."

Suburbia is *an area of cultural tension.* Despite the external indications of peaceful homogeneity there exists below the surface a seething cauldron. More than the city itself, this is a "boiling society." Breadwinners are engaged in ulcer-producing occupations where competition is fierce and relentless. Tensions which build up during work hours are not dispelled during the train or bus ride homeward or even the walk up from the station. Often tensions are carried over into family life in the form of irritability, over-fatigue, and other negative behavior. The tensions spread from person to person in the household. Moreover, the ill-defined role of the modern home-

25

maker under suburban circumstances becomes the occasion for familial friction—temper displays, confusion, misunderstandings, even estrangements. The migration of Jews and Roman Catholics into suburbia has already increased tensions among religious groups. Heretofore the suburb has been regarded as predominantly Protestant. This old generalization is being challenged both by the facts of change and by the growing articulateness of the new religious groups themselves. Colliding values increase the friction. As a result suburbia has become a battleground upon which educational, political, and social issues are hotly debated. Indeed, some faith and sect groups have deliberately set the battle lines and currently prosecute their narrow purposes. The struggle for power increases the cultural tensions here.

Suburbia is *a mecca of comforts and conveniences*. More than in the city the numerous fruits of modern technology are found here—automobile, plumbing, telephone, radio, television, dryer, dishwasher, garbage disposal, and the numerous labor-saving gadgets—automatic heat, garage door openers, cookout facilities. This is a milieu of material good fortune. Nearly everything that eases the burden of homemaking and yard care has been found and installed. Spectorsky as well as J. R. Seeley, R. A. Sim, and E. W. Loosley suggest that suburbia is the realization of a "limited dream." This phrase denotes the technological conveniences which become substitute life goals for some suburbanites. Since the American success dream cannot be fully realized, its material counterpart suffices. Possibly this satisfaction with the limited dream arises out of a prominent orientation of the American culture. In Europe the pattern may be different.

Delineation of these six features provides a preliminary impression of the exciting but complicated existence represented in suburbia. Further, it reminds us of the tremendous task confronting all suburban institutions. Because of spectacular growth trends and the emergence of powerful new perspectives, suburbia now deserves the attention it receives. Beyond this there remain two major problems yet to be considered in their impact upon American suburban life: The cult of suburban criticism and suburban challenges to the churches.

THE CULT OF SUBURBAN CRITICISM

Let the reader of suburban literature beware. A tyranny of ideas exists here. Christianity is shamefully downgraded in suburban fiction. Moreover, it fares little better in serious essays and in research monographs. Throughout the literature one encounters specious attacks based on inadequate knowledge and negativism. Protestantism often receives the full blame for the ills of suburban society. It is treated as an innocuous faith preoccupied with trifling pursuits. Polemical tracts espousing this condemnatory viewpoint feel no obligation to substantiate charges against the denominations. To accuse is to prove. Moreover, wild charges are likely to attract desired public attention to the author himself. Oddly enough, Peter Berger, Gibson Winter, and other popularizers are shrewd enough to exempt Roman Catholicism and Judaism from the attacks. This caution is sensibly grounded. Evidently these two faiths know exactly how to cope with people who make unsupported statements. Such irresponsibility is brought promptly to public attention and the author is discredited. Roman Catholicism and Judaism put the fear of God in the hearts of careless writers. Unfortunately Protestantism has not been as worldly wise and hence unintentionally invites misguided criticism. The time has come when Protestantism should become tough-minded respecting reckless charges.

Possibly the purposes of the present discussion are served best not by responding seriatim to the unsupported accusations but rather by citing several volumes which illustrate the cult of suburban criticism at work. Wherein lies the inadequacy of such materials will soon become evident. Let it be noted here that as a whole *the books do not go far enough* in either sociological or religious criticism. They are timid as a whole about raising fundamental issues. They fail to see the sociological and the religious as confluent aspects of an enormously complicated context in which Christianity functions and has its life.

First, the criticisms found in the literature do not go far enough, *sociologically* speaking. Even a casual scrutiny of suburban fiction reveals a strange mixture of sociology and soap opera.[22] Residents of suburbia since World War II have difficulty recognizing suburbia as described in the fictional accounts. Identification is difficult because the novelist has not sought to portray real life. As an artist he pleads poetic license. However, plot, dialogue, and characterization convey the strong impression that the stories were written with a Hollywood scenario in mind. Surface events treated in a soap opera style is the success formula widely used. Whether

[22] Consult works listed in the bibliography.

27

one peruses *The Clouded Fountain, Make Mine Love, The Devil in Bucks County,* or *The Mackerel Plaza,* the pages unfold a dreary melange of Hollywood-like incidents which contribute little to an adequate understanding of American suburban life. Unfortunately one comes away from the reading of several dozen suburban novels with the conviction that no great writer yet has turned his attention to suburbia. Fiction is preoccupied with a superficial exposé of selected middle-class foibles, stressing succulent marital infidelities and the sating of epicurean tastes. Up to the present American fiction seems to have successfully missed the major sociological aspects of suburban life.

Moreover, when one turns to essays and criticism, the question arises whether sociological insights are presented adequately here. Have the serious books, dissertations, and periodicals dealt sufficiently with the sociology of suburbia? No, the sociological studies likewise are not sociological enough. The soap opera motif appears here also.

Consider, for example, William Whyte's *The Organization Man,* a book which bases its suburban understandings primarily upon surveys of Park Forest (near Chicago) plus Levittown and Drexelbrook (near Philadelphia). It is based upon only three of the nearly three thousand American suburbs. What Whyte really examined are specialized "package" rather than rank-and-file suburbs. A few large development tracts situated in the Northeastern and North central part of the United States are hardly typical of the South, the far West, or even the East and the Midwest. An overwhelming number of American suburbs were omitted from the Whyte analysis although life within them comprises extremely diverse elements. Despite this elementary and obvious fact, Whyte managed to let loose into the world several misleading myths about suburban life; e.g., suburbanites are overwhelmingly white collar, upwardly mobile, young, well educated, socially ambitious, and indifferent to denominational churches.

Unfortunately Whyte's views have been promoted widely by well-intentioned scholars who accepted the generalizations too uncritically. Only recently critics have begun to point out that Whyte is really attacking middle classness generally rather than providing a reliable discussion of suburbia.[23]

[23] See Bennett Berger, *Working-Class Suburb* (Berkeley, Calif.: University of California Press, 1960); William Dobriner, *Class in Suburbia* (Englewood Cliffs, N. J.: Prentice-Hall, Inc., 1963); Herbert Gans' chapter in *The Urban Condition,* edited by Leonard J. Duhl (New York: Basic Books, Inc., 1963).

This belated discovery has failed to curb the ongoing momentum of Whyte's myths.

What the sociological studies should have directed our attention to are: (1) The effects upon community arising from the mass erection of homes, (2) the accumulating pressures upon suburban institutions, including the church, (3) the new challenges to family life, (4) the disturbing consequences of population mobility, (5) the growing heterogeneity of suburbia, (6) the significance of culture clash and tension, and finally (7) the emerging types of suburban residents. It is a disservice to increase the number of myths and misunderstandings about suburbia. What is genuinely needed is an account of the hard sociological realities which must be confronted by Protestant leaders. Scholars of suburban life should *identify reliably the inescapable sociological circumstances,* the special problems deriving therefrom, and the new resources which recently have become available from social science. Suburban literature as a whole has failed to go far enough in its sociological criticism. The reliable findings of the social scientist have not become available to the Protestant churchman.

Second, the criticisms do not go far enough, *religiously* speaking. The caustic comments on suburbia by Peter Berger and Gibson Winter, among other writers, are well known. Yet venom can never be allowed to become a substitute for sound analysis and adequate acquaintance with the relevant religious facts. The shortcomings of the Berger and Winter books disclose the weaknesses of scholars rather than revealing flaws in suburban Protestantism. This is an important distinction. Apparently some serious writers are no more perceptive respecting suburban religion than the aforementioned novelists.

Failure to go far enough religiously becomes evident in at least three ways—in faulty analysis, inadequate data, and a misunderstanding of the church. *Faulty analysis* shows up where Christianity is separated from Christian institutions and Christian agencies; i.e., Christianity is completely divorced from visible expressions of faith. Thus Christianity is defined only in the abstract. Because Protestants commonly make this analytical error, Robin Williams, James Gustafson, and Walter Muelder, have warned against it. Negativism appears among some Protestant intellectuals who have drifted away from vital contact with the work of the local church. Ignorance has fortified an illusory feeling of emancipation. It is a kind of intoxication. Intellectuals who regularly participate in the Protestant church and are intimately acquainted with contemporary religious life find it unnecessary to adopt a pejorative stance. Such persons acquire a firsthand knowledge of church life which informs their opinions. Leaders within Roman Catholicism and Judaism know that faulty analysis yields faulty religious understanding. Apparently some Protestants are unaware of the problem. Berger's irrational antipathy toward the institutional aspects of Christianity entangles him in a faulty analysis from which he does not recover. A pejorative attitude keeps him from going far enough in a religious analysis.

Inadequate data leads Berger and other writers to formulate esoteric and often irrelevant generalizations. Since he has no empirical data of his own, Berger is compelled to rely upon *Crestwood Heights* (a Canadian suburb), *The Exurbanites,* and *The Organization Man,* ignoring the broad sweep of approximately 3,000 suburbs in the United States. Despite insufficient empirical information, Berger proceeds to criticize the Protestant suburban church severely. Mere lack of data yields no personal distress or embarrassment. Although there are many negative references to suburbia, the book contains very little firsthand observation. No adequate empirical study of religious life in suburbia has been utilized. In an attempt to cover up the inadequacy he theologizes over the situation. *Negative criticisms respecting suburban Protestantism remain unproved and unsupported.* Thus it should come as no surprise that his study of suburban Christianity does not go far enough. This embarrassing lack of specific demographic and religious data should be noted in the plethora of shrewd estimations and common sense statements. Protestantism has a right to demand proof and substantiation from her numerous critics. The reduction of irresponsible criticism and the encouragement of reliable analyses of contemporary church life are desirable outcomes. The denominations surely need responsible evaluations.

Misunderstanding of the church emerges from faulty analysis and inadequate data. Because the literature lacks treatments which reliably describe parish life in suburbia, it is difficult to frame suitable prescriptions for action. Prescriptions certainly can be no better than the ingredients which comprise them. This principle applies in the current religious situation. Three examples of church misunderstanding are pertinent here: McCabe's appointment parish visits, Raines's koinonia groups, and Winter's sector ministry.

Joseph McCabe's *The Power of God in a Parish Program* endeavors to restore the pastoral visit to a respected place in organized religion.[24] Based upon pastoral experience in a suburban church near Philadelphia, McCabe's report lists the merits of pastoral calling *by appointment* in a congregation of approximately 500 families. The scheme features a feasible schedule of visits under the direction of the minister. Usually four half-hour appointments in homes in a selected neighborhood per weekday evening are planned. Following this pattern the pastor called throughout the entire parish. Then a second round of evening appointments was arranged by bringing a half dozen nearby families together in a centrally located home. Thus by means of evening appointments the pastor covered the parish systematically with a minimum loss of time and wasted ministerial effort.

McCabe's efforts are directed primarily to the achievement of greater efficiency in pastoral calls, in counseling contacts, and in the use of the ecclesiastical edifice for sacramental and quasi-sacramental occasions. His interest centers in the modest reforms which leave the overall parish organization intact. He raises no great issues which possibly confront 60,000,000 suburbanites, and therefore, his approach betrays a certain captivity to the culture. McCabe accepts uncritically the current structure and the contemporary effort of the church. Apparently nothing significant has happened since World War II which calls for a thoroughgoing re-examination of the church. To envisage no basic change in Protestant strategy is indeed to miss the mark in suburbia. Thus, despite its merits, McCabe's book represents a serious misunderstanding of the church, a misunderstanding which points in the opposite direction from the comments below.

In *New Life in the Church* Robert Raines focuses upon religious conversion in suburbia.[25] Citing pastoral experience in a Protestant church near Cleveland, he urges the universal adoption of *koinonia groups* based upon prayer, Bible reading, Holy Communion, and the sharing of faith and life. Sixty people comprising five groups were drawn from a suburban congregation of 600. The group's objective is to lead individuals into a personal knowledge of God by providing the context for conversion. "Grooves of Grace" and seeing the world "through Christ-colored glasses" are stressed. Raines insists that the small group should take precedence over all other church activity.

[24] Philadelphia: The Westminster Press, 1959.
[25] New York: Harper & Row, Publishers, 1961.

More than a score of savage tirades against Protestantism mar the discussion. Raines asks tolerance for the imperfection of his koinonia groups but is dogmatically intolerant of any flaws in other churches. The koinonia group is evaluated in terms of its ideals and unrealized goals; other Protestant congregations are harshly judged only in terms of their current achievements. Raines overlooks the dominant middle-class orientation of group adherents who possess skill in reading and comprehension, desire to study, and ability to articulate ideas. Evidently the testimonies most prized derive from personnel managers, executives, and salesmen, or their spouses.

Raines unconsciously seeks to substitute one form of social organization for another in the parish. How will he keep the new custom, so narrowly based, from corrupting the reform? Indeed this misunderstanding of the church lies at the opposite end of the continuum from that of McCabe. Raines represents the radical rejection of the church's structure; McCabe is reluctant to part with any of it. Both misunderstand the church in suburbia.

Gibson Winter's proposed "sector ministry" envisages a geographical section of the city extending from downtown out into suburbia yet lying adjacent to a freeway or major street.[26] Hopefully, it furnishes a cross section of the metropolis; i.e., a mixture of people in terms of race, class, occupation, and economic fortune. Within this urban segment all religious work is centralized and co-ordinated under the direction of a representative council of religious leaders presided over by a local bishop, presbyter, or leading clergyman. All parish churches as such disappear, being replaced eventually by several large cathedral-type edifices. Chaplaincies to specific neighborhoods are substituted for the regular pastorate. Worship for everyone will be held only in the "cathedrals." By means of supplementary ordinations of the clergy and an unspecified orientation to Faith ond Order, broadly considered, it will be possible to overcome the Protestant obstacles of pride, individualism, and organization which hinder the immediate adoption of the sector ministry.

This sector approach confuses the real issues, being an inaccurate oversimplification of both urban religious work and the sociology of the city. It is too naïve, sociologically and religiously. A detailed knowledge of urban church work appears to be lacking in the book, although philosophizing about it is abundant. The severe criticism of religious institutions is soon

[26] *The Suburban Captivity of the Churches* (New York: Doubleday & Company, Inc., 1961). Chapters 6 and 7.

forgotten when plans for setting up the sector ministry are unveiled. A sociological understanding of the metropolitan area is but dimly evident and one looks in vain for the specifics which properly should underlie generalization and prescription. Again and again when confronted by the severe limitations of secondary data—drawn primarily from Whyte and Peter Berger —Winter falls back upon common sense solutions to issues, thereby weakening his case. Moreover Robert MacIver long ago pointed out the untenability of the concept "organic" as Winter applies the term to church life.[27] Both systematic and representative knowledge of the suburban church and its community are lacking. Ignorance here is embarrassing since Winter makes *scores of undocumented negative references to suburban life*. What is the basis for such comments? Indeed the entire analysis suffers when Winter offers petulance and a pejorative attitude in place of adequate information and sound analysis. His conception of church contains the flaws (low theoretical estimate of the "visible" church, ignorance of the problem of church order, and the absolute rejection of institutionalism) warned against by Walter Muelder and James Gustafson. The sector ministry appears to present more problems than it solves. Actually the major theme of the book— despite a misleading title—is the promotion of an inner-city ministry. All other aspects are kept subordinate to this goal. Hence *Winter offers an inner-city captivity* to replace the suburban captivity which he so loudly deplores. Why is either captivity necessary? Winter's discussion leaves suburbia an unexplored sphere both sociologically and religiously. This outcome is consistent with the cult of suburban criticism.

According to the literature, three major flaws stand in the way of a reliable evaluation of suburban Protestantism. The studies have not gone far enough. Faulty analysis, inadequate data, and a misunderstanding of the church prevent the casual writer from achieving a reliable appraisal of the situation. Adequate critical studies should furnish reliable information on at least seven problems in suburban Christianity: Recent alterations in the religious composition of suburbia, types of suburban residents, the meaning of neighbor, the nature of suburban sin and suburban crime, the new challenges of Protestantism in family life, the emergence of interfaith tensions, and finally, new opportunities for church extension under suburban circumstances. These are significant areas of concern which stimulate Protestantism

[27] See *Community* (New York: The Macmillan Company, 1928).

to provide a more adequate ministry to the millions of Americans now residing around our cities.

In conclusion, let it be pointed out that suburban Protestantism has no fear of *scholarly* criticism. Yet it is properly suspicious of reckless and unsupported charges. It becomes the inescapable obligation of the critic to produce the evidence which discloses significant weaknesses in religious life. An accusation is not enough. Evidently much of the literature which purports to deal with religion under suburban circumstances is superficial, unrepresentative, and pejorative. Many writers are really unable to provide the constructive criticism which Protestantism urgently needs. Reliable firsthand investigations have not been made. Hence the church awaits deeper sociological and religious analyses. The basic need emphasized here is for accuracy in data, specificity in problems, and constructiveness in possible cures. This book cannot fulfill completely these exacting demands, but it suggests some spheres in which scientific study should be made.

SUBURBIA CHALLENGES THE CHURCH

A defiant challenge originating in the leafy outskirts of the city is hurled at Protestantism today. Suburbia demands attention, respect, and acceptance. It stands ready to supplant any other value or loyalty. Many Americans who otherwise exercise sound judgment become mesmerized and misled in suburbia. Recognizing this inherent danger, we will undertake an examination of two contrasting forms of the challenge: (1) Suburbia viewed as a secular symbol and (2) suburbia viewed as a Christian symbol. Both polar dimensions of the contemporary situation can contribute usefully to an adequate understanding on the part of Protestant leaders.

Suburbia as a Secular Symbol. That suburbia is a secular symbol can be argued for at least three reasons. These points discuss the domination of material values, the centrality of family life, and the politics of suburbia. While not exhausting the topic, these can touch upon several crucial issues which yield a secular outlook. Potentially each can furnish a "pleasing alternative" to the Christian way of life. A man and his faith are too easily parted in suburbia.

First, *the suburbanite symbolizes the successful person* in the modern business and professional world. Materially he has reached an income level which permits home ownership, possession of an automobile, commutation, expensive tastes, and travel vacations. Outwardly he is the acme of confidence and of pleasantness, knowing how to handle himself and how to manipulate others to achieve vocational goals. Persons in a position to promote him are cultivated. He is a company man and believes in its future. Grey flannel suit or not, this man wishes to climb the golden ladder to success and already has subscribed to the values which guarantee realization of the limited dream. Vance Packard, William Whyte, John Keats, and other writers emphasize the prevalence of the success motif in the modern suburban community. Bennett Berger summed up the matter: "Suburbia is the locus of gadgetry, shopping centers, and 'station wagon culture'; its grass grows greener, its chrome shines brighter, its lines are clean and new and modern. Suburbia is America in its drip-dry Sunday clothes, standing before the bar of history fulfilled, waiting for its judgment." [28] Suburbia is the abode of the modern man. He may not know the measure of a great many things but he does know how to succeed in the material world.

Second, suburbia is the scene of *the apotheosis of the family*. This is the new idolatry. Nowhere else in society is the family more important. Here family values on a material and personal plane become the setting for self worship. The suburban family does not have an altar; it is its own altar. Many of the fine values of secular family life are lifted up and exalted. This is pointed out by Dorothy Barclay.[29] Lack of an adequate religious context in the family yields a vast emptiness. Suburbia boasts a very strong emphasis upon family life and family values, including the qualities which make for a good husband or a good wife and children who grow up in a respectable manner. To stay married without nasty divorce proceedings, to be reasonably happy, and to help the children through college and into their own homes appear to be the highest goals espoused by many suburbanites. The dangers of this type of home are cited in *The Split-Level Trap, The Shook-Up Generation,* and *Suburbia's Coddled Kids.* Attention is drawn to a pathetic worship of family values with inadequate awareness of a divine dimension of existence. When the suburban home worships itself it achieves secular values only.

Third, Robert C. Wood regards the modern suburban community as the scene of *the renascence of small-town democracy*. This represents a shift from the town to the suburb, investing the latter with a new political significance. Without a religious context, this is merely secular activity. Here,

---

[28] *Op. cit.,* p. 99.
[29] *Understanding the City Child* (New York: Franklin Watts, Inc., 1959).

despite the awkward and inexperienced manner in which political problems are handled, the suburbanite does express his secular wishes and does set up the form of government which is sensitive to his own needs. This "grass-roots" democracy plunges him into the arena of school problems, the problems of water, electricity, street cleaning, garbage collection, snow removal, and parking facilities for the commuter and the shopper. Lacking the technical know-how in these matters, he often employs an outside expert. The city planner on a small scale is encouraged to bring his engineering skills to bear upon the problems cited above, but he must not seek to merge the suburb with the nearby central city. Robert Wood sees in the imperfect government of suburbia the reappearance of small-town democracy in terms of sound American tradition—a recovery of grass-roots democracy. This becomes a worthwhile secular goal for the suburb. Participation in public life for itself, however, omitting a religious frame of reference, yields secular values.

From the foregoing discussion one gains the impression that suburbia is a strong secular symbol of modern life. It sets goals of aspiration in the success motif, in family values, in technological conveniences, and in local government. A strong case can be made for the suburb as a prototype of worldly success in America. It yields also a shining symbol for the new humanism which is alluded to by Andrew Greeley in *The Church and the Suburbs*. The authors of *Crestwood Heights* call attention to the abnormal emphasis placed upon material values and upon the North American dream. To live under pleasant circumstances in a house of one's own surrounded by his family and served by the comforts and conveniences of modern technological civilization is to realize the dream. Material happiness and familial satisfaction are cited as the goals of modern man. Suburban living represents the achievement of that goal. As a secular symbol suburbia represents the zenith of aspiration and achievement; without faith one can reach no higher.

Suburbia as a Christian Symbol. Who is foolish enough to suggest suburbia as a symbol bearing Christian meaning? Does not everyone know that God made the country and the devil devised the city? Who, then, made suburbia? Perhaps, like Topsy, it "just growed." Regardless of its genesis, here is the place where evil and good currently are locked in mortal combat. Which will prevail is not yet known. God and man, however, newly teamed together in living relationship can accomplish amazing things. To the victor belongs the suburbs. At least four perspectives lend support to the view that suburbia is a Christian symbol.

First, *suburbia can be regarded as a Jabbok*. The word "Jabbok" appears in the Old Testament (Gen. 32:22-32), designating the place where Jacob wrestled all night long with an adversary. Jacob refused to terminate the struggle until a blessing had been received. From this memorable nocturnal engagement he received a new name. No longer was he to be called Jacob but henceforth, "Israel." What is more, Jacob renamed the river's ford where the event occurred, Peniel, in honor of God. Jacob said, "I have seen God face to face, and yet my life is preserved." (Gen. 32:30.) Today, in a profound religious sense, the suburb is the scene of a mighty struggle between God and man. God reminds man of his true nature and destiny but man is prone to pursue worldly values. Suburbia is the place where the best in Christianity encounters the best in modern secular life. A mighty conflict ensues. Beneficial outcome depends upon man's willingness to prolong the struggle until he procures a blessing, until he gets a new name, until he sees God face to face and discovers how his life can be preserved. This struggle discloses that the suburbanite is not spiritually dead. Very much alive, he throws himself into the struggle in which the fundamental issues of life are being settled. This is the Christian meaning of Jabbok. Suburbia is a place where man and God meet in a struggle for mastery.

Second, *suburbia tests faith's relevance in the modern world*. The abundance of civilization accumulates in suburbia. Virtually all of the accolades of praise or tirades of abuse concerning suburban life begin and end with an account of material and physical features. Piled up in home after home, in suburb after suburb, are the remarkable products of modern technology and the coveted rewards of vocational effort. No one underrates the strong temptations of material prosperity. Rather such constitute a hurdle for Christian faith to get over. The Bible reports that Job served God both in days of prosperity and also in days of want (Job 42). This is the supreme test of personal religion. The pilings of Job's faith were driven to depths far below mere economic circumstances, reaching the hidden foundations of human life; hence his faith was demonstrably relevant. God's demands are well-known and vary little from generation to generation. Because the cultural situation changes, each generation must learn anew what it is to be a Christian. Thus, in suburbia faith continues to ask for man's deepest commitment regardless of his other weighty obligations. Nothing matters more.

This demand is hurled in the face of beautiful homes, material prosperity, scientific knowledge, population mobility, public relations, and spiritual indifference. Christianity has no fear of prosperity, modern science, or anything else. In suburbia Protestantism confronts competent protagonists of business success, scientific learning, and cultural sophistication. Does this encounter yield a viable reconciliation between faith and the secular world? Does Christian commitment genuinely suffice for the intellectual and emotional testings of our day? Suburbia furnishes the possibility of an answer. It is a proper place to test the relevance of faith. Beneath the public show of materialism and space-age science, there does exist *an underdeveloped interest* [30] in what Protestantism really has to offer. Thus suburbia is not only a Jabbok but also a place of testing the relevance of one's faith. If faith works here it probably can work elsewhere in the modern world.

Third, *suburbia weighs Christianity's stewardship principle.* Since suburbia represents a triumph over poverty and misery, Christianity asks whether this means a triumph over man's selfishness also. An opportunity to share good fortune is afforded to people who possess material advantages. Inevitably the stewardship question appears. Will the resident here relate himself responsibly to the missionary situations in the city slums and the distant underdeveloped countries? What kind of steward is the suburbanite? Does he fit the stereotype of the barn owner mentioned by Jesus? (Luke 12:16-21.) The New Testament provides a dramatic account of a man who did so well in gaining material possessions that he determined to pull down his storage barns and to build larger ones. Moreover, he determined to keep all of the possessions for himself and shortly to enter into a life of ease, eating, drinking, and merrymaking. Jesus' laconic appraisal of the confused barn owner's dilemma indicates that material things fail as a substitute for being rich toward God. The sad end of the selfish man is known to all readers, but many people fail to see that this parable speaks to the contemporary American suburb. Inordinate love for the material world makes a man forget who he really is theologically. In its own good fortune, does the suburban family see an opportunity to help relieve the misery of mankind? Or does the

[30] Roman Catholic and Jewish leaders detect this interest and are cultivating it. Apparently the phenomenon has been overlooked by the cult of suburban criticism.

prospering family think only of buying a larger house, opening another bank account, and investing in more securities? When the suburbanite acquires a "larger barn" complex, can he be an adequate demonstration of stewardship?

A research study made recently examined the stewardship patterns in 250 suburban Protestant churches. It was discovered that an average of thirteen cents out of each budget dollar is sent from the parish to the outside. But *is thirteen cents enough?* Not for every parish! Some suburban churches prove the point by paying a figure of thirty-three cents. A very few churches as pacesetters contribute fifty cents out of each budget dollar for causes outside the local parish. Deep Christianity is required to implement spiritual concern for others at this high level. The basic issue remains: Will the suburbanite prove to be a good steward of his material blessings? Some indications suggest that he can and will. Suburbia functions as a Christian symbol when it illustrates adequately the stewardship principle.

Fourth, *suburbia symbolizes the church's unfinished task in the world.* Across the United States the most remarkable growth is occurring in the suburbs. Both the outmovement of people from the cities and the bumper crop of suburban babies swell the old towns and villages and bring new communities into existence. Millions of people are buying or building homes out in the city's leafy outskirts. As a result Protestantism finds itself well-nigh inundated. Many older churches need to be expanded or rebuilt. Shirley Greene's *Ferment on the Fringe* depicts this unfinished task.[31] Many new congregations need to be established, according to B. P. Murphy, D. H. Shelhart and other observers. Suburbia has become the greatest religious opportunity of our day; properly understood it means a ministry to approximately one third of the nation.

Moreover, the unfinished character of the task appears in other ways. The oncoming generation needs to be trained in Christian faith; the adults outside the church need to be reached religiously; many church members have not taken Protestantism seriously enough; and many of the faithful disciples need to be renewed and fortified from day to day. Altogether the permanent problem of Protestantism is to labor in an unfinished world. Suburbia symbolizes the church's unfinished task and the need to strive for completion.

In conclusion, this chapter has undertaken a pluralistic definition of

[31] Philadelphia: Christian Education Press, 1960.

suburbia, one which points to the need for sound analysis and new research. As we mentioned earlier, population forecasts indicate that by 1975 one American out of three will reside in suburbia. The mass exodus from the city has been accompanied by revolutionary changes in transportation, in the construction industry, in mortgage credit, and in income structure. By 1975 there are expected to be 100,000,000 registered automobiles on the roads of America, serving a population of 220,000,000 persons. Moreover, the suburbs differ in economic status, in population size, in basic economy, and in forms of specialization. Six features of suburban life were described, and two contrasting views of suburbia were delineated—the territory as a secular symbol and as a Christian symbol. In view of these introductory comments, succeeding chapters will treat the varieties of suburban religion, some types of suburban residents, what the term "neighbor" means, satan in the suburbs, Protestantism and family life, tensions in suburbia, the new spiritual frontier, and suburbia as both Zion and Calvary. Such discussions call the reader's attention to the plight and possibilities of Protestantism in suburbia.

II

New Challenges to Suburban Protestantism

Until recently suburbia has been regarded by many scholars as a major stronghold of Protestantism in the metropolitan community. Prior to World War II the suburbs were dominated by a single religion. Indeed Protestants really pioneered suburbia and hence they feel possessive about it. That drastic change would ever come here seemed highly improbable. The writings of H. Paul Douglass, Ross Sanderson, Martin Marty, Murray Leiffer, William Dobriner, and Walter Kloetzli, among others, illuminate the point. Evidently for some suburban places this clearcut domination by a single faith will continue to be an unquestioned fact into the foreseeable future.

For most major metropolitan areas, however, *noteworthy changes in the religious composition of suburban population have already occurred*. Here single-faith communities are actually on the way out. Strong trends which began during the late '40's and which have continued through the '50's and into the 1960's compel an urgent re-examination of the situation. New challenges, both cultural and religious, now confront suburban Protestantism.

In a preliminary analysis attention can be turned to the post World War II in-migration of the Jew, the Roman Catholic, the sect group, the Negro, and the blue-collar worker. The arrival of these newcomers has added much to the potential richness of suburban life, but it has also introduced disturbing elements into the heretofore placid community. Figuratively speaking, the famous American "melting pot" has shifted from city to suburb. Along with this dislocation have come the turbulence and the encounter of competing values. Whether the impact upon Protestantism will be invigorating or debilitating remains to be seen. Let us now consider who are the challenging newcomers.

JEWS IN THE SUBURBS

Since World War II many thousands of Jews have moved into suburbia. There can be no doubt about it. Albert I. Gordon's *Jews in Suburbia,* among other books, underscores the scope and importance of the movement. This outstanding study embraces eighty-nine suburbs located in metropolitan areas scattered across the United States. One third of the Jews residing around Washington, D. C., moved into the community since 1945. For example, in suburban Montgomery County, the number of Jewish residents jumped from 1,875 in 1946 to over 27,000 at the present time, yielding a fourteenfold gain. Around Los Angeles, following World War II, the Jewish population has doubled in many suburban territories. Over 80,000 Jews now live in San Fernando Valley. Since 1946 the Jewish community in Newton, Massachusetts, has doubled in size. Further, 85 per cent of Cleveland's Jews now reside in five adjacent suburban communities. Skokie, near Chicago, reports 25,000 Jews. With respect to Minneapolis, 34.3 per cent of its Jews reside in the suburbs today. Back east one New York City family out of five who moves into suburban Nassau County is Jewish.

Indeed, currently up to an estimated 400,000,000 dollars are being spent annually for new suburban synagogue construction. Thus, what has been noted above respecting a few selected communities can be projected to include many other metropolitan areas scattered across the United States. Generally speaking, therefore, the Jewish resident in suburbia is a phenomenon of the last two decades. For better or for worse, the Jew is participating in the mass exodus from the American city.

From these selected data it becomes evident that there is a pronounced shift out of the traditional city ghettos into a hoped-for new pattern of existence. While an occasional scholar urges that there are no all-Jewish streets nor all-Jewish neighborhoods, nevertheless distinct Jewish areas of settlement are evident in suburbia.[1] Who can keep his faith a secret from the neighbors? An overall summary of Jewish population in the United States,

[1] See Eugene J. Lipman and Albert Vorspan, *A Tale of Ten Cities* (New York: Union of American Hebrew Congregations, 1962); Judith R. Kramer and Seymour Leventman, *Children of the Gilded Ghetto* (New Haven, Conn.: Yale University Press, 1961).

drawn from many sources, reveals that *approximately 500,000 Jews currently reside in suburbia*. By 1975 the figure is expected to be doubled, climbing from one Jew out of eleven to one out of six. The attraction toward the city's periphery is almost irresistible to the economically able.

Findings from the most recent nationwide poll of Protestant councils of churches disclose that Jews are now well established in the suburbs of more than thirty metropolitan areas.[2] It was learned that the largest number of suburban synagogues are to be found around New York, Chicago, Philadelphia, Cleveland, Washington, Los Angeles, and Miami. But there are also Hebrew congregations in the suburbs of Providence, Boston, Detroit, Pittsburgh, Baltimore, Denver, Springfield (Massachusetts), and elsewhere. Reliable information supports the fact of Jewish residence in suburbia, the postwar dimensions of this development, and the mounting strength of the faith group. At many points these most recent data corroborate and augment Albert Gordon's earlier findings. Apparently many denominational leaders are concerned over the latest arrivals into the traditional stronghold of Protestantism. These leaders do not quite know what the change means. Hence a cordial welcome does not always await the new faith groups.

Gordon fears that suburbia may become solely the home of *all middle-class* Jews. Already a pronounced trend points to this possibility. Many Jews, along with other Americans, have risen in the economic scale. With high economic achievement has come the temptation consciously or unconsciously to adopt as normative the secular values deemed essential to upward mobility. This worldly attitude plays havoc with the suburban synagogue. It worries the rabbinate and places traditional faith in jeopardy.

American Jews will continue to reside predominantly in metropolitan areas, urges Gordon, but residence in suburbia will greatly increase. At the present time 96 per cent of the Jews are happy and satisfied with life in the suburbs. What worries Gordon is the possibility that the Jews will become ghettoized in suburbia. If this eventuality materializes the outcome is merely a shift from an ethnic neighborhood within the city to another area of concentration of Jewish population in the suburbs. Evidently some Jews wish to be amalgamated into the general population but under conditions favorable to their own religious self-determination and expression. They desire to have their matzo and eat it too. Perhaps these are mutually exclusive expectations—

[2] Frederick A. Shippey, "Religious Bodies in Suburbia" (Unpublished manuscript, 1960).

to blend into a general population and yet to remain distinctive from it. Jews wish to identify with other Americans but without giving up their Jewishness. It remains to be seen whether this can be done.

SUBURBAN ROMAN CATHOLICISM

Historically speaking Roman Catholicism is indigenous to the cities of the United States rather than to suburbia. The faith's real strength long has been concentrated primarily in the ethnic colonies whose population originated in Ireland and southern Europe. These ethnic colonies were city situated. Beyond this only a few minor settlements appeared on the outskirts of American cities in early times. Strictly speaking, Roman Catholicism has held only a tiny beachhead in the suburbs for many years. Numerically this outpost has been insignificant. Roman Catholicism became and remained the church of the American city's working class. Greeley reminds the reader that even as late as 1946 66 per cent of the Catholic population in the United States were manual workers.[3] This proportion contrasts with the estimated 45 per cent of Protestantism found in the same socioeconomic stratum.

Now a vast revolution is taking place. A new situation has developed since World War II. To the startled Protestant, there has occurred a spectacular out-movement of Roman Catholic families from the city to suburbia. Indeed, Donald Campion and Dennis Clark estimate that *two and a half million Roman Catholics* have been transplanted to the suburbs since the early 1940's.[4] Moreover, this figure takes on additional meaning when it is realized that approximately one American Roman Catholic out of ten currently resides in the suburbs.

Another source of statistics touching this important change is found in the monographic studies of suburban life. These technical "biographies" of newly established towns call attention to *a new principle of residential settlement;* i.e., housing made available to families on the basis of percentage proportions among the faiths in the city. Although heretofore Jews and Roman Catholics were not numerous in suburbia, under the new principle they now were given a strong beachhead on the periphery of the city. This is evident from a scrutiny of new communities which have sprung up since the end of World War II. One finds significant percentages of Roman Catholics in the local population; e.g., Milpitas, California, 23 per cent; Park Forest, Illinois,

[3] *The Church and the Suburbs*, p. 51.
[4] See "So You're Moving to Suburbia," *America* (April 21, 1956).

25 per cent; and Levittown, New York, 45.3 per cent. Older suburbs such as Greenbelt, Maryland, and Newton, Massachusetts, report 20.9 and 40 per cent Roman Catholic respectively. Similar information is available for many additional communities. Shirley Greene, a Protestant writer, speaks of new Roman Catholic churches in the suburbs of Detroit, St. Louis, Dayton, Baltimore, and Evansville.

A dramatic example of the establishment of Catholic parishes can disclose the dynamic shape of this amazing faith change in suburbia. During an eleven-year period following World War II in metropolitan Los Angeles alone, 70 new parishes and 138 new parochial schools have been opened, according to Greeley. Nearly all this new Catholic work has occurred in the suburbs. Moreover, the diocese has expanded from 690,000 to 1,243,500 souls in the last decade. Many Roman Catholics are recruited from among the newcomers to California who are arriving at the rate of 55,000 a year. Greeley indicates that what already has taken place in Los Angeles will happen in *ten* other Catholic dioceses of the United States within a few years.[5] Indeed, the beginnings are evident in some dioceses now.

Moreover, a study conducted among Protestant councils of churches, embracing sixty-nine metropolitan areas in the United States reveals that Roman Catholic parishes have already been established in the suburbs of fifty-one. If this research coverage is approximately typical and a projection covering unsurveyed places is made, then Catholics now reside in the suburbs of three American metropolitan areas out of four. Protestant leaders contacted in this study almost universally pointed to the remarkably expanded work of Catholicism in the suburbs. Indeed Catholic parish strength really has accumulated in depth around the large industrial cities such as Chicago, New York, Philadelphia, Detroit, Pittsburgh, St. Louis, Buffalo, Providence, Rochester, and Syracuse. Some observers point out that the great number of incoming Negro residents to the inner city has accelerated the out-movement of Roman Catholics, in many cases seriously depleting old inner-city Catholic parishes.

There are several reasons why Roman Catholicism is gaining prominence in the new suburbs. Second and third generation descendents of foreign-born parentage recently have achieved higher levels educationally, occupationally, and economically. Aided in educational advancement by the bene-

[5] *Op. cit.,* p. 65n.

fits of the G.I. Bill, these fortunate people are no longer content to remain in crowded urban neighborhoods and inadequate housing. Their newly achieved economic status makes possible a shift into better residential areas, including the edge of the city. Pressures to leave the old neighborhood also come from another direction. The large in-migration of Negro population to the inner-city section of many industrial communities has hastened the breaking up of many of the older ethnic colonies. What is a port of entry for Negroes becomes the port of exit for people who have improved their economic status.

Protestant leaders are becoming increasingly aware of this new situation. Evidently Greeley is correct in underscoring this revolutionary shift in the place of residence for second and third generation ethnic groups. The move to the suburbs is interpreted here as progress toward material success, toward recognition as Americans. The newly erected Roman Catholic churches mean that the institutions are following their people in order to serve them in the new residential developments. This out-movement reduces noticeably the erstwhile Protestant potential in many communities and calls for a revised pattern of denominational thinking to match the new situation. In many suburbs, however, there are more Protestants than ever before, yet many Roman Catholics now are living among them. This introduces a new element in the milieu. Thus Protestantism is compelled to plan its work more carefully.

While Father Greeley's analysis of American suburban life is conspicuously well balanced, profound, and optimistic, he skillfully calls attention to some unsolved problems. A typical Greeley caveat can illustrate the point:

Two beautiful worlds are growing up in the suburbs. One is the world of the gadget, the lovely world of color TV, deep-freezes, big hi-fis, two cars in the garage and tranquilizing drugs in the medicine cabinet. This world is not of itself bad. The other world is the world of the presumably spiritual: the world of the crowded churches, long lines at the Communion rail, CFM (Catholic Family Movement) meetings, good will, and noble intentions. This world is not of itself enough. The basic trouble is that few suburbanites see any connection between the world of the gadget and the world of the spirit. It never occurs to them to ask whether there might not be some incongruity in the St. Christopher Medal and the Cadillac or the penetential ashes of Lent on the side of a Florida swimming pool. The intimate relationship between the Holy Eucharist and the new migrant in the heart of the city is not evident to them. They are not aware of the connection between their own abundance and starvation in India.[6]

The Roman Catholic Church cannot and does not take lightly her responsibility to serve the newcomers who now have taken up residence on the outer edges of cities. As more and more Roman Catholics become suburbanites that faith is placed under great pressure from new cultural directions. There is spiritual challenge in this annoying problem. The ethical issues demand solution.

The remarkable change has encouraged Catholic leaders now to view suburbia as a promising opportunity for an extension of the faith. Today, one suburbanite out of nine is alleged to be Roman Catholic. Indeed, across the United States four new Roman Catholic churches are reportedly opened each week—many of them on the outskirts of the city. Thus even the general picture is a strongly optimistic one for the faith. Almost everywhere one turns parishes are struggling to finance recently constructed edifices and parochial school buildings. The out-movement of Roman Catholics has given suburbia a new look. Not only are Catholic buildings appearing on the skyline of suburbia but also the appearance of Catholics in the membership of Kiwanis, Rotary, Lions, et cetera, and on the boards of education, community planning, and other important local policy-making groups furnish a powerful reminder of the revolution in religious composition which is occurring. Since World War II Roman Catholics have gained higher and higher visibility in the suburbs.

How propitious is the future? A conservative forecast is likely to be of interest here. According to Campion and Clark Roman Catholics residing in the American suburbs will reach between 5, and 8,000,000 by 1980. This represents approximately one fifth of the members of this faith group in the United States. The phenomenal increase which *doubles the present number* is expected to be focused in ten Catholic dioceses, although noteworthy suburban growth is expected to occur also in other geographical locations.

The Catholic Church already has begun to exercise care in the selection of curates and pastors for suburban parishes. Younger men are strongly preferred. These handpicked clerical leaders are aware of the emergent forces in the suburban community, and they expect to develop new forms of Catholic family life in order to mitigate the frictions which inevitably will be engendered when groups with divergent value systems live together. Greeley,

[6] *Ibid.,* pp. 205-6.

a suburban priest, already has launched the Catholic Family Movement in order to meet this very problem. Its goal is to fortify religiously families living in the new situation. With characteristic thoroughness the Roman Catholic Church has begun a long-range, large-scale program of reaching suburban residents throughout the United States. Possibly this pacesetting example can evoke prompt action on the part of Protestantism. The future in suburbia belongs to those who prepare for it.

SECTS IN SUBURBIA

One of the startling discoveries emerging from the research study— "Religious Bodies in Suburbia" is the variety and abundance of sect groups newly rooted in suburbia. Traditionally sects are regarded as being indigenous to the inner city where they have prospered like the proverbial green bay tree and have multiplied ad infinitum. They emerge from among the urban poor. This congenial city environment and this proliferating process are public knowledge. By way of contrast, the suburb in the past has afforded principally the "old line" Protestant denominations a secluded place in which to carry on a tranquil ministry far removed from the extreme expressions of emotional religion and the esoteric patterns of belief. What a shock and surprise now to discover that the dynamic sect has invaded suburban territory with its disturbing brand of religion. Who believed that it would ever get there? Moreover, it is prospering in the new environment.

Before proceeding further it is desirable to note that the definition of "sect" utilized here derives from Elmer T. Clark's *The Small Sects in America*.[7] According to Clark sects are those religious bodies which exhibit, among other characteristics, pessimism (adventist), perfectionism-subjectivism (holiness), charism (pentecostal), communism (Shakers, et cetera), legalism (orthodoxy), egocentrism (New Thought), and esotericalism (mystic). The appearance of such traits in extreme form suffices here as a general or working definition. This understanding is consistent with the views of H. Richard Niebuhr, Liston Pope, J. Milton Yinger, and kindred scholars. Possibly such clarification here can reduce ambiguity in the discussion which follows.

The survey cited above reveals that the tranquil suburban world is undergoing another remarkable change. Only two metropolitan areas reported no sect groups in suburbia—Great Falls, Montana, and Madison, Wisconsin.

[7] Rev. ed.; Nashville: Abingdon Press, 1957.

Undoubtedly there is some other urbanized territory in the same classification. Within the scope of the research project, however, all the remaining areas, or 97.1 per cent, report at least one or more suburbs containing sect groups. What appears evident is that the larger the major city the more numerous and varied are the sects which appear in its suburbs. The presence of sects in suburbia piques the reader's curiosity. He wants to know about the nature and distribution of these religious bodies.

Among the sect groups now found in suburbia are Advent Christian, Advent Baptist, Apostolic, Assembly of God, Bible Presbyterian, Christian and Missionary Alliance, Church of Christ, Church of God, Free Will Baptist, Free Methodist, Full Gospel, Holiness, Jehovah's Witnesses, Non-denominational, Open Bible, Pentecostal Assemblies, Primitive Methodist, Salvation Army, Universalist,[8] Unity, and Volunteers of America. At least *fifty different sects* were specifically named in the survey responses. Individual sect groups are geographically distributed to the suburbs of the 69 reporting metropolitan areas as follows: Assembly of God, 38; Christian and Missionary Alliance, 32; Christian Science, 28; Adventist, 27; Pentecostal, 24; Jehovah's Witnesses, 23; Mennonite, 19; and Unitarian, 18. Moreover, sect groups not mentioned yet but which are already established in the suburbs of ten or more U. S. metropolitan areas, include Apostolic, Holiness, Salvation Army, and Church of Christ. No sect is found everywhere. The Assembly of God comes closest to achieving nationwide distribution. Most sects possess prominent regional penetrations; e.g., Apostolic Churches in the Midwest; Unity on the West Coast; and Free Will Baptists in the South. The out-of-city trend has grown strong since the end of World War II.

Clearly the "capital" of sectdom in the United States is in the Los Angeles suburbs. At least eighteen sects claim major concentrations of adherents there. In runner-up position is the suburbs of Philadelphia, which appears to be the Eastern capital of sectdom. In the Midwest Detroit is the regional capital, but the suburbs of larger Ohio and Indiana cities also make a strong bid for the honors. In the Rocky Mountain region the leafy outskirts of Denver vie with Detroit in playing host to the sects. Moreover, many cities of both East and West Coasts report hospitable suburbs for heavy concentrations of sects. Thus, the dispersion seems to be nationwide, with a few major urban centers accounting for the largest concentrations.

Evidently Protestantism is challenged on many sides in suburbia today.

[8] Unitarians and Universalists merged in 1962.

With half a hundred sects already in suburbia it is academic to ask whether Protestantism approves the newcomers. Wisdom suggests an inquiry about this new brand of Protestantism which is emerging from the sectarian wing. Jews, Roman Catholics, and sect adherents wonder whether the old-line denominations can match the new conditions of suburban life with adequate spiritual resources.

NEGROES IN SUBURBIA

A scarcely noticed development is the mounting flow of Negroes toward suburbia. Hence the reader is likely to find interesting a summary of available data as reported by selected writers on suburbia, an evaluation of population trends, a delineation of the new status of the suburban Negro, and the relevant observations of local executives of metropolitan councils of churches.

While extensive discussions of suburban residence of nonwhite persons are relatively few in number, some allusions to the subject are very significant. Andrew Greeley regards the Negro primarily as a resident of the inner city. Throughout *The Church and the Suburbs* this author shows no awareness of an out-movement to suburbia among Negroes. Instead, what he highlights is the declining fortunes of inner-city Roman Catholic parishes caused by expanding Negro settlement within the city. Negroes are considered to be overwhelmingly Protestant. Albert Gordon similarly delineates the fortunes of the nonwhite population in *Jews in Suburbia*. Surprisingly, however, he records also the difficulty encountered by a Negro family seeking to establish a home in the huge Levittown community of eastern Pennsylvania. According to Gordon Jewish residents, among others, befriended the Negro family during the crisis. Robert C. Wood in *Suburbia: Its People and Their Politics* acknowledges that some Negroes currently reside in suburbia. Indeed he applies the term "gilded ghettos" in describing those suburban communities where minority ethnic groups have procured housing. These places often merely continue the old urban patterns of discrimination, forcing the people to huddle into ethnic settlements. Where such patterns prevail it is only the city reproducing itself in the suburbs.

In *The Exurbanites* Spectorsky observes that Negroes reside among prominent exurbanites in Bucks County, Pennsylvania, and are accepted strictly on the basis of personal competence and individual personality. A perusal of Dobriner's *The Suburban Community* discloses some awareness of the

Negro's shift into suburbia. Despite brevity of treatment, attention is called to some pertinent facts. Three times as many Negroes live in the inner city as currently reside in suburbia. Reasons cited for the small proportion of suburbanites are essentially socioeconomic. This view is shared by other writers.

Robert A. Futterman's *The Future of Our Cities* devotes an entire chapter to a discussion of Negroes in suburban life.[9] Here attention is focused upon the improved economic fortunes which have opened the way for Negro suburban residence. The building of better roads for motor car use and the federal government backed mortgage loans for the purchase of new homes enter the picture significantly here. A noteworthy alteration of the national ethos has appeared. Today a private house for every family is urged. Minority groups are caught up in these alterations. At first a large lower middle class with many upwardly mobile persons did not exist among Negroes. The condition has changed, however, since World War II. Now Negroes are pushing their way into suburban communities. The shifting of industry to suburban locations now furnishes the working-class Negro an additional reason for migrating to suburbia. Futterman regards the population explosion and outward migration as a mixed blessing since it yields Italian suburbs, Jewish suburbs, Protestant suburbs, and now Negro suburbs. Although this statement has the element of exaggeration in it, the emergence of distinctive ethnic settlements is realistic. Oscar Handlin in *The New-comers* has provided, among other insights, a sophisticated analysis of motives which drive the Negro out of the city into suburbia. Paradoxically the Futterman thesis receives fuller development in Handlin where it is explored with reference to the New York metropolitan area.

In *Negro and White in Connecticut Town* Frank F. Lee provides an account of the difficulties with respect to housing and race relations which confront the Negro in a small Connecticut town and its suburbs.[10] Two per cent of the population is nonwhite. Here in microcosm are found many of the tough problems which are well known to large city residents. Dorothy Slade Williams' doctoral thesis, "Ecology of Negro Communities in Los Angeles County: 1940-1959," delineates Negro residence and other characteristics in 153 census tracts within Los Angeles County.[11] However, only

[9] New York: Doubleday & Company, Inc., 1961.
[10] New York: Bookman Associates, Inc., 1961.
[11] University of Southern California, 1961.

36 of the tracts are located outside the city of Los Angeles. Substantial concentrations of Negroes are found in the suburban communities of Firestone Park, Long Beach, Monrovia, Pasadena, Santa Monica, Watts, and Willowbrook. Smaller percentages reside in Torrance, Dominguez, Gardena, Duarte, Belevedere Gardens, Norwalk, Whittier, and Hawthorne. Since 1940 Negro suburban residents in Los Angeles County—excluding the city of Los Angeles—have jumped from 11,435 to 124,719, yielding a net increase of 113,284 persons or more than 1,000 per cent. Both the Connecticut and California studies report Negroes in the suburbs at the present time and call attention to the increase of Negro suburbanites since World War II.

Continuing the discussion of population trends, one turns attention to an exciting report about Negro residence in suburbia. Abroad in the world is a fresh democratic outlook, possibly originating in a new philosophy of housing and employment. During World War II provisions were made which permitted Negroes to reside in suburbia when a member of the household was employed in war industry; e.g., shipbuilding; tanks, munitions, and aircraft manufacture. Major industrial installations were dispersed widely across the United States permitting Negroes to be housed in the public projects nearly everywhere. This World War II policy established an important precedent with continuing ramifications today.

Under the critical conditions of World War II noteworthy changes occurred respecting the housing of workers. Katherine Archibald described working conditions in the shipyards on the Pacific coast devoting several chapters especially to the plight of ethnic groups. From firsthand observations as professor-turned-plant-employee she recounts the encouragement and improvement of status which eventually came both to Negroes and to female workers in an industry heretofore virtually closed to both population groups. The wartime emergency compelled provision for the suburban residence of Negroes. Some newly erected public housing projects so opened were temporary; others were permanent. This proved to be the initiation of a new arrangement in American society.

Around Portland, Oregon, for example, approximately 12,000 Negroes took up residence in suburbia. Similarly, Negroes were housed in the suburbs of San Francisco, Seattle, San Diego, and numerous other World War II "boom" communities across the nation. Thus, thousands of Negroes tasted life on the city's periphery for the first time as employees of essential war plants. This was a new basis, a far cry from the old pattern of symbiosis.

The new pattern carries over into the present decade. Today the Negro regards it as a normal part of his democratic heritage to choose a place of residence on the grounds of what he desires and can afford. Like new wine this contemporary opportunity has burst some old wineskins.

The national picture is an interesting one. "Trends and Composition," a study I completed of 2,138 suburban places in the United States reveals that Negroes reside in 1,731 of them. If the research project can be regarded as fairly representative of the general situation, then four American suburbs out of five now have nonwhite residents. Density of nonwhite residents within an individual community ranges from a few families to thousands of persons. *Today an estimated 2,250,000 Negroes live under suburban circumstances.* One Negro out of seven now makes his home in the American suburbs. This amazing phenomenon reminds the reader of the unnoticed outmovement of nonwhite population into the city's periphery. By 1975, according to present trends, at least 5,000,000 Negroes will reside in suburbia.

Experiments with mixed and/or all-Negro housing developments are surprisingly numerous: Florida's Washington Shores, Richmond Heights, and Bunche Park; Pennsylvania's Concord Park and Country Estates; Illinois' Rolling Plain; Ohio's Greenvale; California's River Terrace; Georgia's Koinonia Farm near Americus; and others. Such undertakings signify the strong desire of the Negro for better housing conditions. Like so many other Americans, he is attracted to the city's periphery.

Another spectacular alteration is the changed status of the Negro in suburbia. Douglass (*The Suburban Trend*), Lundberg (*Leisure: A Suburban Study*), Tunnard and Reed (*American Skyline*), and other scholars, refer to the symbiotic status of those who took up suburban residence before World War II. The old pattern of Negro dwellers in suburbia can be described as *symbiotic residence.* From the nineteenth into the twentieth century many thousands of Negroes worked as maids, cooks, chauffeurs, governesses, and yard boys on the large suburban estates. Other wealthy homes employed Negroes to aid in the management of the household and/or in the care of the children. While some Negroes lived upon the estate itself, most of them found it necessary to procure a home elsewhere—usually in a neighboring town. Vestigial remains of this symbiotic way of life persist even today in a few elite suburbs near major cities—New York, Chicago, Philadelphia, and elsewhere. Frequently the Negro lived in an adjacent, poorer suburb rather than in the community where he was employed. This

53

symbiotic arrangement led Tunnard and Reed to observe that "beside every Scarsdale there is a Tuckahoe." [12] Lundberg and Douglass echo this comment, showing how prevalent symbiotic residence once was.

Today this way of life has all but vanished. The spectacular rise in wage scales and the skyrocketing property and income taxes have enforced changes. The large estates have disappeared into college campuses, research laboratories, eleemosynary institutions, industrial parks, and housing subdivisions. Such radical changes in land use and in style of life have opened up the way for a new pattern of residence in suburbia for Negroes which amounts to a social revolution.

The emergent pattern of suburban living can fittingly be called *democratic residence*. A diminishing number of Negroes are now employed on estates. Indeed, the Negro has become educated in the professions of law, medicine, dentistry, pedagogy, engineering, research, and business administration. He has risen above and broken out of the menial vocations previously assigned to him. Raw prejudice against his entrance into many high-prestige occupations is on the wane. Along with this general improvement of occupational statue have come concomitant gains in socioeconomic circumstances. Today the Negro is able financially to purchase a home in the better residential areas. He can afford commutation to work via train, bus, or private automobile. The choice is his. Thus, suburban residence is on the new basis of any full-fledged professional or businessman regardless of ethnic background. Just as the Caucasian seeks a suitable separation of place of work from the place of residence so also does the Negro. Both races wish to escape the noise, nuisance, and debilitating effects of city life. Today the Negro possesses the savoir faire, the education, the financial resources, and the consuming desire to settle among the advantaged residents of the suburban community. He now has the requisite socioeconomic credentials. Moreover, he shops in the same stores, banks in the same fiscal institutions, and utilizes the same public parking facilities.

When one turns to a report from Protestant councils of churches a surprise is at hand. Replies deriving from sixty-six United States metropolitan areas becomes the basis for generalization here. Thirty out of sixty-six reporting metropolitan areas indicated that nonwhite congregations already are situated in suburbia. Possibly additional ethnic churches were overlooked. In a few

[12] *American Skyline,* pp. 259-60.

instances the nonwhite congregations comprise Japanese, Chinese, Korean, and so forth. An overwhelming number are Negro, however, and this fact should be borne in mind throughout the present discussion. It is estimated that at least one half of the major metropolitan areas reporting in this Council of Churches study already have nonwhite religious congregations located in suburbia. Definite knowledge of 323 nonwhite congregations is reported in the suburbs of thirty metropolitan areas. If such a ratio holds for the entire United States, there are probably *more than 1,000 nonwhite congregations already located in American suburbs today!* An average of eleven suburban nonwhite congregations exists in the major metropolitan areas of America. Many Protestant observers believe that this trend is gaining strength.

From this modest survey touching Negro residence in suburbia, the reader can gain an impression of its important dimensions. Protestant leaders find in the trends not only a fresh challenge to the ecumenical spirit but also an opportunity to achieve a better understanding of the modern world. Ultimately these significant alterations will affect the fortunes of most of the denominations.

BLUE-COLLAR WORKERS IN SUBURBIA

From the widely publicized discussion of Park Forest, Crestwood Heights, Greenbelt, and Levittown many people have received the strong but mistaken impression that hard-driving junior executives, young engineers, and kindred white-collar personnel on-the-make typify the residents of suburbia. This unfortunate stereotype has been so generally "sold" to the American people that intelligent persons, surrounded by contrary evidence, meekly accept the organization-man image as if it were a divine revelation. However, relief from this distorted situation is on the horizon. Penetrating studies by Bennett Berger, Walter Martin, William Dobriner, and others are helping to correct the one-sided reports. Thus it is necessary to turn to an unnoticed change: Manual workers have moved to suburbia.

Actually thousands of blue-collar workers currently reside in suburbia. This is conspicuously a development of the post World War II period. It began during the war years when great numbers of semiskilled and skilled workers deployed themselves across regional lines into the great centers of essential industry. Robert J. Havighurst and H. G. Morgan (*Social History of a War-Boom Community*) and Katherine Archibald (*Wartime Shipyard*) are among the scholars who have explored important aspects of this remarkable blue-collar emigration.[13] Shipyards and aircraft manufacturers attracted workers and their families to the West Coast. Thus the labor market shifted to meet the needs at war industrial centers situated in Alabama, California, Florida, New York, Illinois, Texas, and elsewhere. After the war the people remained in the community. Today between 20, to 25,000,000 blue-collar workers exist in the United States. How many of these manual workers reside currently in suburbia? According to the best available estimates the figure for the middle 1960's approximates 10,000,000. This represents a phenomenal increase since 1940.

The deployment of workers from one region to another yielded numerous large-scale housing emergencies. Although the private housing industry did its best, the efforts failed to cope with the situation. Admittedly metropolitan areas could not possibly house the hordes of incoming industrial workers and their families. Thus, to meet this crisis large-scale public housing projects of varying types, financed by federal funds, were erected with awesome swiftness. Some facilities were temporary, destined to be dismantled soon after the war ended. Other structures were permanent. Some projects were erected within the city boundaries, but many were constructed in suburban territory.

Possibly a western metropolitan community can serve as an illustration of the phenomena. A quarter of a million people moved into the Portland-Vancouver area during the period 1940-45. Despite the extraordinary efforts of private enterprise in the emergency, it was necessary to erect 32,000 dwelling units under the auspices of the Federal Housing Authority and to finance these facilities largely by government subsidy. Approximately 22,000 units, or 68.8 per cent, were built in the suburban territory around Portland and Vancouver. An additional 5,000 beds were provided in temporary dormitory-type structures. Thousands of families and individuals occupying these suburban housing facilities shopped in suburban stores, patronized the suburban post office, sent children to suburban schools, attended suburban churches, commuted to the distant industrial plant, and otherwise experienced life on the urban periphery. Here many people caught a first glimpse of life in suburbia and developed a liking for it. It is possible that among thousands of blue-collar workers there arose the hope and resolve to own a house some day outside the city. What occurred in the Portland suburbs

[13] Havighurst and Morgan (New York: Longmans, Green & Company, Inc., 1951); Archibald (Berkeley, Calif.: University of California Press, 1947).

probably happened measurably in other wartime suburban housing projects across the nation during subsequent years. The taste for suburban residence acquired during the war or thereafter is being realized today in contemporary America by thousands of blue-collar workers.

Thus, eventually opportunities opened up, permitting manual workers to acquire a piece of the suburban dream. This insight emerges from an exploration of several lines of evidence: Residents in "new tract" and kindred housing; residents in the rural-urban fringe; and residents in mobile houses or trailer homes. From these three sources data support the observation that blue-collar workers are already firmly established in suburban territory. Today more manual workers reside in suburbia than ever before. This new group usually is overlooked and/or underrated in importance by church leaders. The facts warrant a change of viewpoint.

With respect to residence in a *new tract suburb,* the analysis of Bennett Berger in *Working-Class Suburb* serves as an interesting illustration. It is a study of one hundred auto workers and their families residing in Milpitas, California. Among semiskilled workers these employees are the highest paid. Most adults are under fifty years of age and possess only slightly more than an elementary school education. Most homes have children of school age. Seventy per cent are Protestant in background or in current affiliation. Only 23 per cent are Roman Catholic. There are no Jews in the sample. All residents are blue-collar workers, and 87 per cent of them grew up in this type of household. All are home owners. In summarizing the study of auto workers Berger pointed out:

Membership and activities in formal associations are rare; so is semi-formal mutual visiting between couples. There is little evidence of pronounced striving, status anxiety, or orientation to the future. They neither give parties nor go to them. Their tastes and preferences seem untouched by the images of "suburbia" portrayed in the mass media.

These suburbanites have not, to any marked extent, taken on the patterns of behavior and belief associated with white-collar suburbs.

To place a Ford worker, a postman, and a junior engineer at Lockheed in the same "class" represents, if ever anything did, the disappearance of class difference in America.[14]

[14] *Working-Class Suburb,* pp. 92, 92-93, 97.

What Berger succeeds in communicating is that the many blue-collar workers currently residing in suburbia do not reveal the alleged characteristics of the suburban stereotype portrayed in mass media. Rather they appear as normal working people whose value system includes thrift, industry, and happiness of an immediate sort. They are puzzled by the abuse heaped upon suburban living. For them suburbia affords unmistakable advantages. About whom are the critics really speaking?

Evidently, residence in the *rural-urban fringe* is a topic of considerable interest to scholars. Among the research projects which can be listed are Dewey's investigation of Milwaukee's fringe and Blizzard's analysis of the outskirts of Williamsport, Pennsylvania. For our purpose, however, materials from Walter T. Martin's study of the fringe around Eugene and Springfield, Oregon, will suffice to illustrate the phenomena. Martin recorded the occupations of the heads of 832 households. This process revealed that more than 70 per cent of the persons gainfully employed are in the manual occupations. Skilled and semiskilled persons predominate. This finding contrasts sharply with the data treated in Spectorsky's *The Exurbanites,* where most people are heavily concentrated in the high-salaried professional categories. Home ownership on the edge of the two Oregon cities reaches approximately 85 per cent. Income levels for a single year 1948 are revealing. Approximately 71 per cent of the gainfully employed received less than 5,000 dollars income. In summary Martin's study shows that many blue-collar workers reside in suburbia and that they predominate numerically in those portions of suburban territory which are defined as "rural-urban fringe" by Dewey, Rodehaver, Blizzard, and others. This finding is of great importance to Protestant clergymen and administrators who want to discover the church's relevance to all parts of suburbia.

Finally, *residence in trailers* on the part of blue-collar workers completes the range of the present discussion. More than 2,000,000 Americans from all walks of life reside currently in house trailers. An estimated 10,000 trailer parks are in existence, most of them situated in suburbia. Although it is acknowledged that some white-collar people own and use trailers also, our focus here rests upon manual employees so housed. Blue-collar workers during and following World War II discovered the advantages of a home on wheels. Indeed, the James R. Noland and Russell R. Dynes study presents the findings from 239 interviews in a pamphlet entitled *Mobile Industrial Workers and the Church* illustrating in microcosm the problems of trailer life as seen in Ohio's Pike County atomic processing plant.[15] Here the spotlight is put upon men who built the installation. Similarly, mobile construction workers were also attracted to Oak Ridge, Hanford, Los Alamos, Savannah, and Paducah. In Ohio more than thirty different kinds of skilled and semiskilled employment are represented among the blue-collar workers: Cement finishers, welders, plumbers, painters, crane operators, truck drivers, and so on. Surprisingly, 80 per cent of the adults are church members, predominately Protestant. Only 9 per cent are Roman Catholic. Jews are rarely found in trailer facilities. The familiar sight of trailer parks situated in the outskirts of American cities should remind the reader that blue-collar workers also reside in suburbia. According to the best estimate available, more than 1,000,000 blue-collar workers occupy houses on wheels.

Possibly these three illustrations (Berger, Martin, and Noland and Dynes) suffice for an understanding of the numerical prominence of blue-collar workers in modern suburbia. Robert C. Wood in *Suburbia: Its People and Their Politics* presents a study of 106 suburban communities situated in the metropolitan territory of St. Louis, San Francisco, Los Angeles, Philadelphia, Pittsburgh, and Chicago. One important phase of this analysis included the percentages of white-collar persons found in the total employment. When one inverts Wood's analysis, the relevance of the findings for the present discussion becomes more apparent. What is remarkable is that 80 out of the 106 suburbs reported 40 to 100 per cent of the gainfully employed persons to be in the *blue-collar category*. Indeed only two suburbs show less than 20 per cent in the blue-collar category. These facts disclose a prominence of blue-collar suburban residents which constitute a disturbing challenge to the Whyte stereotype. This is an important discovery for the denominations, inasmuch as manual workers still comprise the backbone of Protestant church life throughout the United States. Suburbia is but a continuation of Protestantism's wider ministry to people who work with their hands.

SUMMARY

The purpose of the present chapter is to focus attention upon several important but perhaps little-noticed changes which have occurred in suburbia during recent decades. Five newcomer invading groups have been briefly described—Jews, Roman Catholics, sects, Negroes, and blue-collar

[15] New York: National Council of Churches, 1957.

workers. Such interesting aspects as current status, general trends, future forecasts, and impact upon Protestantism's fortunes were discussed. If beachheads can be established successfully by such groups, then cannot everybody eventually reside in suburbia? It is too soon to answer this significant question conclusively. Certainly the new population elements have participated in a post World War II development which has altered drastically the face of old suburbia. This is a phenomenon of major proportions.

Several considerations emerge. The improved socioeconomic status of the newcomer groups is evident. Cultural ascent comes as a result of the right combination of desire for change plus requisite economic ability. Higher socioeconomic achievement plays a powerful part, fostering within the outgroups the belief that its people are becoming more fully American as they move out of the city and up the salary scale. Taken all together these newcomers disclose how incomplete and how inaccurate is the organization man stereotype as a description of American suburban life. Taken individually each population element craves a fuller portion of the American dream and therefore is ready to fight for the right to live in suburbia. Consequently the current situation is mined with tension and conflict possibilities. Yet social friction is indigenous to change in suburbia. Hence some observers of urban life believe that the "melting pot" has now shifted from the city to the modern suburb. In chapters which follow the dynamic implications of the aforementioned changes will receive further exploration.

III

The Variety of Suburban Residents

More than 60,000,000 Americans now reside under suburban circumstances. This is a great many people. It would be a miracle if they possessed identical tastes, attitudes, and outlooks. Hailing from the remote corners of the nation, the newcomers bring along not only their household goods but also their ways of speaking, spending, thinking, and living. They bring their customs, patterns of action, class orientation, and regional outlook. The "Okies" are not the only people who carry the home state along with them. The sheer accumulation of families of such diverse backgrounds yields a "melting pot" of humanity the like of which hardly has been seen in the city and surely has not been observed in the suburbs before. Scholars have commented upon the varying character of suburban residents. Charles Sears is aware of differences among metropolitan dwellers: "The city is exhilarating to the young, challenging to the prepared, albeit enervating to the weak, frightening to the old and relentlessly hard on the hindermost. If only man never felt fatigue and never grew old, is the long single sigh of the city."[1] This observation has a surprising relevance to suburbia. Since the city's leafy outskirts contain many kinds of residents, the Protestant church is challenged to cope with a wide range of human situations.

Elsewhere, attention has already been called to several new suburban population groups—Jews, Roman Catholics, sects, Negroes, and blue-collar workers. Now the analysis can be pressed much further in order to discover

[1] *City Man*, pp. 11-12.

61

subgroupings of residents which share common cultural orientations important to organized religion. Types of suburbanites emerging from this analysis can be of great interest to the Protestant pastor, aiding him as he ministers to the people's condition in parish life. The type should not be "invented" but rather should emerge naturally out of a penetrating analysis of suburban life. Such aspects of down-to-earth suburban reality furnish insights to the Protestant pastor. Altogether the discussion can help answer the important query, Who resides in suburbia?

HOW TO CLASSIFY SUBURBANITES

Just how one can classify suburban residents into types poses a question which evokes considerable interest pro and con. There appear to be at least two ways of undertaking the task. The *theoretical* approach relies chiefly upon ideas and logic blended together in order to procure a rational construct or type. The *empirical* approach emphasizes the utilization of concrete data on people residing in particular suburban communities. Despite the contrast, neither approach can be dismissed as right or wrong. Both are legitimate. It is a matter of levels of abstraction. The proper criterion for evaluation, however, is really the current need of the reader. Is he seeking a theoretical view of the situation? This means a general view of life, seeing things broadly. Or do his needs focus in the practical sphere? If the latter, then he will benefit from the concreteness and local visibility of the empirical types.

A Theoretical Approach. Let attention be turned first to the theoretical models. Brief reference can be made to several proposals, illustrating how Everett C. Hughes, Robert Park, and William Dobriner approach the task. Possibly these three will suffice to underscore the importance of theoretical considerations in developing a typology of suburbanites. Even in the most thoroughgoing empirical study theory cannot be totally disregarded.

Everett Hughes' perceptive treatment of "Personality Types and the Division of Labor" presents a typology based upon occupations.[2] Whether the occupation is classified under the rubric of missionary, professional, business, art, skilled trades, or just "jobs," a culture and a technique come to be associated with the vocation. Occupation influences the individual's

[2] Paul K. Hatt and Albert J. Reiss, Jr., editors, *Reader in Urban Sociology* (New York: Free Press of Glencoe, 1951), pp. 592-603. See also "The Study of Occupations," *Sociology Today,* edited by Robert K. Merton, *et al.* (New York: Basic Books, Inc., 1959), pp. 442-58.

life organization. If the period of initiation into the occupation is long and arduous, then a greater amount of culture and technique is associated with it. On the other hand, a short initiatory process yields a shallow culture. In any case, Hughes indicates that a set of attitudes and wishes have gathered about the vocation and eventually constellate about a particular occupation within it. In part it is a way of thinking and behaving. This includes ethics, etiquette, and often a group within the occupation which is organized to perpetuate and to defend its interests. The so-called division of labor in the United States has yielded various vocational specialists. For this reason, according to Hughes, personality types emerge. He alludes to such American stereotypes as the clergyman, the professor, the politician, the financier, and the realtor. To this list can be added the commuter, the schoolteacher, and the small businessman. Such are a familiar sight in suburbia. Here then is a vocationally based typology. It is an interesting approach which commends itself in a general way for Protestantism's evangelical ministry.

Robert Park suggests consideration of three types of personality conceived in terms of demonstrated ability to adjust to a changing moral world: (1) *The philistine*—this type of person is conventional and takes over the patterns of life found in the society about him, thereby achieving a consistent life and a stable character; (2) *the bohemian*—this type is the radical, the nonconformist, and hence fails to achieve a stable character or to make a career (as opposed to the philistine); and (3) *the creative personality*—he is able to maintain a consistent life organization in a changing world.[3] This third type widens control over the environment by adapting his purpose to an increasing sphere of social reality. Evidently, Park is distinguishing personalities as they relate themselves to the milieu and then seek to grow. Using a polar type of analysis, he develops the three aforementioned theoretical models. Despite the fine perception of this analysis, its shortcomings for the religious worker lie significantly in the practical sphere. It is difficult to relate these types to a particular parish situation. Possibly a less sophisticated description of people can prove more useful at the congregational level. Generalizations which are overconceptualized fail to provide concrete access to the problem. Park's typological insights should not, how-

[3] See *Methods in Social Science,* edited by Stuart A. Rice (Chicago: University of Chicago Press, 1931), pp. 171 ff.

ever, be ignored in a constructive approach to suburban life. They can supplement other understandings.

With a noteworthy assist from Tönnies' classic theory of *Gemeinschaft und Gesellschaft,* Dobriner proposes a typological approach to residents of suburbia, utilizing a continuum which extends between the two polar positions of "locals" and "cosmopolitans." [4] These two poles are identified further as "old timers" and "new suburbanites," respectively. Thus Dobriner classifies persons who reside around the edges of the city according to several features—place of nativity, local cultural orientation, and the dominant locale of one's major interests (vocation, social life, et cetera). Taken together these criteria distinguish differing polar types of persons and hence possess an aspect of empirical significance. Indeed Dobriner has tested the relevance of his analysis in suburban Huntington Village, Long Island, New York, by means of a sample study embracing 275 residents. The community's history extends backward prior to the American Revolution. Before the post World War II suburban migration Huntington Village was a relatively isolated, homogeneous, semirural community. By means of an exploratory scale, a measure was sought of the suburbanite's internalization of the modal pattern of social relationships within the social system. From the study Dobriner is convinced that the polar types of locals and cosmopolitans are clear-cut. Actually the distinction demonstrated is akin to that which lies between oldtimer and newcomer. Religious and ethnic status do modify the outcomes significantly, however. In spite of the empirical dimension of this study the types are too broad to afford much help to the Protestant church in the practical situation.

The foregoing examples of the theoretical approach are exciting and significant. Yet each suggests the possibility of an empirical approach to suburban residents which can both test theory and also can yield a typology of persons which will aid the church in a general appraisal of its ministry.

A Practical Approach. "Practical" here means types which emerge from the analysis of empirical materials drawn from specific communities. Theoretical elements may be involved, to be sure, but only as they facilitate the appearance of an easily identified type. The practical involves a lower level of abstraction. To draft the types in terms of concrete data prepares the way eventually for a relevant Christian ministry. It is a non-pejorative approach wherein the positive is accented.

[4] See *The Suburban Community,* pp. 132-43.

Protestantism needs to make identifications quickly and reliably in the suburban parish. The individual likewise should be able to achieve a trustworthy self-identification. Accurate self-identity is sought even though the individual may exchange roles during residence in a particular suburban community. Moreover, the relative stability of identification is an important factor also.

The typology presented in the following section is based upon empirical data yet it points specifically to *kinds of relationships*. The meaning of relations is crucial. In the sixfold practical typology which is discussed below these points should be noted: *Marginal* describes the suburbanite's relation to vital religion; *pioneer* delineates his relation to contemporary society; *stranger* defines his relation to the local community; *organization man* describes his relation to the business world; *pagan* designates his relation to God; and *churchgoer* specifies his relation to Christianity. This typological approach places the stress upon significant relationships. Protestantism does need to identify the suburbanite in order to serve him. The church seeks to ascertain the manifold needs of suburban dwellers. Upon the evidence available and the classifications noted above a relevant ministry is shaped by the denominations. In the succeeding pages six types of suburbanites will be presented for evaluation. As will soon become evident, the major emphasis, intentionally, falls upon the practical rather than the theoretical.

SIX TYPES OF SUBURBAN RESIDENTS

Since the objectives here are practical fairly obvious distinctions among people will be utilized. From observation of and experience among suburbanites, it becomes apparent that a delineation of various kinds of such residents is possible. Each designated type exhibits the essential characteristics of a group of suburbanites. There is no desire to press the classification beyond this point. Neither a naïve nor a pejorative approach is used here. Moreover, the focus falls upon the unfinished task of the church, including the underdeveloped evangelistic responsibility. The six types noted below can serve as handles of concern for Protestantism.

1. *The Marginal Protestant.* Suburbia furnishes an ideal hiding place for the marginal Protestant; i.e., the individual who assigns low priority to religious matters. This is the person who rarely attends worship, rarely contributes to the church budget, rarely holds a church office, rarely serves on a committee, rarely affiliates with a church organization, rarely reads

the Bible, rarely has grace at mealtime, rarely holds family devotions, rarely subscribes to religious periodicals. Little or no time is allotted for these matters. All such activity is viewed as quite unnecessary for bolstering or nourishing one's inward life. It is regarded as old fashioned since the individual considers that he has outgrown the need to practice his childhood faith. Marginality, as the term is used here, refers to the inadequate relationship maintained with both the visible and invisible church. The individual occupies the borderland which lies between Christian faith and nonfaith. He is very close to the lower limit of qualification to be included as a Protestant.

Despite so formidable an array of negative attitudes, the marginal Protestant still insists upon self-identification as a "Protestant." By criticizing the church, the minister, and the members of the local congregation the marginal Protestant thinks that he affirms a continuing interest in Christianity. It is strange logic. The divine right to tell the world what is wrong with the church unfortunately does not include a report on the good that it does. Apparently this individual has drifted out from under an ecclesiastical discipline and away from an up-to-date knowledge of life within the church. Possibly the current pejorative posture is but a vestigial impression carried over from younger days. Now, however, it remains unsupported by responsible church participation and the public practice of faith. Hence there exists a haunting hollowness about the person, indicating why he has acquired the status of a marginal Protestant.

Some interesting facts emerged from a research study I recently completed covering fifty marginal Protestant households situated in selected suburbs of New York and New Jersey. In three cases out of five job requirements conflict with hours of normal church participation. Most marginal Protestants studied here had been more active in the congregation during earlier years. Yet the homemaker in 45 out of 50 families was still in the child-bearing age. On the average, the marginal Protestant is several years younger than active church members. Perhaps this is a surprise. For manifold reasons they now attend Sunday worship infrequently and avoid holding offices. At home a feeble attempt is made to retain the rudiments of a religious practice—grace at meals, Bible reading, and prayers. Usually one or another of the practices is followed irregularly. However, strong conviction is shared in the underlying philosophy expressed by a marginal Protestant: "You don't need to practice Christianity, you just have faith."

Unfortunately many people subscribe to the logic of this dangerous antinomianism. They fail to discover a connection between faith and practice.

Three fourths of the marginal Protestants make concrete suggestions respecting the church's responsibility for unmet needs in the community. Moreover, there was no holding back over specifying the minister's role and task in suburbia; he is to stand for something, to be an example, to visit the sick, to reach new people, to call on members, to attract youth, to preach the gospel. This stereotype is quite conventional. Approximately one half of the respondents lacked enthusiasm in appraising how well the job was being done by the present pastor. Even so brief an exploration reveals that the marginal Protestant regards himself a Protestant still, although his relationship to the church has been vitiated.

A profound challenge is presented to Christianity by the existence of the marginal Protestant. This type of person varies in age, can be either male or female, blue collar or white collar, married or single, and even can shift from his current inactive religious role to one of exemplary participation and spiritual maturity. It is a dynamic pluralistic role. Moreover, the existence of this type of suburbanite reveals the phenomenon of socioreligious distance in congregational life. Some people by personal effort and commitment attain levels of spiritual appropriation which exceed the normal reach of others. Why cannot all members of the congregation attain significant religious stature? Why do some fail to make the effort?

Possibly three unsolved problems are posed by the marginal Protestant: (1) How can the church member reconcile the contradictory values and patterns of conduct found in the church and society? (2) How does the relativity of social situations affect the Protestant's idea of goodness and badness? (3) In what ways does the social structure of the congregation interfere with the Christian fellowship of the church? This type of suburbanite challenges Protestantism to remove every ambiguity from its witness in society.

2. *The Pioneer.* In discussing the hundreds of families which moved into suburban Greenbelt, Maryland, George Warner indicates that they thought of themselves as pioneers of a new way of living.[5] The individuals making the shift out into suburban life believed that they possessed an internal hardiness and determination which would carry them through every trial in the new community. There were many trials—muddy streets, lack of fire

[5] *Greenbelt: The Cooperative Community* (New York: Exposition Press, 1954), p. 66.

and police protection, inadequate political and social organizations, faulty mass transportation services, poor schools, no churches, and so on. Walter Martin, Shirley Greene, and others join Warner in acclaiming the rough pioneerlike life during the early months or years of existence in many suburban communities.

Moreover, the authors of *The Split-Level Trap* found a "frontier" type of person residing in suburban Bergen County, New Jersey. William Whyte refers to "the spirit of frontier communities" as he describes the new housing developments around the edge of the city.[6] David Reisman speaks of the "private inventiveness" which characterizes the residents of suburbia.[7] Life in the Canadian suburb of Crestwood Heights utilized references to the term "pioneer" in order to detail the phenomena. Evidently one does not need to search the literature very far before uncovering data on the pioneer type. The reference to Warner, Whyte, Reisman, the Gordons, and others, suffice to underscore the importance of recognizing this type.

The pioneer in modern suburbia is the individual who is willing to accept responsibility for himself, who will undertake heavy vocational assignments, and who will take risks in order to advance self and family. He will even carry the idea of venture into the life of the local church. He is frontierlike in his rugged individualism. He is a doer, and very often he will clash with the person who wants merely to organize a committee whenever a job needs to be done. Often he is rough and impatient with the slow wheels of progress. In the local church he is hard to get along with or without!

In recapitulation several unsolved problems emerge: The pioneer raises questions for the Christian church to answer. (1) He expects the church to do *new* things, to lead the way, to set the pace. If Protestantism does not, then he is disappointed. What new trails should be opened up or new standards of life need to be set today? Is there an opportunity for spiritual pioneering? (2) He is a man of action who likes to see something happen as a result of the expenditure of his energies. What Christian action do the denominations intend to enter into? What religious practices need to be established? (3) He responds best to big demands and large challenges. What Herculean tasks are laid upon the Protestant church by the contemporary world? Why are these challenges not being met now? Thus

---

[6] *The Organization Man,* p. 438.
[7] "The Suburban Dislocation," in *The Annals* (Fall 1957), pp. 123-46.

the pioneer reminds Protestantism that there exist hardy souls who are willing and able to plunge into the unknown future in pursuit of mankind's unrealized goals. Protestantism is thereby challenged to undertake the largest unfinished tasks in the world. It must become a church of action, standards, and Herculean labors.

3. *The Stranger.* An essay by Georg Simmel under the title "The Stranger" is widely regarded as one of the classic treatments.[8] Here Simmel focuses upon several considerations of interest to the religious leader in suburbia: The stranger is the ever potential wanderer; the stranger is not tied to the soil; the stranger is regarded by the native as a type rather than as an individual; the stranger represents freedom of movement; and finally reciprocal tension is embodied in formal relations to the stranger. Simmel associated the stranger with trade and with urban life. Due to strong mobility trends in the American scene the stranger has emerged as a prominent type in suburban life.

Evidently the concept of stranger is significant in sociology and has implications for Protestantism in suburbia. Under the title "The Stranger and the City" Julie Meyer surveys recent developments in the American situation.[9] The results are somewhat parallel with Simmel's. Here are the relevant findings: The stranger is a migrant; his past is unknown; he cannot change completely from stranger into native; the city is really a conglomerate of strangers; the concept of stranger is essential for an adequate understanding of action and interaction between city and country; the stranger is regarded as a menace to established values and ways of life; membership in an association can lead the stranger into community acceptance; and finally, the stranger is not readily accepted in suburban, town, and village communities. Meyer presents a dynamic city-oriented concept which recognizes that the stranger can come into a suburb with a high or low status depending upon his personal qualifications. To Meyer, this type of person exists in large numbers in the modern metropolitan community.

According to Blanche Housman Gelfant, strangers communicate through the symbolic language of fashion, dress, manners, level of consumption, and possessions.[10] In this manner they indicate who they are, usually re-

---

[8] Kurt H. Wolff, editor and translator, *The Sociology of Georg Simmel* (New York: Free Press of Glencoe, 1950), pp. 402-8.
[9] *American Journal of Sociology* (March, 1951), pp. 476-83.
[10] *The American City Novel* (Norman, Okla.: University of Oklahoma Press, 1954), p. 26.

vealing their social status or orientation. It thus becomes possible to "read" a newcomer, to size the person up, to estimate who or what he is by means of external clues. While it is not possible thus to assess every newcomer individually, arrangements can be made to incorporate strangers into local community institutions. This is a group approach. Such affiliation can reduce enormously the strangeness of the strangers.

"Each time a family moves a new pattern of life is formed," urges Kenneth Miller.[11] This principle applies in suburbia. New friendships must be made, new associations have to be formed, and very often new daily and weekly schedules have to be worked out. Old routines are disturbed and scrapped. In this new situation erosion of worthwhile habits often takes place. It is altogether too easy for the mobile person to diminish participation in the life of the church, substituting in its place a lazy Sunday morning with the newspaper, an afternoon with friends, and an evening at the theater or watching television. When rural persons move into the metropolitan area they often drop their church activity patterns. Likewise people who shift from the cities to suburbia often take a vacation from church participation. They shed old patterns. The unsavory fact must be faced that suburbia is full of mobile persons, people who move around extensively. Mobility did not end with World War II. Whether Protestantism now can develop a ministry adequate to men and families on the move is one of the great challenges confronting the church.

There is a danger that urban conditions exalt mere movement into a cult. People do not reside very long in any particular neighborhood or community or state. They are restless. They move around. Sociologists remind us that more than 25,000,000 Americans change residence each year. This process produces many strangers. Seven out of eight of the movers are city and suburban dwellers. There can be no doubt about the fact of mobility. The comments of one writer respecting the public school situation are relevant here:

One youngster had lived in forty-six . . . states. A second grader had already attended fifteen schools, and during the year had moved away from Seneca. One high school girl had attended five different schools during [an academic year], while another had attended fourteen different high schools.[12]

[11] *Man and God in the City* (New York: Friendship Press, 1954), p. 42.
[12] Havighurst and Morgan, *Social History of a War-Boom Community,* pp. 133-34.

While this statement obviously illustrates an extreme situation, experienced church leaders are aware of the turnover of membership and the shifting character of urban population. Many suburban communities are prominently characterized by a shuffling of the population.

According to *The Split-Level Trap,* some personal and familial problems would never have appeared if the person had remained in his natal community. Mobility exposes the individual to stresses and strains he would not ordinarily have encountered. Mobility uncovers basic weaknesses among the individual's skills. Preparation for life in the childhood community was inadequate. Apparently the mobile person has to possess a special toughness and flexibility suitable to the new way of life. Transients know this. The person needs to be prepared for difficult experience lest he acquire a needless cynicism and "hardness." Thus, the church has an obligation to help mobile people.

Finally, an overlooked fact respecting strangers is that often the suburban newcomers are Negroes or representatives of some other minority group. This point is underscored by Frank F. Lee in *Negro and White in Connecticut Town.* Here attention is called to all persons of "non local background." To achieve eventual acceptance it is usually necessary to break through an aloofness, suspicion, prejudice, and even outright hostility. That it is often difficult for the well-intentioned oldtimer to rise to the occasion is illustrated in Havighurst and Morgan and in Oliver C. Cox *Caste, Class and Race.*[13] When the stranger is a man of color the situation may be more difficult to meet. Much time has been spent discussing the Iron Curtain and the Bamboo Curtain. Church leaders working in suburbia find the "ethnic curtain" rather difficult to penetrate also.

Evidently the stranger confronts the Protestant church with at least six troublesome problems. The denominations are expected to know how (1) to understand reliably the culture and expectancies of suburban newcomers, (2) to reconcile the liabilities and assets of mobility, (3) to exercise influence on the new patterns of life which are forming, (4) to bolster persons who bear the heavy strains of suburban life, (5) to provide particular church experience to transient-minded newcomers, and (6) to hasten the abolition of the "ethnic curtain" in suburbia. Thus the stranger symbolizes a constellation of problems to which Protestantism must direct its healing ministry.

[13] New York: Monthly Review Press, 1959.

4. *The Organization Man.* According to Frederick Allen the salesman was "canonized" in the United States about 1935.[14] This vocation was "invented," among other reasons, in order to pull business out of a slump. Since the 1930's, however, the role of the salesman has expanded, making the vocation virtually indispensable to society. Today most Americans take him for granted. He is a uniquely urban product with a consuming passion to sell himself over and over again to the American people. What used to be the best-known prototype of city life, however, is now being replaced rapidly by another type.

From the salesman has evolved the organization man. New business structures and the managerial revolution have brought this change. Whyte defines the organization man as a middle-class individual who is neither a white-collar clerk nor a salesman in the customary usage of the term but rather is placed at the junior-executive level. Having taken the vows of organization life, he sets his mind upon not merely working for the organization but rather on *belonging* to it. According to Whyte's definition, one must include strongly motivated persons who are engaged occupationally in research, politics, business, and religion. The organization man is found in all these fields. In describing the implications of this vocational posture, Whyte urges that:

Man exists as a unit of society. Of himself, he is isolated, meaningless; only as he collaborates with others does he become worth while, for by sublimating himself in the group, he helps produce a whole that is greater than the sum of its parts. There should be, then, no conflict between man and society. What we think are conflicts are misunderstandings, breakdowns in communication. By applying the methods of science to human relations we can eliminate these obstacles to consensus and create an equilibrium in which society's needs and the needs of the individual are one and the same.[15]

Herewith is given the rationale of the organization man, disclosing the importance which Whyte attaches to this new type. As a working philosophy it is taken with the utmost seriousness. Commitment, consensus, and conformity appear as normative goals. The individual does not count.

The organization man possesses such traits as high educational achieve-

[14] *The Big Change* (New York: Harper & Row, Publishers, 1952).
[15] *Op. cit.,* pp. 7-8.

ment, upgrading of self, mastery of personality skills, loyalty to the corporation, the apotheosis of the organization ethic, mobility, rootlessness, conformity, and budgetism. Corporation life shapes the outlook, directs the personal preferences, and dictates the vocational objectives of the person. He loses much of his individuality and conforms increasingly to the demands of the group, of the corporation. In this present age of organization it is surprisingly easy to recruit persons to keep the wheels turning routinely. Whyte notes that the fault does not lie in the organization but rather in the worship of it. The individual is imprisoned in a brotherhood of conforming people. Unless he conforms he is "washed" out.

Suburbia is the home of the organization man. Residence here signifies that he is "getting ahead," and at the same time furnishes the individual some opportunities to practice in community life what is being learned in the business world. Whyte shrewdly comments upon the exercise of expertise in suburbia: "But it is the young organization man who is dominant. More than others, it is he who organizes the committees, runs the schools, selects the ministers, fights the developers, makes the speeches, and sets the styles." [16] This type of resident knows how to take charge of the suburbs and how to move into the situation with zeal and ideas. While other people are holding back because of shyness, lack of leadership experience, or whatever, the organization man takes over and soon has a hum of group activity going on. Thus, John Keats, Auguste Spectorsky, Vance Packard, William Whyte, Shirley Greene, and other writers speak of suburbia as a mecca of organization men and their families.

Kenneth Miller reports that the city fringe attracts people who are propelled through life by the strong desire to get ahead. Among the suburban dwellers who have this drive prominently are the young executive and other high-level white-collar personnel. Promotion to a higher position depends upon the proper combination of deportment and talent; yet one must fit the stereotype also. The individual manifests strong interest in getting ahead, and this drive becomes the matrix for a number of day-by-day practical decisions. He must reside in the proper neighborhood, associate with the right people, affiliate with the right church, belong to the right club, entertain the right people, purchase the appropriate automobile. In John Marquand's novel *Point of No Return* this tantalizing drama unfolds.

[16] *Ibid.*, p. 295.

Decision after decision was made holding in mind its possible contributions to getting ahead in business. All life appeared to be organized around this principle. Progress and success came to be measured almost wholly in material terms and hence the person's outlook came to be focused primarily upon material values. Charles Sears has warned against such "a deadly economic and social determinism" under which vast numbers of people live. William Whyte shrewdly points out that the well-rounded organization man is "loyal to the company and the company to him." This is a kind of economic love at first sight!

From the foregoing remarks it is not surprising that the organization man and his family sometimes regard the church as scarcely more than a badge of respectability. Thousands of such suburban people attend suburban churches not for what the church truly has to offer but because it is the respectable thing to do. Later on they wonder why the church wanders astray from her true purposes or gets largely swallowed up in the secular concerns of suburban life. It is good business to go to church. Some of the local church officials derive from this type. The individual brings his vocational perspectives into the life of the church, insisting that the church become like him. The organization man knows how to steer around every controversy and how to "handle" everybody in order to keep himself in power. Inadvertently the church really can furnish social connections which possibly serve the interest of the social climber, the prestige hunter, and the newly established business or professional man. How suburban living polishes the outside of the proverbial cup!

The organization man and his family present a powerful challenge to the church in suburbia. As Protestantism plans for the future, however, it should bear in mind Andrew Greeley's disconcerting prediction that "the organization man will be dead by 1980, replaced by the far more efficient and far less neurotic digital computer." [17] As a noteworthy successor to *The Death of a Salesman,* some rising playright, hereby alerted, can prepare a dramatic script entitled *The Death of an Organization Man!* Until that day of demise arrives, however, Protestantism would be wise to make salvation accessible to the self-sufficient organization man.

Finally, in recapitulation, this type of suburbanite constitutes a disconcerting challenge to the Protestant church. Hedged about by skillfully executed public relations and the practice of personality skills, he is difficult

[17] *The Church and the Suburbs,* p. 163.

to reach. The denominations must evaluate (1) the low estimate of the individual held by business organizations, (2) the spiritually inexperienced but aggressive church leaders, (3) the dominance of the worldly success motif in appraising church life, and (4) the future of the organization man. How difficult it is really to confront this suburbanite with the rigorous demands of the gospel. So often he thinks you mean the man in the next pew.

5. *The Wistful Pagan.* In suburbia people are exposed to a powerful pagan influence. It is a pervasive threat. The resident is tempted to be neither a Christian, nor a Mohammedan, nor a Jew but rather to become a heathen, an irreligious person, an idolater. He is attracted into the ranks of those who do not acknowledge the God of the Bible. Although the individual often is charming, gracious, intelligent, and thoughtful, the major orientation of his life remains that of the wistful pagan. He is nontheistic yet usually does not hold a pejorative attitude toward Protestantism. Though uncommitted, he remains wistful. Seeking an adequate conception of the universe and ultimate reality he frequently ends up in humanism. He fears to take genuine religion seriously.

Instead of turning to Christianity, he develops a deep and often worthy interest in humanity, in the perfectability of man's nature solely through his own efforts. Thus he starts in the posture of paganism and moves toward a humanitarianism. As noted in *Crestwood Heights,* he acquires a vast confidence in man's powers. All about in the suburban milieu are the instances of man's ingenuity, intelligence, and prowess. Suburbia is the showcase of man's capacity to deal adequately with the world. The bulldozers level the land; the new homes spring up; green lawns and shrubs cover the scarred earth; and a Garden of Eden appears on the countryside. Moreover, air conditioning and heating control the temperature within the homes all year round.

The Crestwood child never experiences physical peril from the elements in the sense that the child of the prairie farm feels it when exposed to the terror of being lost with his family in a January blizzard. He must, it is true, learn the hazards of automobile traffic, but these are gadget-driven threats, and hence, to him ultimately controllable. To this child, nature is seldom either beneficent or threatening.[18]

[18] John R. Seeley, *et al., Crestwood Heights* (New York: Basic Books, Inc., 1956), p. 62.

In the suburbs, more than elsewhere, one finds people possessing a profound interest in humanitarianism. Individuals who regard religion lightly will often turn with great enthusiasm to eleemosynary enterprises. Such people comprehend the importance of relieving hardship or misery among fellow men. They are often quite generous in gifts of time and money. When called upon to consider the work of the Protestant churches, however, some suburbanites draw back, disclosing a fear of personal involvement or shunning the Christian ethical demands. On the contrary, when the matter of social service is broached, they brighten up again with interest and speak with swift-paced enthusiasm. Such activity often consumes considerable time and money while permitting the individual to live a private life without religious standards and without reminders of them. Freedom is featured. A favorite charity can always be cut off; social service can be discontinued. After all, social status and social applause is available to those who help the needy. Do not people applaud good deeds? But Christianity urges that the deed without the doer is bare. What salvation inheres in good deeds alone?

Suburbia is a haven for pagans. Kenneth Miller speaks of the American city as being filled with "wistful pagans." This does not mean that pagans are necessarily people of bad morals. Usually they are neither crude nor vulgar. The personal dilemma of such suburbanites lies in the fact that they are out of touch with the resources of Christianity, but they are unaware of their dilemma. What suburban pastor does not know laymen who are big healthy pagans, yet who are friendly and courteous toward the church. They drive a nice car, reside in a beautiful home, and want their children to receive an excellent education. All life's secondary goals are achieved without an encounter with Christianity. Hence, the suburban church's concern must reach out far enough to include the pagan. Ministry to this group is so important that Kenneth Miller reminds us that "every city has been a Babylon, and every city has been a New Jerusalem." So much depends upon what the suburb represents to the resident. Is it a center of secularism or a divine community?

In Ernest G. Lee's book *Christianity and the New Situation* attention is directed to the growing number of people who remain outside the influence of the church.[19] These are the wistful pagans. Yet it is not a new problem.

[19] Boston: The Beacon Press, 1954.

The Apostle Paul attempted to bring Christ to every city of the ancient Mediterranean world. The intrepid traveler told about his Lord to the pagans of city after city. All but Alexandria knew the sound of his voice in the streets. Paul presented the city as a potential New Jerusalem to people who regarded it as a Babylon. Today Protestantism should seek out the suburban pagans and bring the pressure of Christ's life upon their lives. Just as Paul refused to permit city dwellers to regard the community as merely a Babylon so Protestantism must lift up the divine possibilities of suburban life. Many of the pagans are not opposed to the church; rather they lack adequate knowledge of its true nature.

Yet the appeal of religion is winsome. Protestantism maintains a wide range of social service—hospitals, orphanages, homes for the aged, projects among delinquent youth, et cetera. But Christianity places eleemosynary work in its proper context. The Protestant suburbanite does not participate in charity for social rewards but rather out of a deep faith and concern over the spiritual welfare of fellow men. This is a normal extension of a religious life. What Protestantism says to the resident of suburbia is that this is God's world and that all men are brothers. As brothers, needy people anywhere are encompassed in the suburbanite's concern. Therefore no mere humanism can ever substitute for the charity and good works which originate in Christian faith. True charity begins with the religiously committed person. Therefore, the humanitarian lacks adequate motivation and a suitable frame of reference for deeds of mercy. Only commitment to Christianity can remove the lack.

6. *The Churchgoer.* That a revival of religion has occurred in our time and in suburbia can hardly be disputed according to Greeley, Gordon, Herberg, Greene, and other writers. Yet, that the spiritual renewal to have taken root among the middle classes is a source of amazement for many Americans. It should not be. Did not Christianity in Japan first take root among the elite? In how many other lands is this a familiar pattern? Thus, what really matters is that a renewal did occur, lifting religion once more to the respectable level of interest. Greeley emphatically states that there are no atheists in the postwar suburban communities. Thus the basic question is not whether a religious revival really occurred but rather what kind of revival has taken place? How deeply did it penetrate the American suburban milieu?

At least two contrasting observations can be reported here; one acknowledges the external dimension of religious expression, and the other estimates the internal aspects of personal faith. A connection between the external and internal aspects is known to some leaders but remains undiscovered for others.

Certainly a great many suburban people attend church services. Most writers report a vast increase of suburban church activities, even to the point of suggesting that a bad parish is one in which there is "nothing going on." Some of this busyness probably falls short of intended religious ends. Possibly if activity were thought of as either a point of beginning for newcomers or else as the outward and visible expression of an inward and genuine expression of a divine relationship, then the suburban situation could be interpreted in other than a pejorative mood. Indeed, many suburban churches in which abundant activity takes place, manage to retain a lively concern respecting the deeper aspects of Christian life.

Therefore the existence of the church's institutional activity should not preclude the possibility of the Holy Spirit's working in the suburbs. While it must be urged that Protestantism is concerned with both the outward and inward expressions of faith, to keep them both alive ultimately the external must be buttressed by an adequate inner relation with God. On the other hand, is it possible to be a Protestant Christian without participation in the visible fellowship, or in deeds of mercy in a needy world? Probably not. The greatest Christians were unable to prevent the two spheres from intermingling with one another.

There are churchgoers and church participants who are the salt of the earth and the backbone of the Kingdom. They believe that: "The customs and taboos derived from centuries of human experience deserve better consideration than to be heaved out the window of an apartment house." [20] Some church people tithe all their adult lives, never miss a worship service, and maintain homes which are as nearly Christian as any anywhere. Often these people truly are church leaders, rather than merely officers armed with personality skills. These, a minority of living saints, are the spiritual pacesetters in the life of the congregation. They are part of the solution rather than part of the problem of religion in suburban life. They possess the courage to depart from the ordinary routine of life in order to participate in Protestantism.

[20] Sears, *op. cit.*, pp. 193-94.

Therefore, it is appropriate to direct attention to the relatively small number of solid, dependable people who have perceived the church for what it truly stands, have accepted the commitment personally, and are utilizing New Testament insights in daily life. Day by day they are living the life in Christ at home, at the office or shop, and at the level of community relationships in suburbia. Thus, no account of the types of suburban people would be complete without mention of those exceptional followers of Christ. The much maligned churchgoer may turn out to be the only full-fledged Christian which the Protestant church possesses. It is always easier to find fault than it is to be a participant in the imperfect suburban church.

Certainly the account of these six types—the marginal Protestant, the pioneer, the stranger, the organization man, the wistful pagan, and the churchgoer—does not exhaust the subject. Limitation of space precludes a discussion of the intellectual, the complacent, the unprepared, the ambivalent, and the authoritarian personality—additional legitimate types of persons who reside in suburbia. Knowledge of their characteristics and how they challenge Christianity is essential if Protestant church effectiveness is to be achieved in suburbia. Enough has been said in the present discussion, however, to open the subject for a more extensive treatment. A wider ranging analysis can come later. What is currently before us can provide some useful understandings of the practical situation.

IMPLICATIONS FOR PROTESTANTISM

The aforementioned list of types of suburban residents suffices in terms of the chapter's objectives. Its purpose is fourfold: (1) *To call attention* to the fact that many people with nonsuburban backgrounds reside in the suburb. Persons came to the city's periphery before organizations and institions arrived. The people themselves organized and set up appropriate social and economic structures. Suburbia means people rather than places or things. (2) *To delineate* the situation of people in quandaries. The types disclose human dilemmas. Problems are never really solved; they just shift around, eventually giving way to other critical issues. People move from one quandary to another. This is illustrated in the well-known situational programs of television and radio. In one lifetime how many personal crises does a suburban resident survive? The person alone is the constant; the issues come and go. Man is a tougher creature than he is often supposed to be. (3) *To discover* the church's responsibility and perspectives in the community. Types of people can reveal Protestantism's broad range of obligation. Certainly Christianity can always see the person for what he really is and where he is in the midst of his quandaries. (4) *To prepare* the way for more profound analyses of personality types and human problems which can be undertaken by qualified scholars and interested pastors.

Surely it becomes evident that the minister truly must speak to the condition of the suburban resident. This can be done through preaching, through personal counseling, through church administration, and through small group activity. In the suburb, the church stands for such values as the sacredness of the human personality, faith in man, love as the motive of life, the reality of Christian fellowship, and the responsibility of society to provide opportunities for the abundant life. The gospel need not be muted in the suburb. Indeed, it will not be silenced if the preacher catches a glimpse of suburban people in quandaries and hears their insistent query, "Who will speak to my condition?" No man need walk alone in suburbia. Christ is ever available as the great companion and friend. Through the improved witness of laymen and pastors each suburb can become a hundred avenues leading to God. The varieties of suburban residents can become a multipronged challenge to Protestantism. No matter what posture man takes God will find him and call him into fellowship with Jesus Christ and his fellow men. This is the ultimate relationship.

IV

Who Is
My Neighbor?

The tremendous growth of the American suburbs along with the
arrival of new population elements has precipitated a crisis in community. Once upon a time geographical proximity of people implied neighboring, but this is no longer so. The old homogeneity which made neighboring almost an automatic process has vanished from hundreds of suburbs.
Conditions have changed. If neighboring occurs today the suburbanite must
intend that it come to pass and then implement the intention assiduously.
Hence it becomes necessary to investigate the crisis of community, seeking
a rediscovery of meanings in neighborhood life and an adequate motivation for human contacts. This exploration proceeds with an awareness
of the deep crisis which underlies all questions considered here.

Who is my neighbor? Before World War II the question was answered
quite simply: My neighbor is any Protestant family residing along a suburban
street. Or possibly, my more distant neighbor is the Chinese, African, or
Indian who qualifies as a heathen. *Neither answer makes sense today.* Since
the prewar years a suburban revolution has swept across the nation, leaving
in its wake a changed world. No simple answer can be given in the 1960's
and 1970's. Who has not discovered that his suburban neighbor now is a
Jew, or a Roman Catholic, or a Negro, or a pentecostal? Is it not clear
now that overseas neighbors have been granted religious franchise by
scholars and statesmen? This vast turn of events makes answering the
ancient question a much more difficult matter today.

Yet probably no question possesses greater relevance and poignancy. It encapsulates into a single forlorn query the meaning of new life in the suburbs. Not only have millions of new families taken up residence here since World War II, but also the newcomers are of divergent faiths, divergent ethnic backgrounds, and divergent socioeconomic circumstances, thereby challenging indigenous Protestantism to do some new thinking. How can the crisis in community life be resolved? The world watches expectantly to discover whether Christianity really can cope with the polyglot situation. The out-movement of Jews, Roman Catholics, sect groups, Negroes, and blue-collar workers has brought the unsolved problems of Western civilization to suburbia, and dumped them into the lap of suburban Protestantism. Thus the fiercest challenge truly occurs in the religious sphere. The church ought to do something about this crisis! In order to procure insight and new understanding let the denominations re-examine the meaning of *community, nigh-dwelling, neighbor* (in biblical sources), and *brotherhood*. Such a responsible exploration can introduce new ideas and dynamics into the adequate answer awaited by the contemporary world.

NEIGHBOR IN COMMUNITY

Community is found wherever *a group of neighbors* share a common life together. This definition recognizes that people residing in close proximity can share a sufficiency of interests held in common to allow for the interactivities of life. They become an aggregation of individuals residing in a specified locality endowed with a degree of political autonomy. They generously support primary institutions such as schools, churches, government, and so on. Thus, in the chief concerns of life they function together. Baker Brownell's well-known definition regards community as a group of neighbors who know one another face to face.[1] This valuable insight sees neighbor always in a social situation. People live in community, and hence the concern for others naturally falls across their shoulders. In terms of suburbia community usually comprises a locality grouping of people with personal contacts occurring among the residents. The community is not simply an area; it is a geographical territory in which people have important experiences and ideas in common, including participation in primary institutions and other important aspects of group life. Without community the concept of neighbor has no meaning.

[1] *The Human Community* (New York: Harper & Brothers, 1950), pp. 198 ff.

Of particular interest here is the truism that while a suburbanite may affiliate with various associations, social organizations, and institutions, he really belongs to but one community. He belongs where he lives. He has no other geographical roots. He is a neighbor in a particular neighborhood. Usually a number of his friends and acquaintances reside along the street or reasonably nearby his residence. Upon this point virtually all definitions of community agree. The community consists in the interplay of suburban activity through the patterns of the institutions. When this activity is wholesome and vigorous the neighbors are stimulated and emancipated. It is a boon to personal growth. The opposite obtains when the neighborhood malfunctions. "Neighboring" occurs most perfectly among homeowners, reports John Kinneman.[2] Thus, suburbia, which features the highest incidence of homeownership, affords an excellent opportunity to test fully Christianity's neighboring idea. Protestantism can capitalize upon it.

Life in the suburbs can be interpreted in manifold ways. Some writers designate it as a *struggle between conformity and community.* Those who espouse the views of William Whyte urge that the major activity of suburban life focuses upon conformity. John Keats explores this thesis, stressing the similarity in dress, tastes, conversation, and level of consumption among residents in the large development suburbs. Unfortunately, patterns of conformity really are present and do exercise undue influence upon the decision making of people. The standards of behavior and of human relationships are forced into a uniform mold. This procrustean bed makes it difficult for genuine community to emerge.

Hence there arises a conflict between conformity and adequate community life. Their very presence creates tension. How can both goals be achieved? Field studies delineate community as the place where people complement one another's activity vocationally, and otherwise, in a pattern of mutual service and helpfulness. Heterogeneity in occupation is necessary in order to achieve a high degree of local self-sufficiency. Moreover, heterogeneity in age, marital status, and so on exists. The needs of people living in the same neighborhood are really broad in range. A true community cannot be adequately described by the term conformity. It is a misleading idea. Therefore, where a strong trend toward conformity exists it carries suburban residents away from the achievement of community. Where com-

[2] *The Community in American Society* (New York: Appleton-Century-Crofts, Inc., 1947), p. 8.

munity is lost the neighbor issue is irrelevant. The one depends upon the other.

To ask the question, "Who is my neighbor?" is to raise an issue of fundamental religious importance in suburbia. In any thoroughgoing analysis of suburban life this is the crucial question. The issue encompasses both the expectations of the newcomers and the standards of the oldtime residents. It includes the family, the school, and the church. It embraces the hidden possibilities for the community. The neighbor must involve himself in appropriate processes, however. The suburbanite is forced into a responsible consideration of human relationships both within and beyond the edges of the community. Under such conditions personal encounters open up the richness of community life to him.

NIGH DWELLER OR NEIGHBOR?

The meaning of the word neighbor comes into sharper focus when a contrast is provided with the term "nigh dweller." Kinneman, Brownell, and other writers have given attention to this interesting comparison. By definition, as the term is used here, a "nigh dweller" is a suburbanite who resides adjacent to people with whom he does not intermingle socially. Rather, friendships and social activities are established among people elsewhere in the metropolitan community. Physically he and his family reside alongside potential friends. He is physically near but socially distant. In this strange role he is a nigh dweller who lacks local friends and/or acquaintances.

In sharp contrast, the true neighbor readily socializes with other suburbanites up and down the street. What Brownell calls "the stubborn wholeness of one another's life" obtrudes into the situation. This means the confrontation of whole personality with whole personality, rather than merely touching at the point of some minor interest. Neighbors are whole persons interacting with one another. Moreover, in times of personal or family crisis, whether great or small, one turns to the neighbors for assistance. He borrows tools, food, and seeks advice about yard and house care. Further, it is a reciprocal relationship. The people help each other. In this manner a pattern of mutuality becomes established in which there occur many exchanges of help, experience, confidences, gossip, and the time of day. Out of such giving and receiving of assistance, plus the personal association itself, does the word neighbor take on significant meaning. Many small things and occasional large concerns accumulate to yield the phenomenon of neighboring.

S. F. Fava's study of contrasts in neighboring between city and suburban residents is important here.[3] This investigation based upon samples of residents taken in New York City and suburban Nassau County yields interesting insights: (1) Basic differences do exist with respect to neighboring; (2) neighboring increases with the distance from the major city's center; (3) social-psychological factors are important for interpretations here; and (4) migrants to suburbia exhibit greater friendliness and interest in community participation. Fava concludes that while some neighboring exists in the city, it predominates in the suburbs. However, the process of neighboring is complicated by religion, ethnic background, and place of nativity. Dobriner's research studies generally reinforce Fava's work.

Because mobility is a prominent feature of suburban life some attention should be given to the process by which a stranger matriculates from newcomer to neighbor. Various writers point out that the role of a stranger is a temporary one. But of what consists the transition? Descriptions are provided in *The Split-Level Trap, The Crack in the Picture Window,* and *The Organization Man* especially. All three cite the profound difficulties encountered in shedding the role of the stranger or newcomer. The difficulties are in several spheres—physical, social, and psychological.

Consider the ordinary burdens of the newcomers. During the early days of residence, the newcomer has to find the bank, the post office, the school, the shopping center, and many other institutions necessary to ordinary life. Merely to locate places of business is not the entire problem. Rather, the issue is to find a store or bank which approximates the one which was patronized in the previous community. What looks somewhat familiar is desired. In the midst of working out these necessary business arrangements the housewife has the heavy burden of settling the family in a new household. Salesmen start ringing the doorbell. Residents up and down the street commence dropping in. Thus, a situation already burdensome and confused acquires more confusion and strain. If somewhere during this adjustment process someone's patience snaps the unpleasantness can remain a scar for years. First impressions persist a long time.

Who knows how long it takes for the newcomer to become a neighbor? The metamorphosis is an intricate one. Perhaps the first week is ample time

[3] "Urban-Suburban Contrasts in Social Participation: A Study of Neighboring in New York City and Nassau County" (Ph.D. dissertation, Northwestern University, 1956).

for some people; for others a year may be too short a period. Some new-comers wonder why any effort should be taken to be neighborly. They are undermotivated or had unfortunate previous experience. Others plunge into a pattern of friendship upon the day of arrival. Along the same street one encounters a wide range of attitudes, mores, religious convictions, and expectations for the future. Some people are more aggressive or more experienced than others. The newcomer probably will behave in the suburban situation the way he has conducted himself elsewhere. The outcome also may be the same as before.

One must press beyond the definitions to content and outcome. What is more important is an exploration of the consequences of being a neighbor. Some consequences are formation of friendships, involvement in other people's problems, increased local sociability, concern for neighborhood needs, and sharing of common interests. The comparison of nigh dweller and neighbor is a helpful one. It brings out the remarkable possibilities of the neighbor.

NEIGHBOR: A CHRISTIAN DEFINITION

A *Christian* definition of neighbor is needed in suburbia. Most readers are already familiar with the strictly human ingredients of the word and its horizontal dimension. What they know less about is the vertical dimension involving God. To procure a Christian definition it will be necessary to draw upon both biblical and parish resources. These twin tap roots render possible ultimately a transcendence over suburban culture. The definition becomes grounded both in the gospel and in the witnessing Christian community.

The New Testament specifies that whoever loves his neighbor fulfills the law. (Rom. 13:8; Gal. 5:14; Jas. 2:8.) This affirmation encourages the Christian neither to harm nor to judge his neighbor. Indeed, biblical sources generally furnish a lengthy catalogue of attitudes and behavior which are unworthy of the Christian. He must not kill, slander, oppress, rob, bear false witness against, nor sin against his neighbor. He must not covet his neighbor's house, nor his neighbor's wife, nor his neighbor's servant, nor anything else which belongs to the neighbor. How relevantly this counsel rings out across the modern world! Both in fiction and in real life covetousness is king. Positively stated, the suburban Christian should extend toward his neighbor honor, truthfulness, mercy, affection, and understanding. So important is the relationship between the religious man and his neighbor that the Bible provides explicit suggestions in more than 150 different verses scattered across 28 different Old and New Testament books. Both the negative and positive sides of the matter are spelled out.

How much love should be extended to the neighbor? From the pages of the New Testament comes a reply: "Love your neighbor as yourself." This is clearly and strongly stated. Anyone who does not know how much to love himself is probably dead or mentally incompetent. Hence Paul urged, "Let no one seek his own good, but the good of his neighbor" (I Cor. 10:24). The epistle to the Romans stresses, "Love does no wrong to a neighbor" (Rom. 13:10). James calls the love-of-neighbor principle a "royal law" (Jas. 2:8). Such a deep religious affection edifies and pleases the neighbor. Always one must seek the good of his neighbor. Love is so significant that the Christian can never knowingly wrong his neighbor nor ever cease from seeking the latter's welfare in all things. Genuine love of neighbor is worth much more than "all whole burnt offerings and sacrifices" (Mark 12:33). Rather than a worship experience, love of neighbor is an inescapable implementation of personal faith. It is Christ in action working through human personality.

The importance of this Christian relationship can be explored still further. Proverbs regards the obligation to be stronger than blood ties:

> Better is a neighbor who is near
> than a brother who is far away. (27:10.)

Here is a principle which should be utilized in every community across the United States. Consider how much the New Testament makes of the matter. The *neighbors* are called in to help a family rejoice in at least two parables told by Jesus—the lost sheep (Luke 15:6) and the lost coin (Luke 15:9). Moreover, the neighbors were active in the rejoicing over the birth of a son to Elizabeth, Mary's cousin (Luke 1:57-66). These people stood in awe of this tiny son who was named John and upon whom God looked with favor. Other instances of concrete involvement with neighbors could be cited, however, these will suffice to show that this responsible relationship is embedded deep in Christianity and is treated with the utmost respect throughout the Bible. Indeed, one of the two great teachings of Christ deals with neighbor (Mark 12:29-31). The Master expected his followers to take this teaching seriously.

The contemporary witnessing community (i.e., the local congregation) further strengthens the importance of Christ's teaching about neighbors. Here the ideal is practiced to some extent. In a recent research study of 500 suburban Protestant parishes it was found that more than two thirds of the church members reside as neighbors close around the church edifice. Many of the people live side by side along the same streets. These people encounter each other many times between Sundays—at the market, at the commuters' railroad station, in neighborhood activities, and elsewhere. This practice of seeing one another, of exchanging favors, is the outward and visible sign of a deeper inner relationship called "neighboring" by Dobriner. The clustered-parish pattern of suburban Protestant churches is typical for both members and church-school enrollees. It is fact not fiction. Physically this concentrated parish provides an excellent opportunity for suburban Christians to practice faith within the congregation and also to become Christian neighbors in fact toward other local residents. Each Protestant has a definite responsibility to show love toward the new neighbors who are now migrating into suburbia. Many of these newcomers are of another faith or of another race. Neighboring here needs to be reciprocal, with both parties competing vigorously in the display of genuine love and concern.

Finally, the quest for a Christian definition of neighbor has led to a discovery of the importance of the biblical and parish elements. Moreover, it points to the all-important culture transcending quality. Without such the spiritual dimension would be missing. The role of neighbor in relation is so important that it is placed along with one's very obligations to God according to the teachings of Jesus Christ. The Protestant congregation in suburbia persists predominantly as a neighborhood institution. Neighbors as members confront one another in many of the ordinary and extraordinary activities of life. It becomes second nature to consider one's obligation to the neighbor in affection, honor, and a concern to share the highest joys and ideals. The Christian definition thus transcends suburban culture because God is in it. Church members are expected to raise the level of all human relationships. Without this lofty principle it would be very difficult to face the incoming groups with behavior appropriate to Christians.

AM I MY BROTHER'S KEEPER?

Regardless of the socioeconomic circumstances of residents in the suburbs it is necessary to raise the question of being a brother's keeper. Is not the suburbanite responsible for his brother? What are the duties and opportunities which present themselves to twentieth-century suburbanites? The familiar biblical passage (Gen. 4:8-16) is ever a reminder of religion's larger demands which have persisted across the centuries. Cain enticed his brother Abel to go out into a field where he then slew him. When the Lord inquired concerning the whereabouts of Abel Cain shrewdly said, "I do not know; am I my brother's keeper?" This context of violence should not hinder us from taking account of the Lord's imperious question: *Where is your brother?* The implications for contemporary life need to be made clear in all the churches. For the suburban congregation the specific meaning needs to be delineated. To what extent does being a brother's keeper demand a sharing of time, talent, and material resources? What are the terms or conditions of this sharing? To what extent does it mean a sharing of faith itself?

It is very important that the suburban Protestant church *know where its brother is.* One denomination finds its brother among minority groups, among migrants, among inner-city residents, among inhabitants of prisons, among college students, among homeless children, and among the aged.

The concern for others is implemented by the suburban church in a variety of ways. Allusion has already been made to the standard and well-nigh universal approach of benevolences, but the concern is manifest also in the maintenance of slum missions, settlements, community houses, Goodwill Industries, and programs in penal institutions. At least one half (49.1 per cent) of the suburban churches are involved in programs for needy people. This is evident in the placement of Displaced Persons' families, aid of Negro centers, and the financing of Mexican missions. Sponsorship of work among migrants, alcoholics, homeless children, and elderly people comprises another sphere of implementation. Student programs and youth groups attract aid from a number of suburban churches. Apparently Thanksgiving and Christmas baskets are still needed across the United States.

The burden of launching new congregations is shared by 70 per cent of the suburban churches. They are deeply interested in church extension, not only for themselves but also for others. Amounts up to 8,000 dollars per year are given by individual churches. One congregation even mortgaged its building in order to secure a 50,000 dollar loan needed by a new church for urgent construction. Only a few suburban churches fail to be "brothers' keepers" in any of the ways cited above. Because of the widespread propensity to implement concern for others in practical ways a reassessment of the unselfishness and ecclesiastical vision of the suburban church is in order. In some quarters this is still a much maligned institution.

Gibson Winter, Peter Berger, and others, have pointed out the importance of the suburbanite's accepting an adequate share of caring for the world's needs. There is always a danger that the suburbanite will remain insufficiently informed with respect to the nature and extent of social and spiritual needs. Because of this possibility the suburban congregation needs to be reminded that it should carry as heavy a load as possible of the world's needs. This means more than financial aid; it means also the loan of personnel and the sharing of faith itself. Being a brother's keeper is very serious business within Protestantism. It is linked up with salvation itself.

BASIC CONCERNS OF THE SUBURBANITE

An overview reveals that the suburbanite needs a reminder of the concerns which implement personal faith and corporate life in the Protestant church. While it is possible to prepare a long list, it will suffice here to suggest a few of the prominent concerns. There are at least four of them.

1. *Concern for the inner city.* Foremost among the responsibilities of the suburbanite is concern for the inner city. There remains an unfinished religious and social task within the boundaries of the nearby urban community. It will be unfinished for many years to come. Each generation must find God. Although the suburbanite has moved out of the city he cannot dismiss this concern. His responsibility extends not only to his capacity to contribute materially to the support of adequate work, but also involves his personal attitudes toward minority groups and toward the urban poor. Who will minister to their condition in the name of Christ? In J. Milton Yinger's terminology, there are vast areas of "disprivilege" in the American city.[4] Many of these rundown neighborhoods are unable to find hope or the way out by themselves. Hence the burden comes back upon the shoulders of the fleeing suburbanite. He cannot hide from human need.

2. *Concern for spiritual achievement.* Many suburban congregations have become aware of the possible pacesetting character of their religious life. To the cynic the church only sets the pace in erecting new edifices and in furnishing the structures with all available comforts and conveniences.

---

[4] See "Religion and Social Change: Functions and Dysfunctions of Sects and Cults Among the Disprivileged," *Review of Religious Research* (Winter, 1963).

Other observers note that the suburban religious groups report enviable statistical trends and conspicuous institutional success. One must acknowledge such achievements. This, also, is a kind of pacesetting. However, attention can be directed to the pace set in the spiritual realm. Suburban congregations lead the way in the support of missions and virtually all other important social-service enterprises. Moreover, they pioneer in the formation of small-group activity which undoubtedly deepens the religious life and commitment of the congregation. Surely the suburban church has an obligation to be a pacesetter in the highest and most relevant sense according to its Protestant goals and purposes. This leadership role, however, unless properly understood and humbly pursued on the high level will do nothing but evoke envy, jealousy, and criticism. Perhaps it is not inappropriate to urge that the suburban congregation make a search for additional meanings in order that the leadership potential be not swallowed up in modern urban life.

3. *Concern for denominational growth.* Many suburbanites look around at the acres of new homes along with many new school and church buildings. From observation comes a reminder of the obligation which each suburbanite has to contribute importantly to the growth of his own denominational group. This is a concern for evangelical outreach. When a new church needs to be started in an adjacent housing area he should reach for his pocketbook and contribute money. More than this, he needs to be willing to recruit leadership and find other volunteer labor to aid the new congregation. Surely this does not mean that he should withhold support of the struggling suburban church of which he is now a member. The church in his own community needs his responsible assistance. This is noted in all three faiths by such writers as Greeley, Gordon, Greene, Kloetzli, and others. Stress is placed upon local church loyalty. It is not an end in itself.

4. *Concern for ecumenical relations.* A fourth concern to which the suburbanite must give attention is the obligation to co-operate across faith and denominational lines. For the Protestant this means co-operation in the local Council of Churches which seeks to focus the religious task upon issues of importance year after year. The individual congregation has an obligation to participate in this ecumenical process, taking as much initiative as is possible according to denominational polity. It must be borne in mind that there is a mandate in our time for all religious groups to relate themselves effectively with one another. This mandate cuts across faith lines,

calling all religious people to find the highest expression of the religious life in co-operative endeavor.

These several concerns can facilitate and undergird the type of attitude and sensitivity which will give meaning to what a neighbor is and who is Protestantism's neighbor. The latter is needful today. Not all of the present-day neighbors in suburbia are Protestant any longer. Now being a neighbor means relations with people who are different both within the suburb and elsewhere. Let then the Protestant church scrutinize her relations well and pursue the concerns which will bind up the wounds of humanity and make Christ known among all people.

V

Satan in the Suburbs

Some years ago Bertrand Russell wrote a book with the startling title *Satan in the Suburbs and Other Stories*.[1] The initial story occupies nearly one half of the slim volume. It recounts how Dr. Mallako, the villain, exerts evil influences which eventually wreck the lives of five suburban residents. A doctor, the respected manager of an important bank, the stolid secretary of a Bible distribution society, a professional photographer, and the wife of a leading scientist find themselves hopelessly compromised. By the time it is over there have been three suicides and one murder.

Curiously enough, there are some observers who fail to find evidence of Satan in the suburbs. For them no significant hidden problems, disorganization, or brokenness characterize the internal life of suburbia. Andrew Greeley, for example, mentions the exploitive propensities of a few real estate brokers and builders. He comments on the need for pastoral consultation on a wide range of problems, making occasional referrals to a psychiatrist. However, he regards the suburban teenager as rather docile and unlikely to go on lawbreaking sprees. Seeley, Sim, and Loosley, authors of *Crestwood Heights,* concur. Greeley discovers no crime, no delinquency. Indeed, the seamy side of suburban life scarcely appears in his book. Although there are hints and glimpses, so serious a subject remains untreated. Albert Gordon takes approximately the same posture. He recognizes that some juvenile delinquency exists and further laments the presence of some anti-Jewish and anti-Negro feeling in suburbia. Apart from this slight

[1] London: Allen & Unwin, Ltd., 1953.

passing notice, Gordon leaves the area of crime and delinquency undiscussed.

Fortunately, or unfortunately, Protestantism cannot be content with silence on the subject. The findings of a special research study covering 292 suburban Protestant clergymen leave no doubt respecting Satan's presence in suburbia.[2] Over a twelve-month period more than half of the ministers were called upon to deal with juvenile delinquents and one third with adult criminals. Clearly a wide range of serious hidden problems exist here—alcoholism, adultery, stealing, frauds, violations of trust, to mention but a few. Moreover, fiction writers who probe the suburban milieu disclose gruesome behavior and great need. Professional novelists occasionally put the spotlight on profound human problems. Whether John P. Marquand, Sloan Wilson, Peter DeVries, Edmund Schiddel, or someone else, writers point out hidden troubles in heavenly suburbia. Although debate rages around the question, a factual analysis calls for a practical and more realistic approach.

Indeed, it should occasion no surprise to find that the age-old struggle between good and evil is carried on amid the rows of trim, colorful homes, well shrubbed and set down on green lawns. It is no longer possible seriously to hold the popular theory in criminology that delinquents and criminals are the products of the lower socioeconomic groupings. Edwin Sutherland's studies compel a revision of this viewpoint, showing that people of high socioeconomic status also run afoul of the law.[3] Both Norman Jaspan and Frank Gibney, among other writers, support this viewpoint.[4] In the field of juvenile delinquency, Harrison Salisbury is emphatic in indicating that teenage crime occurs in suburbia.[5] A beautiful home in suburbia is no guarantee that a person does not or will not enter into criminal activity.

TEMPTATION, TENSION, AND TROUBLE

Crime and trouble come to suburbia. The suicide of a young wife whose marriage was about to break up is depicted in Sophie Treadwell's novel *One Fierce Hour and Sweet*.[6] Drunkenness and sex irregularities are woven into the frustrating story of troubled home life. A variation on the sex-and-drink theme is furnished by Edmund Schiddel in *The Devil in Bucks*

---

[2] "Suburban Pastoral Activities" (Report, Drew University, 1960).

[3] Especially *White Collar Crime* (New York: Holt, Rinehart & Winston, Inc., 1961).

[4] Jaspan and Hillel Black, *The Thief in the White Collar* (Philadelphia: J. B. Lippincott Company, 1959); Gibney, *The Operators* (New York: Harper & Row, Publishers, 1959).

[5] *The Shook-Up Generation* (New York: Harper & Row, Publishers, 1958).

[6] New York: Appleton-Century-Crofts, Inc., 1959.

County.[7] Here both grownups and teenagers are caught up in a lurid account of adultery in the suburbs. Many other novels make use of what apparently has become a standard theme.

Serious danger arises when the reader regards this material as merely fiction. When a suburban pastor from metropolitan Philadelphia, Joseph McCabe, in *The Power of God in a Parish Program* drew up a list of occasions upon which laymen should call the minister, he included four items touching the seamy side of life—alcoholism, separation and divorce, difficult decisions, and spiritual depressions. This list is reminiscent of that of many other suburban experts. Indeed, Edgar N. Jackson, who has spent twenty years in suburban church work, adds insecurity, guilt, tension, immaturity, and fear.[8] Both McCabe and Jackson have much in common with Richard and Katherine Gordon's *The Split-Level Trap* in the diagnosis of temptations, tensions, and trouble which harass residents of suburbia. Writers of novels and nonfiction appear to have no difficulty in the detection of evil.

Moreover, there is another way of exposing the situation. Jackson describes a suburban congregation of 500 people. Scrutinized from the viewpoint of problems, it is reasonable to assume that at least one hundred members have been recently bereaved, one third of the married persons are facing important adjustments, at least one half of the congregation has problems of emotional adjustment to school, work, home, or community. Others may have neuroses from alcohol addiction and from lesser obsessions and anxieties. Another hundred may be suffering from feelings of guilt or fear. The remainder of the congregation bears other types of problems. Obviously some people are harassed by more than one of these problems. According to Jackson, only the rare individual has complete peace of mind and soul. Thus it is realistic and necessary to regard the suburban congregation as made up of a great many persons who are carrying heavy burdens. To be sure, Satan is in suburbia.

When it comes to teenage difficulties, nearly every expert in the suburban field includes some of the following: Auto theft, car burglaries, sex clubs, crashing parties, drinking to excess, rowdyism, breaking into and entering public buildings, traffic violations, running away from home, and vandalism. Some of these activities are predelinquent; others are misdemeanors for which police arrests can be made. While the percentage of boys and girls

---

[7] New York: Simon and Schuster, Inc., 1959.
[8] *How to Preach to People's Needs* (Nashville: Abingdon Press, 1956).

involved remains relatively low, nearly every American suburb knows the tragedy of youth in trouble and the consequent parental anguish. No account of suburban life is complete without information on what the Hechingers call "teen-age tyranny." [9]

Apparently there is a kinship between Bertrand Russell's story and *The Split-Level Trap,* the report of a team of psychiatrists on suburban Bergen County, New Jersey. Both books call attention to the breakdown of individuals who carry "unsharable" problems. While Russell describes five suburbanites, *The Split-Level Trap* presents eight case studies of temptation, tension, and trouble in suburbia. Respecting the latter, Richard and Katherine Gordon, a husband and wife team, detail the genesis of each common problem, the trauma of crisis and breakdown, the necessary readjustments in the situation, and finally, the outcome. What therapy was utilized and how the breakdown could have been avoided are discussed fully. This challenging book contrasts the environmental strains of suburban living as seen in a suburban New Jersey county with the slower-paced life in a rural New York county. Perceivable differences are cited in terms of psychosomatic medicine and patterns of life adjustment.

From extensive studies the Gordons selected family case histories which illustrate the range of problems characteristic of modern suburban life. These are the problems most commonly handled in psychiatric practice. Difficulties arise from a wide range of circumstances—company transfers, cultural intermarriage, teenage delinquency, defeated middle age, inordinate ambition to climb socially and financially, social erosion of marriage, and exceptional economic success. According to the Bergen County study the suburban temptation is to live beyond one's means, to seek and accept promotions without adequate experience and preparation, to cover up inadequacies with lavish public-relations activities, to permit one's self to be overmatched in work responsibility, and so on. In substance this pattern of action, or "skating on thin ice," is reiterated by Frank Gibney in *The Operators.* Elsewhere in the literature the theme receives additional treatment.

Moreover, the Gordons insist that suburbia possesses many of the features of the early American frontier. It is so. The modern individual is expected to bring to the contemporary situation the qualities of self-reliance, aggres-

[9] Fred and Grace Hechinger, *Teen-Age Tyranny* (New York: William Morrow & Company, 1963).

siveness, independence, personal confidence, willingness to move, and a wide range of competences. Suburbia is hard on those who do not come adequately prepared to compete on this twentieth-century frontier. In the fierce competition for business and professional advancement the devil takes the hindmost. Unfortunately, wives and children are caught up in the satanic maelstrom also.

Tension, temptation, and trouble emerge from mobility, overwork, inordinate ambition to get ahead, value codes in collision, rootlessness, commutation pressures, burdens of homeownership, insomnia, the speculative way of life, overreaching one's income, worshiping the cult of popularity, spoiled children, overloaded people, youthful marriage, too many defeats, discontented spouses, and self-ignorance. To this environment the Gordons assign the term "Disturbia." Indeed, the word is used in numerous places as a synonym for suburbia. Life on the periphery of the city is disturbed in manifold ways.

TEENAGE MISCHIEF, VANDALISM, AND THRILL-SEEKING

John Marquand's *Life at Happy Knoll* describes teenage delinquency among the country club set in Connecticut and Westchester, New York.[10] Youngsters on occasion were permitted to hold parties at the Happy Knoll Country Club. Marquand recounts some illuminating details. As an evening wore on and the drinking increased the teenagers looked around for something interesting to do. Previously they had thrown the silver into the swimming pool. Then they wrecked the club's fancy bar by throwing glasses and bottles against it until everything in sight, including the mirrors, had been smashed. On another occasion they determined to have a tug of war on the tennis courts. Failing to find a rope the resourceful youngsters cut the Persian rug into strips and tied them together. Oddly enough, some older members of the club took a dim view of such "harmless" activity.

In *The Shook-Up Generation* Salisbury calls attention to the fact that much delinquent and quasi-delinquent behavior goes unreported in suburban communities. Neither the police nor the parents want records kept or prosecution pressed. This confirms the findings from special youth studies I conducted in Northern New Jersey. Suburban newspapers do not print all instances of juvenile crime. Yet, frequent reference is made to the middle-class context and to what Salisbury designates as "the shook-up generation"

[10] Boston: Little, Brown and Company, 1957.

residing in the American suburb. William and Joan McCord wrote *Origins of Crime* to report an evaluation of delinquent youth in two Boston suburban communities—Cambridge and Somerville.[11] Moreover, the findings of Guy L. Roberts on 150 Protestant delinquents in and around Pittsburgh is an interesting account of kindred problems in another metropolitan area.[12]

While it is pointed out that youthful offenders are often arrested, booked, and sometimes punished for their offenses, there exists a range of behavior which is properly identified as "predelinquent" or "fringe" behavior. Teachers, school administrators, guidance counselors, and police officers warn about these phenomena and their possible serious consequences. Here misbehavior ranging from petty larceny to teacher assaults is hushed up by parents, particularly those from upper income brackets. Many cases are first instances of public rebellion, destructive or delinquent activity. Frequently, as a solution, the obstreperous child is sent by his parents to a private school or placed in the hands of a counselor.

It cannot be said that poverty alone breeds problems. Delinquency usually ignores economic barriers; however, a difference appears in apprehension and treatment. The poor boy is likely to be arrested promptly and punished. On the other hand, a boy from a locally prominent family is likely to be scolded and given another chance, provided his parents take responsibility for the situation. In each case defective family life behind the youthful offender is the key. Delinquent youth come from homes where love, understanding, and parental care are lacking.

Some instances of destructiveness on the part of suburban teenagers are noted by Harrison Salisbury. School property was broken into and vandalized in Maplewood and Passaic, New Jersey; in West Islip, Uniondale, and Valley Stream, New York. The library at Bellmore, Long Island, was broken into and set afire, causing 65,000 dollars damage. Near Merrick, Long Island, a teenage gang killed swans in the reservoir by hurling lighted sticks at them. Other youths spent entire evenings smashing school windows and street lights. At suburban parking lots teenagers have smashed windshields, slit tires, and mangled convertible tops.

Elsewhere teenagers have wrecked diners and held up service stations "for kicks." With or without the stimulation of such mixed alcoholic

[11] New York: Columbia University Press, 1959.
[12] *How the Church Can Help Where Delinquency Begins* (Richmond: John Knox Press, 1958).

beverages as "sneaky pete," "thunderbird," et cetera, youths have sought illicit sex fulfillment through the establishment of "anti-virgin" clubs and schemes of white teenagers "dating" Negro girls from the city. Car "borrowing" is another name for auto stealing. Beating park squirrels and birds to death with their shoes is another way some suburban youths amuse themselves. Other activities include the rotten-egging of convertibles parked at public restaurants, stealing hub caps, beating up Jewish and Negro boys, traffic violations, uprooting tombstones, and other forms of mischief, vandalism, rowdyism, and thrill-seeking.

Evidence of teenage delinquency and gang activities in suburban communities is most convincing. Novelists and writers of serious documents report many instances in lurid detail. It is not a figment of anyone's imagination; it is fact, not fiction. Salisbury concludes that instances of juvenile delinquency in recent years have been unusually destructive and vicious. The activity as well as the argot have a remarkable similarity between teenagers in the suburbs and teenagers in the blighted inner city. However, suburban delinquents have the advantage of automobiles and reluctant police authorities. The suburban aspect of the problem deserves serious attention.

WHITE-COLLAR CRIME

According to the novelists adult life in suburbia is a dreary round of alcoholism, country-club lechery, family disorganization, adultery, human greed, anomie, and personal surrender to material values. In *The Thief in the White Collar* Jaspan and Black delineate a variety of white-collar crimes—embezzlement, stealing of merchandise, theft of company secrets, frauds to maintain job or community status, sabotage, padded expense accounts, manipulation of inventories to conceal stock shrinkage, and so on. In case after case persons placed in positions of trust succumb to temptation. This appears to be an American counterpart of Bertrand Russell's short story cited earlier. It defines white-collar crime.

On the other hand, in *The Operators,* Frank Gibney speaks of the frauds imposed upon suburban residents—the fake humus racket, the bogus termite expert, the phony tree surgeon, the lawn seed gyp, the fly-by-night roofers, and the crooked fire alarm demonstrator. Gibney concurs with John Keats's (*The Crack in the Picture Window*) strong attack on the exploitative tactics of real-estate developers and new home builders. In concluding the discussion of fraud in suburbia Gibney speaks rather bluntly about "sins against quality and fair dealing." He warns against the con man in the gray flannel suit. Further, in speaking of "fallen" suburbanites he traces the condition to immoderation and self-delusion. The term "fallen" here refers to adults who commit crimes.

Novels utilizing the suburban milieu direct some attention to white-collar crime. Edmund Schiddel's *The Devil in Bucks County* constitutes an exploration of infidelity and adultery. Other novels, such as *Make Mine Love* by Faber Birren, treat the theme of alcoholism as an occasion for the disintegration of personal character and family life in suburbia.[13] Some outstanding themes treated by suburban novelists include racially integrated housing, marital adjustment, vocational advancement, and society. Such stories as "The Housebreaker of Shady Hill" by John Cheever deal with stealing and kindred topics.[14] Always the report includes an account of good men and women of suburbia gone wrong.

White-collar crime properly is receiving ever more attention by scholars and law enforcement bodies. The writings of Frank Gibney, Norman Jaspan, Edwin Sutherland, and others show that the cost of white-collar crime alone probably exceeds by several times the financial cost of all of the crimes usually regarded as the "crime problem." Sutherland pleads for a more adequate theory of crime, insisting that some persons from advantaged classes do engage in criminal behavior. Sutherland's definition takes this idea into account. "White collar crime may be defined approximately as a crime committed by a person of respectability and high social status in the course of his occupation." [15] This definition can be applied to the materials written by Bertrand Russell and Norman Jaspan. It also approximates some of the nefarious behavior described by the Gordons in *The Split-Level Trap*. There can be no doubt about the existence of white-collar crime among suburbanites nor of its increasing significance today. Conditions call for a drastic revision of the outmoded theory that only poor people run afoul the law. White-collar crime costs the employers about 4,000,000 dollars per working day in cash and property.

[13] New York: Frederick Fell, Inc., 1958.
[14] *The Housebreaker of Shady Hill and Other Stories* (New York: Harper & Row, Publishers, 1958).
[15] *Op. cit.*, p. 9.

HOW SUBURBAN LIVING AFFECTS PEOPLE

An analysis of the foregoing materials can yield a useful delineation of problems. Some residents of suburbia get into deep trouble which affects the welfare of community life, the home, personality, and social institutions. Despite exceptional material advantages and pleasant surroundings, which surely ought to satisfy all man's essential needs, some suburban people manage to fail. This personal tragedy befalls both teenagers and adults. Why? Evidently something is fundamentally wrong with life here. This wrongness creates a "ferment on the fringe" of American cities, a profound suburban disturbance which bears a satanic aspect. The condition leads residents away from the pursuit of the good, the true, and the beautiful and discourages aspiration to spiritual goals.

What does suburban living do to people? Why do individuals from privileged homes get into trouble? Why is Satan here? Failure in suburbia causes difficulty not only to self and family but also to neighbors and friends. It has far-reaching personal and social consequences. This calls for an exploration of at least six facets of the problem: (1) The temptations of materialism, (2) rejected traditional values, (3) education's new messianic role, (4) broken homes, (5) wayward children, and (6) the contagion of delinquency.

1. *The Temptations of Materialism.* Residence in suburbia exposes people to fabulous materialistic temptations. A powerful milieu of "things" and "thing getting" dominates life here, making it easy to cultivate a desire to possess this world's goods. Marketing experts regard the suburbs as a plush market for quality merchandise and expensive personal services. This earthy environment ever confronts and ever tempts the suburbanite. There is no escape. Private ownership of property and of the public symbols of success predominate in the primary orientation here. Both among children and adults intense peer group competition for material things forces the lazy, the undisciplined, the unprepared, the maladjusted, and the clever to resort to manifold forms of deception, dishonesty, fraud, and outright crime. Possession regardless serves as the norm. Ownership of the outward symbols of success is regarded by too many as a suitable substitute for character. The siren call of materialism is wafted out across the ranch-type, split-level and Cape Cod rooftops. For children and youth suburbia affords numerous situations of temptation. Parental example and daily encouragement to strive after material goals and rewards yield a deleterious effect. If

parents and other suburban adults make this "limited dream" normative from whom will young people receive encouragement to aspire higher? Suburban contentment with merely "getting things" in life seriously shortchanges the rising generation and creates havoc in the institutions of society—the home, school, and church.

2. *Rejected Traditional Values.* Residence in suburbia erodes traditional values commonly associated with home life and personal character. Some people soon lose their ethical outlook and their religious standards in the scramble to get ahead. Values are sacrificed upon the altar of vocational advancement. This erosive process subordinates mankind's tested norms to a succession of contemporary fads and fashions. An inordinate emphasis is placed upon the erection of a public-relations facade rather than upon the building of character. Intense cultivation of the "personality crafts" illustrates the unfortunate contemporary trend. Overeagerness to conform, to please everybody, to keep in step with modern patterns of conduct, has encouraged some suburbanites to turn away from traditional values and tested patterns of discipline in personal and social life. Parents themselves are often part of the problem rather than part of the solution. They seek an escape from the restraints of conventions and moral codes. This rebellious attitude is the dominant theme of the suburban novels. Some spouses seek to shed moral responsibilities in order to lighten the load of adult life. Parental burdens are dumped into the community's lap. In this regard husband and wife behave very much like residents of the city's slum, exhibiting a refusal to accept parental responsibility. When this occurs children in the household are deprived of a dependable environment of discipline, recognition, love, and religious insight within which to grow up. Satanic behavior, delinquency, and crime are among the unwelcome results deriving currently from irresponsible parenthood. Children do not learn to espouse tested values or to apply ethical norms to the problems of living. Where traditional values are rejected crime and delinquency flourish, regardless of socioeconomic status. The ethical rebellion begins with the adults and spreads to the children.

3. *Messianic Role of Education.* Residence in suburbia places people in a secular power struggle wherein religious perspectives are progressively de-emphasized. The growing power and importance attached to the suburban school betokens the emergence of a secular "church," replete with its "priests" (experts) and laymen (parents). Contemporary education evokes

and generates a feeling of reverence and awe. Moreover, in many communities the suburban school has gained virtually a monopoly upon the child's time, attention, and energy. During the years since World War II home and church have been elbowed rudely aside. Meanwhile this growing secular goliath has taken over major responsibilities for the youngster's personality development, vocational choices, recreational interests, citizenship training, and morals, as well as his education. The unwelcome outcome is that the home, the church and other social institutions are assigned to a lower, perhaps even optional, status among suburban children. Preoccupied with its own interest and perpetuation, the suburban school spreads like a green bay tree across suburbia. What is overlooked, however, is that education must eventually bear its full share of responsibility for deviant behavior. Some schools do not. Top priority assigned to education is neither warranted in terms of the general welfare nor is it congruous with the true nature and destiny of man. Excessive emphasis upon education in suburbia to the penalty of religion leads to a mistaken view of life. The messianic role is an awkward one for true education to assume. Only religion can deal truly with the life before, during, and after the school experience.

4. *Broken Homes.* Residence in suburbia often produces "psychologically broken homes," which are as truly broken as some households in the inner city. Commutation and business travel take the suburban father out of the home a great deal. Although he returns regularly and supports his family, often he is as truly "absent" from the household as is the father in the slum. Preoccupation with business concerns consumes considerable energy and time. Since this condition continues over a crucial span of years, a loosening up of parental authority occurs. If the wife also is engaged in an active social or business life out of the home the problems are compounded. No material advantage in terms of comfort and convenience procured by overwork can make up for this brokenness. Psychological absence imposes a weakness upon family life. The absence of either spouse, the overworking husband or the oversocializing wife, contribute to the emergence of a broken home. When the home becomes weak additional problems arise from the condition. Broken homes produce delinquency and yield criminal behavior. This is the lesson taught by urban experience.

5. *Wayward Children.* Residence in suburbia deprives some boys of an adequate male model during the crucial maturation years. Family experts urge that a son needs someone of his own sex to guide him in the process

of becoming a man. No one can really supplant the father in this child management responsibility. Faring much better, a suburban daughter is normally exposed to a healthy range of adult female models—mother, school teachers, scout leaders, and other women of the community. Regrettably some suburban boys are not as fortunate. They are compelled to rely abnormally upon *father substitutes;* i.e., peer group selections of the athletic hero or the movie and TV star. Such choices rarely suffice, since they lack the down-to-earth reality of a man who resides in the local community. This deprivation on the male parental side robs the son of an important dimension of reality and guidance that are crucial as he matures. Suburban boys so deprived often become delinquent. Recent studies disclose that suburban boys get into trouble from three to eight times more frequently than do girls. A survey of the revelant literature leaves little doubt respecting the unwelcome consequences of "absentee" fathers. A boy deprived of his father's presence and adequate involvement is at an overwhelming disadvantage. Grave ramifications for suburban life and American society derive from the unsolved problem of wayward children. In the provocative book *Delinquency: Sickness or Sin?* Richard McCann refers vividly to this phenomenon as "the stain of juvenile delinquency." [16]

6. *The Contagion of Delinquency.* Residence in suburbia sometimes inadvertently glamorizes and nurtures deviant behavior. Adults fear to restrict so-called "creative" expression in their children. Hence immature teenagers are furnished automobiles and are granted unlimited freedom of activity. Parents indulge spoiled children, subsequently ignoring *the danger signals* of predelinquent behavior. What teacher, social worker, or minister does not know these signs? Confronted by real indicators of trouble, irresponsible adults dismiss the evidence nonchalantly. Patterns of antisocial conduct which heretofore have been associated with the lower classes have now spread to suburbia, yielding "gimme kids," "joyriders," and "split-level delinquency." These youngsters are lazy, irresponsible, and shockingly destructive. As noted earlier in the chapter, such activity has acquired an aspect of boldness, frequency, and extent which is frightening. While instances of delinquent behavior have been observed previously in suburban communities, a giant wave of satanic behavior has appeared recently. There is no hiding place from it. This spread of antisocial conduct deeply affects suburban life.

[16] New York: Harper & Row, Publishers, 1957.

This brief discussion touching six spheres of suburban trouble hardly exhausts the matter. The treatment, however, can direct attention to a fierce ferment on the city's fringe which betokens Satan in suburbia. The failures in a changing society become apparent. Delinquency and crime exist because the conditions of life here fall far short of the ideal. Circumstances permit the possibility of deviltry, recklessness, rebellion, irresponsibility, and sinfulness. The secular pressure upon persons is unprecedented. Evidently suburban living does things to people, causing some to fall into deviant behavior and sin. The acids of suburban life eat deep into the character of man and into the structure of family life. Something there is which pulls down the weak and the ill prepared. People fail in an environment which portends so much happiness and well-being. Suburban living affects some people negatively.

PROBLEM SOLVING IN SUBURBIA

Because the problems of suburbia have not always been widely publicized it should not be supposed that these problems have been ignored. Suburbia has frequently faced its problems unobtrusively, yet effectively. To solve problems of delinquency and adult misbehavior without reliance upon publicity is not altogether new. This method is favored by various experts in the treatment of youthful offenders. Generally speaking, police officials are not eager to arrest teenagers. Rather they prefer to counsel with the young person, hopefully expecting the misdemeanor will not be repeated. Parents are called in for conversations and asked to take responsibility for the youth's future behavior. Thus, many instances of mischief, vandalism, and delinquency are handled without the onus of arrest and unfavorable publicity. Suburban newspapers often co-operate in the process, believing it is in the public interest to leave some juvenile misbehavior unreported. Wherever responsibility is properly assigned and accepted the journalists have been willing to omit mention of youngsters who run afoul the law.

A second way of solving problems is achieved through pastoral counseling. A suburban minister of twenty years' experience reveals that an astonishing number of persons have received help in working out problems of alcoholism, marital infidelity, betrayal of trust in business, and other serious problems. This is not exceptional. "Suburban Pastoral Activities," a study of the counseling demands made upon 292 suburban Protestant ministers, revealed that *every* clergyman in the sample was asked for help in dealing with serious personal or social problems. Protected by the traditional secrecy of the counselor's office, persons guilty of misbehavior ranging from social indiscretion to crimes of violence have confessed wrongdoing and found a way to salvage that which is worthwhile in life. This process affords the client an opportunity to make restitution and to correct his own attitude and behavior patterns. Thus, a solution to burdensome problems can be found without the deleterious effect of damaging publicity. Pastoral counseling does not relieve the individual of his responsibility in wrongdoing. Rather it opens the way for reconciliation and a new life while protecting the innocent members of his family.

In yet another manner does unpublicized problem solving go on. Richard and Katherine Gordon have demonstrated dignified ways of seeking solutions to persistent and serious problems. In suburban Bergen County a group therapy approach has been developed which has proved beneficial to clients. It has been used with expectant mothers and other homogeneous groups. Only doctor and clients are witnesses to and participate in the process. Persons who need more individual attention because of deeper-seated problems receive help through supplemental therapy. Many communities now provide mental health clinics and kindred services.

SUNDAY IN SUBURBIA

This realistic appraisal of the existence of Satan in the suburbs should not leave us with the feeling that religion no longer has any force in the suburbs. Recently an interesting cartoon appeared in a magazine of national circulation. The cartoon depicted an absent-minded organization man who started out from home to go to the office. As he closed the door behind him he looked up and down the street of the suburban subdivision. What a sight he beheld! Men attired in work and sport clothes were everywhere. One neighbor was washing his auto; another was mowing the lawn; yet another was carrying golf clubs out to the car. The absent-minded white-collar man pulled himself up short with the comment, "Oh, my gosh, it's Sunday!"

The cartoon is probably an accurate portrayal of the popular estimate of the significance of Sunday in the suburbs. Fiction has much to say on the negative side. In Faber Birren's novel *Make Mine Love* a society woman turned alcoholic and prostitute sent word back to her former neighbors in suburbia assuring the resident clergyman that she attended church every Sunday. Sophie Treadwell has a young suburban mother of two children state her reason for attending Sunday religious services—to procure an extra hour of relaxation from the grueling work regimen at home. On this low level of interest in the sabbath, the remaining characters in the novel arranged themselves.

McCready Huston's *The Clouded Fountain* reports Sunday as the day when women attend church services and children go to Sunday school.[17] Men, on the other hand, choose golf, socializing, and sleeping late as essential sabbath-day activities. That this goes on with the knowledge of the local Episcopal clergyman is patent. Occasionally he chides a parishioner whom he has not seen in church since the previous Christmas or Easter Sunday.

What emerges from a brief survey of recent suburban fiction is the strange impression that Sunday has declined in religious significance. It has become just another day, a kind of second Saturday. It fails even to achieve the importance of a workday. Leisure, lassitude, and liquor comprise an espoused trinity. Hence for many residents of the city's leafy outskirts the "lost" weekend has become a distressing reality. So many other activities fill the hours that no place is reserved for the person who genuinely seeks to recharge his spiritual batteries, to renew his life in God. The fiction writer who utilizes the suburban milieu bluntly reduces religion to a very minor status.

When one turns to the nonfiction writers he finds a completely different picture. Even a reply from William Whyte is not completely pessimistic. Moreover, Bennett Berger in *Working-Class Suburb* points out that attendance at worship services is a normal weekend experience. Auto workers' wives generally attend more frequently than their husbands. Yet, in the total sample only 30 per cent of the suburban residents attend regularly. Baptists show an increase in activity since moving to the suburbs, whereas a slight decline is reported among Roman Catholics. Moreover, an empirical study of church attendance in a suburban Protestant church of 1,000 members disclosed that more than one half (55.3 per cent) of the members attended Sunday services frequently. This congregation is situated in a stable middle-class suburb. Whether the novelist knows it or not a great many people are interested in the religious significance of Sunday. Too often the

[17] Philadelphia: J. B. Lippincott Company, 1959.

professional writer projects his personal value system into the story and hence overlooks the fact that the sabbath still possesses intrinsic spiritual value. The sabbath is a resource for solving many problems.

SELECTED IMPLICATIONS FOR PROTESTANTISM

A recapitulation of the materials covered in this chapter encompasses the manifold ways in which the demonic appears in suburban life. Where there is juvenile delinquency, white-collar crime, trouble, temptation, tension, misuses of the sabbath, personal and social disorganization, and manifold forms of behavior deviation the satanic is present. Protestantism cannot ignore the seamy side of suburbia. Indeed, the church must develop an interest in human difficulties and share its ministry with all who need it. Is there any kind of trouble which can separate a man from the Protestant church? Or from God? The Bible (e.g. Rom. 8:31-39) seems to think not.

Because of the wide range of problems it is patent that religion's solution must of necessity be pluralistic. No simple or single formula will avail as a panacea. Rather, a variety of solutions must be sought which are adequate to the varying types of sin, stress, and trouble. Since Protestantism is deeply interested in each person, its approach must provide a way of helping persons in the midst of concrete circumstances. There is a personal aspect to each kind of trouble. When "Satan" enters a situation he endeavors to capture the total man or women rather than merely an aspect of behavior. Eventually the individual is corrupted as an entity, as a whole. For this reason Protestantism renders succor to the total person caught in a distressing dilemma.

No matter whether individuals, committees, or local congregations grow concerned about Satan in suburbia, some constructive suggestions can find acceptance. Indeed, the church wants to know what can be done. The foregoing discussion of the central problem opens the way for some relevant prescriptions which are suggestive rather than exhaustive. Thus the following ten categories cover a range of concern which is appropriate currently in suburbia. Beyond this the reader will need to work out specific practical application to a particular suburban community. This is the task of Protestantism.

1. *Identify the stresses of suburbia.* This identification should include the profound strains which arise from mobility of population, the role of stranger, exposure to new patterns of living, challenges to one's values, the

accelerated pace of life, buying on credit and mortgage financing, pressure to become too busy, temptation to omit the sources of ethical and spiritual insight (religious especially), and so on. Perception and experience are twin helpers here. All these stresses tend to slip up on the suburbanite largely unnoticed. Always there is a combination of stresses which close in upon the unheeding individual or family. The customary stance is to ignore the strains and stresses on the ground that such could never affect the observer. This unwise posture is severely criticized in *The Split-Level Trap*. Later the ignored pressures turn out to be the chief source of difficulty. Adequate diagnosis of the stresses can lead to an accurate identification of problems. Identification can be followed by awareness of possible personal consequences and the adoption of necessary precautions. Hence the individual, knowing the healing propensities of church life, may organize his suburban living to permit regular attendance and participation in religion. Church life is not eliminated or subordinate to anything else. Identification raises the question of criteria in dealing with stresses. To wend one's way safely among the latter requires definite standards of personal life and high purposefulness in living. The Protestant church should furnish aid in this sphere.

2. *Recognize modern vocational dangers.* It is very difficult to remain Christian in the present work-a-day world. More in suburbia than elsewhere, more in the modern world than previously, vocational pursuits have a deleterious impact upon the breadwinner. Fewer primary satisfactions reside in the work itself. Attention is focused increasingly upon the rewards of work—fewer hours, better working conditions, and more money. To this modern development is affixed an unnoticed price tag. Hidden strains emerge from the vocation. The tensions surrounding procedures for advancement, jockeying for position, selling oneself over and over to the representatives of the power structure, anxiety to be considered indispensable, concern for financial security—these are among the dangers arising from suburbanite occupations. More and more suburbanites, whether blue-collar or white-collar, are compelled to rely upon the "personality skills" in order to retain jobs. Many advance too rapidly, too recklessly, and then sink in the strain of overwork. Apparently mere technical competence and dedication to task are not enough. In order to be secure in employment the suburbanite must "butter" his superiors constantly and ever renew publicly an informal "loyalty oath" to the company. Something within the intelli-

gent suburbanite rebels against this vicious personnel policy. Something within resists the general cheapening of vocational activity. Thus some suburbanites become deeply frustrated and disillusioned. An awareness of modern vocational dangers must be achieved and retained. Overwork, overworry, overstrain, and overmatching lead to personal breakdown. To understand work and employment in the midst of life's wider perspectives is necessary. Heavy reliance upon the perfection of *means* to the neglect of long range *ends* is dangerous for society and the suburbanite. New dire dangers have arisen in the career world.

3. *Reinforce the Christian Home.* Parenthood challenges the suburbanite to re-evaluate the personal experience of growing up and then to seek adequate Christian ideals for family life. Yet often Protestant parents feel that they are working alone. If they erect standards for their children with respect to companions, home chores, study time, limitation on parties, rules for dating, and so on, they discover that few neighbors make analogous demands. The Protestant church has an obligation here. These embattled suburban parents need help with respect to standards. So often the Protestant church has little or nothing definite to say touching the ideals of Christian parenthood and the Christian home. It fails to support parents who are doing right. Even the most elementary discussion of crime and delinquency in the suburbs underscores the cruciality of the home and the continuing merit of its values. This means standards of conduct which are fit to become universal. This means home discipline and personal behavior which are not only an extension of the New Testament ideals of the church but also her intentional reinforcement of Christian home ideals. The church should not be a nervous bystander but rather a sure-footed ethical leader. This is an overlooked and underestimated ministry. If the home receives adequate reinforcement the incidence of sin, crime, and delinquency in the suburbs can be greatly reduced. Parents need insights and spiritual reinforcement from the Protestant church and from Christian neighbors. Without such aid Christian parenthood becomes a very heavy and often frustrating burden.

4. *Train youth to cope with trouble areas.* Many suburban youth fall into trouble because they have not been taught the rules and requisite disciplines in the primary trouble areas. Fire, guns, alcohol, sex, and autos hold a proverbial fascination for many young people. Usually both the home and the church institutions which have had an opportunity to touch the youngster's life, have failed to help him here in the process of growing up.

While heavy responsibility should continue to be focused in the suburban home, the suburban church has an obligation through its youth program to share in the task. Each institution complements the other. At as early an age as possible and in an atmosphere of love and understanding, youngsters need to be taught the role of fire, guns, alcohol, sex, and autos in human life. More than this, the youngsters need to acquire the necessary discipline which will support an understanding of such matters. Neither adequate knowledge nor requisite discipline can be achieved quickly. Rather, time and patience are needed here. Experts urge that virtually every youngster can master these essentials if the responsible adults will patiently teach him. If parents really knew how important this training is, and that it can be done with patience, what a transformation would occur in many suburban communities! This is a necessary task the outcome of which will surely affect the general welfare of suburbia. Parents and Protestant church leaders must resolve neither to deny young people the opportunity of experience in these spheres nor to abandon the rising generation without wise counsel, discipline, and control.

5. *Recognize signs of predelinquent behavior.* Early evidence of predelinquent behavior can be detected. At least one writer indicates that the signs appear as early as kindergarten. What are the signs? They include inordinate rudeness to parents, temper tantrums, irresponsibility in school homework assignments, impatience and lack of perseverance, disregard for the rights of others, cruel bullying of younger children, refusal to discipline self, exceptional laziness, acquisition of dissipatory habits, et cetera. Conversations with truant officers, principals, school counselors, social workers, and police officials can aid interested parents in distinguishing the clues which warn of possible delinquent behavior. Salisbury speaks of "the shook-up generation" in suburbia; the Gordons refer to "gimme kids." Both references signify the youngsters who grow up without adequate guidance from parents or church. If the children had received proper direction during the crucial years of maturation much of the delinquency in suburbia could have been avoided. Moreover, if parents, teachers, and youth leaders had been alert they could have been forewarned by the telltale danger signs. Recognition of the meaning and direction of children's behavior can lead attentive, loving adults to nip trouble in the bud. Remedial action and guidance can alter the outcome for many youngsters.

6. *Develop challenging youth programs.* Any program which leaves youth

unchallenged should be avoided. Suburban churches should be wary of activities which fail to capture the attention of teenagers. Youth are antagonized by elements in society which fail to meet their needs. The question arises naturally, In what areas should youth be challenged again and again at each level of emerging maturity? Several areas can be suggested—brotherhood, ecumenicity, service, vocation, science and religion, faith, world peace, and social justice. This line of thought should suggest also that a large attendance at a meeting or the mere popularity of a topic may not be suitable as criteria. Challenge must go deeper than this. It should reach the level of talent and engender concern. The positive must be accented in dealing with these youngsters. Moreover, youth's integrity must be respected. The church should rely upon intellectual understanding rather than exhortation and direct appeal. During the stress and storm of the teen years youngsters will need all the help available from an open and supportive fellowship in the church. Top priority must be given to youth. In a setting where the value of persons is elevated above institutional values youth really can hear a call to confront the great issues of our time. Normally the challenge must be hurled by someone who actually is engaged in such creative activity. The program must be dynamic and relevant.

7. *Provide for church members in trouble.* Many Protestant churches take no responsibility for their adherents who run afoul the law. The burden is dumped upon the social agencies. Adequate provision should be made by Protestantism at least for its own church members of all ages who are in trouble. Both adults and youth fail in life. What is "trouble"? Edgar Jackson, Joseph McCabe, and the Richard Gordons in the lists cited earlier have provided an interesting catalog of suburban problems. For our purposes here "trouble" is defined as all of the kinds of crime, sin, and delinquency alluded to in the present chapter. There can be no mistaking the tangled problem of acceptance within the general congregation which emerges here. The individual who is in trouble needs to be received by his church. Church members find it easier, however, to accept people in hardship situations (Luke 10:25-37) than in cases where guilt is associated with theft, crime, or wrongdoing. Evidently it is easier to donate money, food, and clothing than it is to provide friendship and understanding. Yet a deeper acceptance must come if the healing support of the church fellowship is to sustain the person in trouble. Provision for distressed church members does not involve fellowship alone but also opportunities to par-

ticipate in the organizational activities, possibly even in leadership roles, as well as backing in the community also. It means giving the person a chance to make good, to prove himself. The friendliness and confidence of the church is needed to bolster the morale of the troubled individual. Somehow local Protestantism should see this opportunity as truly a part of its legitimate ministry as is the training of children in Christian education. When the guilty are repentant Protestants need to remember Christ's example on the cross. Individual church members can take the initiative in laying this priority upon the heart of the congregation. The Protestant community must learn how to help troubled members.

8. *Adopt an inner-city church obligation.* It is common knowledge that many of the Protestant congregations in the inner city are struggling and handicapped. Here is a significant focus of concern for the suburban church. It should rank in importance along with India, Africa, and Latin America. Suburban Christianity is called upon to participate responsibly in the process of serving underprivileged people. This obligation can keep the congregation sensitized to human need. Because the inner city represents a place where serious personal and social disorganization is lamentably commonplace, where human needs pile up to an awesome height, and where people are overmatched in terms of ills and needs, a working relationship with suburban Protestantism can be of mutual benefit. Slum churches need the insight, encouragement, and material help which can become available from suburban Protestantism. Further, the inner city is today an outpost of Christian social concerns, raising in dynamic form the great issues of our time. It has a yeasty effect upon all society. Suburban Christianity truly needs to address itself to these crucial issues inasmuch as such are no longer merely academic concerns rattling around college halls. The adoption of a working relationship with an inner-city church can furnish the suburban congregation a continuous confrontation with the unsolved problems of poverty, second-class education, unemployment, and kindred stormy issues. The slum is trying to say something which suburbia needs to hear. Adoption of an inner-city obligation should be investigated and arranged through denominational and ecumenical channels. It can mean religious salvation for many a self-centered, captive suburban congregation.

9. *Co-operate with community agencies.* The local Protestant church needs to discover what associations and social agencies are concerned about suburban crime, sin, and delinquency. Religion is not alone in the field.

Many problems are too complicated to be handled by a single agency alone. In particular, the church should relate itself to law enforcement bodies, the school system, alcoholics anonymous, employment and child care agencies, and other eleemosynary institutions. In some suburban places such a relationship already exists on a casual basis. What may remain to be done is to work out patterns of specific co-operation which will co-ordinate the activity of concerned groups seeking to help people in trouble. A pattern of co-operation needs to be specific and long-range rather than vague or on a year-by-year basis. Deep-seated troubles cannot be dealt with adequately in a short time span. Continuing concern combined with remedial action yields desired results. Even this co-operative relationship should not bind the church to mere perpetuation of palliative measures. Rather, a more constructive and imaginative way of handling the community problems should be sought. Co-operation should never stand in the way of the achievement of improved community conditions. The church's relationship to community agencies should round out an adequate program of concern and genuine help.

10. *Mobilize church resources.* Thus far in the present discussion attention has been focused largely upon the problems themselves. This remains an important emphasis. Yet it does overlook the broad capability of the religious institution. Why cannot the total resources of the church be mobilized in a grand and meaningful way? Crime, sin, and delinquency in suburbia present such a formidable problem that Protestantism should put its strongest foot forward. Great power lies in concerted effort. Mobilization of church resources should possess at least four dimensions: (1) The congregation's leadership should function as a detective committee to make sure that none of Satan's victims are overlooked or uncared for; (2) the local church organizations should utilize their power to help, scheduling women's organizations to help troubled women, men's organizations to help men, and youth organizations to help young people; (3) the congregation's counseling capability (medical, psychiatric, vocational, spiritual, recreational, et cetera) should become available regularly in needy situations; and (4) the material resources of the local church should be focused upon the needs of the family of the troubled person. Certainly the suburban church should be willing to mobilize all her resources wisely in order to meet the needs of suburban residents who fail in personal and community life. The church needs to become a united, dynamic, and dedicated body of conscientious

persons which will take a stronger hand in the shaping of community life. All the resources of the church need to be brought to bear upon the brokenness of suburban life.

The materials treated in this chapter should not convey the impression that suburbia is either a crime center or a cesspool of civilization. This would be untrue. Rather, some working knowledge of the indigenous troubles as well as the remarkable advantages of suburban living are needed to provide a fair appraisal of the thousands of new communities which afford homes for 60,000,000 Americans. People who reside in suburbia know that life flows on in a channel lying somewhere between the two extreme sides or banks set by the critics.

Certainly Protestantism stands in a very important relation to modern suburban life. This faith has thousands of indigenous congregations. Because of its evident anchorage in Christian history and the New Testament the church can transcend any cultural pattern and speak significantly in every situation. It possesses unusual resources for meeting the issues of suburban life. Protestantism knows human conduct and human relationships. This knowledge helps the church retain its prophetic role and healing ministry.

Certain implications emerge from our discussion of Satan in the suburbs. Protestantism can certainly examine the evil, the crime, the delinquency, and other types of unsavory behavior. From a thoroughgoing inquiry it can determine its responsibility in serving the people and in preparing them for the kingdom of God and for the world of tomorrow. The committed Protestant is a good citizen in the kingdom and in the world.

VI

Protestantism and
Family Life

For a discussion of family life in suburbia there exists a wide
range of relevant materials—a score of serious analyses plus several
dozen novels and scores of periodical articles. What does an exploration
of such literature yield? Possibly the question can be answered under the
seven meaningful rubrics: Family life behind a picture window, blue-
collar and white-collar families, institutional mobility of families, the omnipotence of mother, major suburban family problems, the lost ministry
to families, and new family life and suburban Protestantism. This brief
treatment can delineate the main issues, indicate several lines of constructive action, and serve as an antidote to the unwarranted cynicism of some
writers.

FAMILY LIFE BEHIND A PICTURE WINDOW

Ever since the rash of books about suburbia began to appear high
visibility of its family life has been assured. From the biting rakish satire
of John Keats through the distressing maze of interdisciplinary opinions
of *Crestwood Heights,* to the patient constructive concern of the authors
of *The Split-Level Trap,* the matter of conjugal life under suburban circumstances is definitely of interest to a great many people. In addition to
the nonfiction, several dozen novelists have lifted up aspects of personal
and family life over which the public can either gloat or despair. Generally
speaking, negative treatments of suburbia outnumber the positive discussions. How then can one actually discover what family life is like behind
the picture window?

There can be no doubting the public spectacle which is presented by the appearance of new tract and development suburbs. Such housing projects range from a few hundred to thousands of new homes—often very much alike in design and color. These dormitory or bedroom communities displace the forests, the fruit orchards, and the fields of waving grain which up until a few years ago covered the countryside. The residential structures are often jammed so closely together that the view from one picture window looks right into the picture window of the development house across the street.

Moreover, these acres of look-alike houses often provide shelter for look-alike, think-alike, and live-alike residents. What these families have in common are debts, mud, gynecological problems, and conformity. The compulsion to neighborliness often arises out of the situation of physical contiguity and the attitude of "misery loves company." Under conditions of such intense interaction, which often omit the dimension of true friendship, a pressure builds up to keep pace with the Joneses—in house furnishings, in dressing the children, in building a backyard fireplace, and so on. These features of suburban life most easily catch the attention of the general public. Such are described colorfully and with great vigor by William Dobriner, John Keats, John Liell, Auguste Spectorsky, George Warner, William Whyte, the journalists, and the novelists.

Suburban social devices for procuring conformity include the daily lawn date for mothers of young children, the adult cocktail or bridge party for the dissemination of obscene jokes and small talk, and finally the "cookout" in somebody's backyard. Through these informal gatherings the resident catches up on the latest scuttlebutt and the choice morsels of gossip which make the rounds of the suburban community. Because families are jammed so closely together, especially in the economy suburbs, everyone finds out everything about everyone else's household almost as quickly as it occurs. As a result some wife, or husband, or child is always on the spot with the neighbors. Close friendships are usually difficult to develop under the circumstances. Evidently too much "visibility" for suburban family life is not wholesome. The inevitable imperfections of the home become too widely advertised and criticized. Curious spectators often violate the integrity of sound family life. Some household matters are private whether the gossipmongers recognize this fact or not. Indeed, since no home is perfect whatever its geographical location no useful purpose is served by holding up for public view and criticism the suburban family. The diatribes against suburban life are often misdirected, being really aimed at middle-class values and attitudes. Irresponsible attacks produce a needless self-consciousness and confusion within the family circle.

A glimpse of suburban family life as depicted by several representative writers can illustrate the range of domestic phenomena behind the picture window. On one end of the socioeconomic continuum is the gracious family life of upper middle-class suburban residents exhibited in *Crestwood Heights*. Through the picture window here are displayed luxurious furniture and excellent taste in décor. Social activity is extremely important among these homemakers. Every labor- and time-saving gadget has been installed in the ample house. Child rearing is turned over largely to the experts—teacher, psychologist, guidance counselor, religious educator, recreation director, and so on. The delegation of these many burdens releases the upper middle-class wife for *a career of social activity,* which becomes a goal of major proportions. Despite pleasant surroundings and freedom from taxing responsibilities, however, tension, heartache, and frustration pursue even the privileged family. It is no surprise to learn that happiness, recognition, and peace of mind elude the advantaged individual also. Wealth cannot purchase some values.

Near the other end of the socioeconomic scale is family life behind the picture window in an auto worker's suburb, disclosed in Bennett Berger's *Working-Class Suburb*. Here the breadwinners are hourly wage factory employees. The house is much smaller and furnished in quite an ordinary fashion. The television set, the automobile or two, and the numerous material gadgets are taken for granted. There appears to be no status anxiety, however, since life is lived pretty much in the present. Social activities are minimal and informal. Little ambition to climb the prestige ladder is evident. Vocational aspiration is not very high. A glimpse through the picture window here may be a bit disappointing for some readers.

Between the socioeconomic extremes noted above is family life in a white-collar suburb as portrayed by John Keats. Husband, wife, and several children are seen stuffed into cramped quarters which are mortgaged to the limit. What a miracle it will take to convert this tiny, boxlike house into a home! The structure is situated in a large development suburb where families reside briefly and then move on. This white-collar family is upwardly mobile. A visible mark of success here is the outmovement to a "better" suburban community. Many white-collar families of modest circumstances long fervently for that day. Finally, *The Split-Level Trap* presents vignette studies of eight households in which the rigors of suburban life have yielded psychosomatic illness. These cases will be discussed in a subsequent section. The authors point out that domestic love, understanding, and meaningfulness had eroded away. When the stricken persons eventually recover normal outlooks and adequate attitudes again, we see how rich and meaningful family life can be in suburbia. Indeed, *personal recovery was not possible without the restoration of healthy family life*. At best it is difficult to escape the strains, the stresses, and the pitfalls, the trap which is hidden in contemporary suburban life. The situation is complicated by the new values emerging here.

In recapitulation, patterns of family life behind the picture window as noted in development housing, in blue-collar territories, and in upper middle-class suburbs differ just as the external features of the communities are conspicuously dissimilar. Families reside in all types of suburbs. Sixty million Americans make their homes here. These households bear the responsibility for a vast amount of homemaking, child rearing, and character development. Because the culture of the United States is in flux, family life is caught up in some drastic alterations. The nature and scope of these changes and their impingement upon Christian discipleship deserve serious attention.

BLUE-COLLAR AND WHITE-COLLAR FAMILIES

The foregoing comments on family life behind the picture window have prepared the way for further discussion of the differences which possibly exist between blue-collar and white-collar suburbanites. To carry this necessary orientation further one should observe that studies of suburbia can be divided for purposes of analysis into two general groupings: (1) *Middle-class suburbs*—Chatham, Crestwood Heights, Englewood, Greenbelt, Levittown, and Park Forest, for example; and (2) *working-class suburbs*—Milpitas and Autotown, for example.

Under the first rubric one encounters the familiar stereotype of suburbia so widely advertised in novels, periodical articles, and "popular" books. Insights here derive from the writings of Keats; Spectorsky; Whyte; the Gordons and Gunther; Seeley, Sim, and Loosley; and others. Suburbia is the home of the organization man, the residence of the social striver, the domestic retreat of the hard-driving, public-relations conscious, ambitious man. Among the prominent features of the white-collar suburb are the effects of geographical and social mobility upon the family. This means the impact of frequent change of residence, high priority assigned to vocational advancement, secondary concern attached to activity which does not have public relations value, and the primacy of social conformity.

Some suburban families change their places of residence as many as *ten times* during the child-bearing and child-rearing years. The home is caught up in and swept along by a relentless pursuit of vocational success and financial security. Security soon becomes defined in terms of material wealth rather than in terms of permanent residence. Mobility permits only time enough to develop short roots in the community life in each place, whether the relationship is to church, school, club, or association. The entire family has become a rolling stone. A young woman who had grown up in a mobile family was asked to name the place of her nativity. "We have resided in so many cities and suburbs since I was born that I really don't know," she admitted reluctantly.

Family life under middle-class circumstances imposes upon each member of the household the necessity of learning the personality skills and the know-how requisite to establishing instant friendships, instant credit, instant status, instant church relationships, instant recreation, and above all, instant departures. What must be accomplished has to be done quickly. Since bank services, shopping facilities, transportation, community affairs, have become standardized across the nation, it has become easier to move from suburb to suburb, from community to community. The speed of movement plus the everlasting urge to get ahead puts the white-collar family under debilitating pressures. Out of these modern tensions arise the causes for psychosomatic illness and spiritual exhaustion. Over the many pleasant features of white-collar family life there hangs the ever-present threat of personal failure and breakdown. White-collar family life is a stressful existence.

The second category of suburbs refers to manual employees, the hourly rate factory workers, and kindred employees. Somehow the fact of suburban residence for such people has been almost overlooked in the literature, although H. Paul Douglass' older study mentions it. Oddly enough, blue-collar families are not interested in social prestige and economic mobility as defined by the organization man. Rather, satisfactions derive from a differing round of activities and a varying set of values.

Respecting blue-collar suburbia, one observes evidence of unabashed material prosperity American style. The families who completed the move from the city neighborhoods and elsewhere now reside in their own split-level houses, wear attractive clothes, have television sets, and may even possess two automobiles. Is it not remarkable that a factory worker can receive such ample rewards for his labors? To earn approximately 5,000 dollars or more a year from blue-collar employment yields these astonishing suburban advantages.

Contrary to popular expectation, however, Bennett Berger's findings show that the blue-collar worker transports his previous milieu out into the suburb with him. The moving van which carries his furniture to the outlying community also transports much of his old way of life. These people from a drab industrial neighborhood do not learn middle-class behavior, beliefs, and aspirations as a result of the suburbanization process. Rather they simply reproduce important aspects of their previous lives here in the newly settled suburb. The suburb is a place, not a way of life, according to Bennett Berger's study.

The so-called suburban context leaves the blue-collar worker largely unaffected. Some convincing evidence can be cited. Membership and activity in formal associations, semiformal mutual visiting between couples, cocktails before dinner, giving and going to parties, social striving, and status anxiety are rarely found here. In Bennett Berger's judgment: "Their tastes and preferences seem untouched by the image of 'suburbia' portrayed in the mass media." [1] Surprisingly, the blue-collar suburbanite is well-aware of his own educational and technical limitations and has made a realistic estimate of his prospects of achieving a larger share of this world's material advantages. Both he and his family are grateful for the present rewards of his labors. They do not expect much more. Caught up in the new-found convenience and pleasures of suburban living, they fix attention upon the present and are satisfied. Here is the focus of their interests, concerns, and pleasures. In this respect they retain the outlook carried out with them from the city. Undoubtedly many of the findings of Bennett Berger's study would apply to other booming cities around

---

[1] *Working-Class Suburb*, p. 92.

which the suburbs are populated dominantly by well-paid industrial workers. Indeed Walter Martin's analysis of the suburban fringe of two Oregon cities, Eugene and Springfield, tends to support Berger's findings.

In summary, blue-collar and white-collar suburbs differ markedly with respect to both external and internal features. This contrast is exhibited in family life—the barometer of significant living. Blue-collar families live in the present, know their educational limitations, hold limited vocational ambitions, are relatively unmoved by status anxiety, and have their own distinctive way of life replete with cultural preferences, child-rearing practices, and noncommunity participation. Church relationships are often exemplary. By way of contrast, the white-collar family is often more aware of public relations and the worth of personality skills, more interested in getting ahead in the economic and social realms, more sensitive to public opinion, and likewise has a distinctive way of life spanning the gap between cultural preferences and psychosomatic illnesses. As a result of genuine differences the families are conditioned to divergent types of beliefs, values, and customs. Woe unto the local Protestant church which fails to take into account these differences. Suburban families are mobile families predominantly. Discussion of the struggle to get ahead points up the importance of socioeconomic mobility. Today modern suburban residence is almost synonymous with promotions, salary raises, and climbing the success ladder.

INSTITUTIONAL MOBILITY OF FAMILIES

The ancient maxim "a rolling stone gathers no moss" has been rewritten in the modern world to read, "a standing stone gathers no moola!" Movement is equated with success. That there is significant mobility in suburbia appears to be an established fact according to the experts. Walter Martin asserts that consistent with the traditions of American society are *freedom of movement* and *freedom of location*.[2] Citizens have a constitutional right to move around at will within the United States and to select places of residence as they desire. Clearly these freedoms are exercised at the present time by the highly mobile American family. The importance of mobility in suburbia is seen in a discussion of two kinds of movement —geographical mobility from one community to another and socioeconomic

[2] *The Rural-Urban Fringe* (Eugene: University of Oregon Press, 1953), p. iii.

mobility which entails upward economic achievement or "climbing." In modern business the two have been united, forming a strategy of personnel training and advancement. Thus, *mobility has become intentionally institutionalized.* As such it profoundly affects family life.

First, what is the nature and extent of *geographical mobility* in suburbia? One out of five Americans will probably be residing in a different home next year. That the typical mover in the United States is the suburbanite may be evidenced in part by the surprising turnover in homeownership. Duncan and Reiss report that the percentage of families which move is greater in the suburbs than in central cities.[3] John Keats emphasizes the inadequacy of many suburban houses, especially those situated in the large-scale developments. Crowded, unsatisfactory living conditions in economy suburbs evoke the dream of selling out someday and of moving elsewhere to a better house in a better neighborhood. At best the development house can be regarded as a temporary expedient, making mobility both inevitable and endemic to the situation. Andrew Greeley speaks of a powerful internal compulsion which drives Americans to purchase a home of their own. This homeownership expectancy is one of the legitimate ends of the American success story. People believe that they have a right to escape to the suburbs from the ugly and debilitating complexity of industrial cities.

Martin's study of the rural fringe areas adjacent to Eugene and Springfield, Oregon, disclosed that 76 per cent of the families had moved into the territory during the previous five years. Moreover, the last previous residential location for 88.4 per cent of the families was in cities or rural nonfarm areas. Only one family out of eight came directly from the farm to the fringe. Richard Dewey's comparable study of the residents of Milwaukee's suburbs shows approximately the same percentage ratios.[4] Predominantly the people originate in the city or in other suburbs. Ernest Mowrer reports[5] that four fifths of the families residing in the Chicago suburbs studied originate as noted by Dewey and Martin.

The situation in a New Jersey suburban community is relevant here. Among the seventy-six families interviewed last year several important

[3] Dobriner, editor, *The Suburban Community,* pp. 45-66.
[4] "Peripheral Expansion of Population in Metropolitan Milwaukee" (Ph.D. dissertation, University of Wisconsin, 1946).
[5] Dobriner, *op. cit.* pp. 147-64.

facts appear. It was discovered that only 11.6 per cent of the husbands and wives were born in the suburban community where they now reside. Further, 38 per cent were born in the remainder of the state. Summarizing the matter, eight spouses out of nine are not native to the suburb of current residence.

Moreover, the findings of a research study I completed in 1960 included 109 interviews of selected families residing in ten New Jersey and New York suburbs which disclosed that only one person out of fifteen is native locally. Four out of five families have resided in two or more suburbs since the spouses spoke their nuptial vows. On the average, a family sojourns in a suburban community 8.4 years before moving on. This figure compares favorably with that of Mowrer. By way of contrast, a small minority of suburban families had resided in the present community for thirty years or longer. Predominantly, however, suburban families remain but a short time and then move on. Geographical mobility is a strong pattern.

Second, *socioeconomic mobility* refers to climbing the ladder of worldly success. In a recent penetrating discussion of family life Ernest Mowrer speaks of suburban mobility as being generated by at least three sets of factors—material prosperity, governmental encouragement of homeownership, and the suburban vision. Such factors underlie the contemporary flight to suburbia. Accumulated savings, low interest rates on mortgages, and small down payments as incentives of homeownership and the phenomenal increase of the birth rate since World War II have combined to produce a spectacular shift in American community life. By the term "the suburban vision" Mowrer means the well-known struggle for status and economic advancement in metropolitan communities. Mowrer finds in suburbia an increased emphasis upon "living it up," upon reaching after more income.

The restless, never-satisfied, job-hopping, middle-class consumer is not only the backbone of American growth but also the chief participant in mobility. He drags his family into the maelstrom. Job transfers, salary increases, the desire for more adequate housing, are several of the causes for the intercommunity movement of suburban families. The typical suburban family is a "climber" family according to Whyte and other writers. The white-collar suburbanite expects to climb the socioeconomic ladder. Movement geographically means, for him, vocational advancement and increased income, two rather interesting rewards deriving from mobility.

Above all, the single-family dwelling emerges as the symbol of the sub-urban vision. To own a home in the suburbs indicates that the family has "arrived," is actually getting somewhere. Martin frequently points the reader's attention to the clash of rural nostalgias and urban appetites, a clash which has a disturbing effect upon family life. Eagerness to possess a home in the suburb is accompanied by the strong desire to have the conveniences of urban civilization—garbage collection, paved streets, mass transportation facilities, and so forth. John Liell stresses this point also.[6] Moreover, homeownership reveals the starved character of the household which strives so hard to get ahead in the material realm. Desire can be-come a very powerful force. Thus discussion of the upward struggle ac-knowledges the importance of socioeconomic mobility. Today suburban residence exudes the impression of promotions, salary increases, and ascent of the success ladder. How profound are the consequences of economic mobility for family life—access to cultural advantages, levels of consump-tion, and class identification!

Third, the two types of mobility mentioned above lead naturally to a recognition of *institutionalized mobility,* the emerging strong pattern of the business world. One is familiar already with the pattern of itineracy among clergymen who shift from parish to parish. This is a normal re-quirement of the profession. What is new currently, however, is the ap-plication of the principle to the business world. Young men who desire to make advances in career must accept itineracy. Either they are deployable or they are expendable. Thus geographical mobility has been invested with added meaning. A man must move around in order to move up the socio-economic scale. Who has not seen the anguish, dismay, or joy written upon the faces of personal acquaintances who are involved in the new corpora-tion deployment system?

This itinerant pattern has an impact upon family life, as is noted by various writers. The transfer of families from one part of the United States to another often creates agonizing problems of adjustment for spouses and children. Repeated company transfers rob the family of its community roots and its deep emotional anchorages in familiar places and among tested friends. Distress emerges over questions of loyalty, institutional af-filiations, and participation in community life. How can one make a transition from loyalties left behind in the little church, the little town,

---

[6] "Levittown."

and the region? Where can one find help now in procuring larger loyalties which will enable the family to transcend its left-behind local affections? Where will one find an overarching loyalty of adequate dimensions for the new situation? Who will teach these itinerant business personnel and their mobile families what it means to be a Protestant Christian in the new situation? Can they find the right way without the church's help?

Due to mobility few suburbanites have established deep roots in the local suburban community. When these people think of home their thoughts turn nostalgically to some place across the plains or over the mountains many miles away. Contemporary existence has acquired a nomadic aspect. Thus, *the itinerant family is modal for modern suburban life.* Despite such patterns of mobility, Rodda remains optimistic: "Actually, the suburban community has resisted, more successfully than the central city, the forces working for the dissolution of family life." [7] This observation leads one to realize that in spite of the enormous pressures upon the suburban family, it manages somehow to retain a surprising integrity, coherence, and spiritual potential. From Protestantism it needs all of the help it can get. The denominations must learn to render a more significant ministry to the harried, mobile suburban family.

THE OMNIPOTENCE OF MOTHER

A new power and significance attaches itself to wife and mother in suburbia. The importance of the homemaker is exalted here. The children —two, three, four, or five—in nearly every household have invested her role with a heroism heretofore unnoticed. The husband and father, being increasingly absorbed in his vocation, relinquishes many responsibilities traditionally borne by the male spouse in homelife. This shifting of domestic burdens to his wife's shoulders arises from the increasingly competitive character of his employment. Whatever may be an adequate explanation for the juxtaposition of home burdens and responsibilities, today's suburban housewife finds herself saddled with a vital new and significant role to play—she has become *the living center of home life* in suburbia. She now focuses the dynamic process so essential to the rearing of children and the management of the household.

Although the suburban mother is not a superwoman, when viewed in

[7] "An Exploration of the Response of Organized Protestantism in an Expanding Commuter Suburb" (Ed.D. dissertation, New York University, 1953), Chapter VII.

terms of her accomplishments she comes very close to deserving the appellation. She is a capable woman who is often overloaded in the early
and middle years of marriage with the tasks of childbearing and training,
and frequently underloaded in later years after the children have grown
up. Across the childbearing and child-rearing years her burdens and her
capabilities are phenomenal; she functions as cook; housekeeper; nurse;
counselor of children and youth; slave driver; prosecutor; protagonist of
education; planner of vacations; director of youth's work experience; super-
visor of chores; chauffeur to school, dance class, and music lesson; socializing force; home manager; shopper; and many other things. She is often
asked to play the role of both mother and father to the children. In addition to running this three-ring circus charitably called a suburban home,
she assumes the role of sweetheart and intellectual companion to her husband.

In *The Split-Level Trap* the suburban mother is cited for her pioneerlike
qualities. Usually she has pulled up her roots from the place of nativity.
Now she is very much on her own, being separated by many miles from
relatives and from childhood friends. She is independent and does not
want to be a burden to others. Along with her husband she has established
a home in a new community filled with strangers. While the new house
may possess many time- and energy-saving gadgets, these conveniences
merely release mother for more chauffeuring of the children, more shopping, more socializing, and more community activity. Because the young
mother functions without the help and counsel of nearby relatives, because the demands are physical and psychological as well as mental, the
book cited above considers the suburban mother as a kind of pioneer, revealing the qualities of strength, toughness, resourcefulness, and courage.
Dorothy Barclay observes that *the suburban mother is more exposed to
outside claims* upon time and energy, to other grueling strains of life
than is the city mother.[8] Sometimes she is inadequately prepared to meet
the demands of suburban parenthood. Often she has to learn to deal with
loud, pushy people and to develop qualities of firmness, toughness, and
self-reliance.

On the other hand, she may already have winning qualities. Spectorsky
described a mother in exurbia who dealt with a crisis at home when her

[8] See *Understanding the City Child*, pp. 15-16.

young daughter fell out of a tree and sustained a skull fracture. She rushed the child to the nearest hospital sixteen miles away for x rays and a medical examination, and after all the excitement died down she telephoned her husband at the office to report what had happened. The suburban mother has to cope with daily emergencies alone. In instances of automobile failure she may have to decide whether to buy a new battery; quick action with a pail of water by a young mother quenched a fire at home and averted a tragedy; she may have to care for the coal burning furnace after it has exploded or summon the plumber to fix leaky pipes; et cetera. It is all in the day's work. Suburbia's multifarious demands draw out the mother's pioneerlike qualities. In this role she experiences many of the heartaches and loneliness of frontier life.

Thus, motherhood has been invested with a grand new aura of importance. Among Jewish suburbanites, Albert Gordon finds that the mother has more responsibility than ever before. Today her ideas, her opinions, and her values clearly dominate. She drives the car, makes the medical and dental appointments, organizes the dancing and music lessons, keeps the checking account in balance, and generally manages the home. Under her penetrating surveillance the children are corrected, goaded, encouraged, congratulated, and punished. The weeds are pulled from life daily, in order that the children grow up properly. Gordon concludes that the suburbs actually have strengthened Jewish family life.

What has the suburb done to Roman Catholics? While the woman's place continues to be in the home, she has grown into a new stature with respect to added responsibilities and increased influence in decision making. Suburban residence gives rise to a special kind of parenthood. Mother supervises the achievement of good grades at school and generally oversees social adjustment. Mother exercises strong influence upon what house to buy, what schools are suitable for children, what vacations should be taken by the family. Meanwhile father settles the questions of presidential elections, peacetime uses of atomic power, and intercontinental ballistic missiles. She makes the little decisions; he makes the big ones!

Among Protestants residing in suburbia one discovers that the wife inherits the responsibilities which her husband abandons. Hence the young mother runs suburbia, among other things, during her eighty hour work week. She has to switch in role from housewife and mother to sweetheart of Sigma Chi daily. She handles the money, perpetuates home "rituals" during appropriate seasons of the year, balances the rights and responsibilities of the child, and many other things. There appears to be little doubt about the dominant influence of Protestant mothers in suburbia. With respect to many issues, however, the spouses jointly agree that the wife should take charge and work matters out. It is really a mutually acceptable delegation of authority. Such all-around competence and activity does give suburbia the aspect of a matriarchy, albeit a benevolent one. The "omnipotence" of mother emerges from even a brief evaluation of her activities and accomplishments.

MAJOR SUBURBAN FAMILY PROBLEMS

What appears to escape the attention of many mobile families is the disturbing impact of tensions and stress. Suburbanites foolishly underrate or ignore such ever-present dangers. Under the halo of a driving ambition to get ahead these tough young climbers seem to regard themselves as immune to the ravages of stress and strain. They suppose that the disastrous thing can happen only to the other person; yet a casual examination of suburban hospital records for the incidence of such psychosomatic illnesses ("a physical disorder with emotional roots") as high blood pressure, peptic ulcers, and coronary thrombosis (heart attack) yields a shocking discovery. Grave danger lurks just ahead along the path of the overburdened suburbanite and his family.

The Gordons and Gunther matched the incidence of these three disorders in the records of a rural county hospital versus a suburban county hospital. What does the comparison reveal? The respective percentage figures speak eloquently for themselves: Heart attack: rural 2.4, *suburban 11.7;* high blood pressure: rural *6.7, suburban 143;* duodenal ulcers: rural 2.8, *suburban 9.6.* Evidently there is a convincing factual basis for urging that something is troubling residents in suburbia. Heart attack occurs five times more frequently in suburbia than in the rural county, while ulcers are three times more frequent. *The Split-Level Trap* provides the interested reader with a detailed discussion of psychosomatic disorders. Such findings deserve the attention of all those who are concerned about family life in suburbia. Tensions and stresses exact a fearsome toll; they comprise the unacknowledged price tags of life in the get-ahead communities. These and kindred woes lead the Gordons and Gunther to coin the nickname "Disturbia."

To explore the situation deeply the Gordons selected eight case histories of families residing in suburban Bergen County, New Jersey. These cases illustrate some of the major problems endemic to modern suburban life. Specifically they disclose *the problems and personality-types most commonly treated in suburban psychiatric practice.* As such they have much to say to the Protestant church. The list includes a family involved in each of the following categories: The social climber, the chronic failure, a teenage delinquent, the big success, a company transfer, a mixed marriage, a broken home, and defeated middle age. These situations disclose the range of troubles which harass modern suburban life. The well-being and happiness of the family is at stake in each situation. The last four problems noted will be discussed briefly below.

The adjustment of *the company transfer* often works out more smoothly for the husband than for the wife. When he arrives at the new office or industrial plant an escort usually is waiting to show him around and otherwise acquaint him with the personnel and operations in the new situation. The family is not as fortunate, however; it must shift for itself. Such is the case presented here. Upon arrival in the new suburb the family was thrown immediately upon its own resources. Although the housing question already was settled, the wife had to locate convenient shopping facilities, establish credit at a local bank, get the children started in school, drive about the streets of a strange community, commence relations with neighbors and potential friends, ward off a succession of salesmen, and handle a multitude of other weighty responsibilities. Due to her husband's preoccupation with new duties, she had to shoulder a personal burden much heavier than usual. The two small children and the household required close and continuous attention. Moreover, it was not easy for a newcomer to break into the local social life and to make new friends. The young wife, an attractive, cultured Southern person, was not invited to join the woman's club in town. Strangers were not welcome everywhere. Moreover, she was ill prepared for the tasks and altogether too shy to handle the burdens in a strange community. The pace of living was too fast for her, and her husband was too busy and too frustrated to realize what was happening. The Gordons and Gunther show here how a housewife broke down under these heavy stresses. After a perceptive discussion of the problem they point out the kind of therapy which was required in order to secure recovery. There is a devastating matter-of-factness about this analysis, but there is also a deep spiritual sensitivity to the worth of persons and to the value of a good home. Recovery was not achieved without the restoration of sound family life.

A mixed marriage can become an occasion for psychosomatic illness. When a mobile young couple starts out with a wide cultural gap between them, and things do not go so smoothly, the result may be a breakdown for one spouse or the other. Cultural diversity is even more serious than faith difference according to *The Split-Level Trap*. In the case of a Protestant married to a Roman Catholic girl whose parents came to America from southern Europe differences in up-bringing complicated the usual adjustments in marriage and parenthood. To frustrate matters further, religious and national prejudice on the part of the husband's parents raised its ugly head. "Baby blues," failure to find other young housewives with whom to share her problems, sex maladjustment, perfectionism in housekeeping—these produced tension, insomnia, outbursts of anger, and eventually breakdown. Both geographical and economic mobility figured as troublesome aspects of this situation. Mobility increased the normally heavy stresses to a breaking point. The cultural gap between husband and wife was difficult to bridge and to keep bridged. Hence love and understanding lacked ways of getting back and forth between the marriage partners.

The broken home is another hidden cost of suburban living. In the United States the divorce rate has more than tripled since 1900. But several times as many marriages end in separation as terminate in divorce. The peculiar stresses of suburbia disclose the lurking weaknesses of numerous marriages, especially if the spouses took their nuptial vows at a very young age. By the nature of suburban existence the woman remains at home absorbed in the care of children and household and in community activities. Her friendships arise locally out of these tasks. Meanwhile her husband goes off to work in the city. There he forms friendships and develops interests, living and moving in a different world. As a result the spouses often grow apart, or one lags behind the other in social development. At the beginning of marriage they shared experiences, exchanged views regularly, made decisions together. As the years passed, however, the heavier vocational demands plus suburban mobility have caused the marital bonds to weaken. Suburban cocktail parties and other social activities tend to furnish stimulation and opportunities for extra-marital interest and experience. With the aid of alcoholic beverages and scenes yielding estrangement they eventually reach a breaking point. Obviously the process has a debilitating effect upon family life. This juicy aspect of suburban living is widely circulated by modern novels. Unfortunately popular fiction writers have capitalized upon a situation which is all too frequently characteristic of homelife in Disturbia.

Defeated middle agers comprise another serious problem in suburbia. Both spouses face grave emotional dangers at this stage of life. Possibly here the climber makes the alarming discovery that he can no longer keep pace with a fast-changing or highly competitive business, or perhaps that promotions are given to younger men. A vocational assessment at middle age leads the breadwinner to see that he has gone about as far as he can go career wise. It is depressing to witness classmates passing by in the upward climb. The case reported indicated also the manifold concerns of the middle-aged wife. Health was problematic; the children had left home; death had taken close friends; she began to fear the loss of husband to death, divorce, another woman, or his business. She felt lonely, neglected, and jobless. She sought refuge in her church. Unfortunately, after several years the elderly clergyman died suddenly. Her depression deepened, and she often thought of suicide. Likewise her husband grew more discouraged as business moved to the verge of failure. Unable to face the hard realities of the situation, he turned to drink. Both spouses came to feel that they were nobodies, and hence they lost the will to go on living. They felt out of step with things, unwanted, and useless. She tried to commit suicide. He sustained injury in an automobile accident. The defeated middle ager is not a pleasant sight to see. Many reside in suburbia.

Obviously the foregoing account of problems does not exhaust the list of difficulties endemic to suburban family life. Rather it suggests the broad range and depth of major difficulties which keep the urban periphery from being mistaken as heaven. Suburbia is a place of family troubles. To each of the troubled situations Protestantism should bring its intelligence, understanding, and succor. It can team with medicine in a program to heal the harassed residents of Disturbia. It can pick up where psychiatry leaves off. It would be unfortunate if Protestantism were to turn its back upon the distress and frustration of suburban family life. The major situations noted above challenge church leaders to work out a spiritual program for crises. If the authors of *The Split-Level Trap* urge that *these break-downs of family life do not need to occur,* what then is the church's obligation on the preventative side? A new kind of Protestant home is called for in order to escape the corrosive effects of suburbanism on family life.

THE LOST MINISTRY TO FAMILIES

An important perspective concerning suburbia is the relation which can or should exist between Protestantism and family life. Unfortunately the church's ministry is still focused upon the individual rather than directed toward the family as a sociological and spiritual entity. This approach through individuals, to some extent, is inevitable and meritorious. There are at least two significant ways in which the church can influence the person—by direct approach on an individual basis and by direct approach to the family as a unit. Oddly enough, in suburbia, where the family is so important, the second approach is inadequate or missing. Neither the Jewish nor Roman Catholic leaders equivocate on the second approach. They are not prodigal with respect to this great opportunity which encompasses the individual's life with the influence of a religious home. Its potential is too rich to ignore.

Protestantism has a stake here but has failed to provide a well-conceived ministry in this sphere. Of course there is some attempt to use counseling care in preparing a young man and a young woman for nuptial vows. Many ministers refuse to solemnize a wedding without premarital counseling sessions. Who does not know about this significant approach to marriage? It is very important. Then eventually the wedding day arrives, and the couple is married. What happens now? After the wedding what is the ministry of the church toward the newly established home? Past experience indicates that a ministry of some sort to each spouse will continue strictly on an individual basis. Yet what does the church now do respecting the home upon which her blessing has been placed? Usually nothing! This oversight is the focus of our concern here.

This is a lamentable situation. Protestantism has almost completely overlooked the unique influence of a Christian home. Indeed there is a great gulf fixed between the publication of national magazines and other printed materials treating the subject and a concrete program of ministry to families at the local-church level. The oversight and chief neglect persists at the level of the local community. In the local church the ministry consists of hardly more than a celebration of the rites of passage—birth by baptism, conjugal decision by marriage, and death by funeral service. The family as a functioning unit receives scant attention apart from these traditional ceremonies. Hence the embarrassing question naturally arises, Is there no need for close relationship between *family* and church? Is the family unit, self-evidently so important in suburban living, merely an addressographical convenience to the church which utilizes it for delivering messages and materials to individuals who happen to be housed under the same roof? This is a serious question. It should reopen for consideration the possibility of a Protestant ministry to the home as a sociological entity.

Just how does the home manage between the peaks of nuptial bliss and death or divorce? Does the church have anything to say to the household during all of the thousands of ordinary hours of living? Ironically enough, life goes right on under the aegis of secular influences, during which time the church alibis, equivocates, and neglects its opportunity. Is there a way to have a Protestant home in truth and reality? *This is the lost ministry which merits recovery.* The current unwarranted reliance among Protestants upon indirect influence upon family life is not enough. The very family itself must become a center of Christianizing influence upon individual persons charged to its care. The local church must see the family as an auxiliary arm, as a "little church." Since the local church cannot win the community by itself, it must welcome the spiritual ally which the suburban family can become.

NEW FAMILY LIFE AND SUBURBAN PROTESTANTISM

Turbulent suburbia can yield a newer, stronger pattern of American family life. Such an outcome is desirable and possible. Religion can gain a new importance in the home if the church will speak directly to the needs of suburban residents. Roman Catholicism and Judaism have made this discovery; Protestantism is beginning to. The mobile hearth can be transmuted into a center of spiritual insight and development, thus reinforcing the work of the church in the local community. Under the aegis of Christianity, a better-disciplined household, yielding mutual confidence, love, and happiness, can emerge. It can be community oriented, functioning as an ally of the best which manifests itself in the suburb. Integrity, responsibility, and service to others can be the constant goal toward which the mobile family can grow. Its power and attractiveness cannot be delineated fully in terms of visible externals or mechanical processes however. Yet as an entity it can be discerned to possess a quality which is new and significant.

In the present chapter the task remaining is to set forth ways in which suburban families can receive assistance from Protestantism. At least six concrete suggestions can be found under the following rubrics: (1) New interest in family life, (2) serving the family as a whole, (3) marks of marital success, (4) Protestantism's word on child rearing, (5) dealing with religious pessimism, and finally, (6) new values for old. Rather than being exhaustive, this list can emphasize the importance of Protestantism's practical concern for suburban family life.

1. *New interest in family life.* Throughout America a vast renewal of interest in family life is apparent today. Not for many decades has there been such profound searching for the essential physical, social, and spiritual ingredients of a household wherein children can be reared and happiness found. This new interest focuses in suburbia. For thousands of couples the welfare of the family is of paramount concern. How well acquainted is Protestantism with this fact? Like the suburb itself, the indigenous church reflects the accumulation of young and middle-aged families who have fled from the city seeking to fulfill, in a pleasanter environment, the responsibilities of parenthood. Underlying this migration is a profound interest in family life.

This is an interest which the Protestant church can recognize, encourage, and guide. Whether or not the mobile people ever achieve satisfactory roots in local community life, it is very important that they retain, nourish, and develop long and adequate roots in Protestant Christianity. Some people acquire long roots in the community and short roots in religion. Christianity is always greater than the environment in which it manifests itself. Even in the mobile suburban community where population turnover is spectacular Protestantism has a stake in and a message for the modern, nomadic household. What specifically is the message? Protestantism welcomes the vast renewal of interest in family life and pledges its physical, social, and spiritual resources to the achievement of an equally vast renewal of family faith. Faith and family belong together.

2. *Serving the family as a whole.* The aforementioned sharp focus of concern upon family life in suburbia possibly suggests a new ministry for Protestantism. Why not serve the family as a whole, as a distinctive

entity? Of course, this approach cannot replace the traditional attention fixed upon individuals but rather can supplement it. Joseph McCabe considers this a viable possibility and has endeavored to implement the ministry in *The Power of God in a Parish Program.* The authors of *The Split-Level Trap* promote interest in the suburban family as a distinctive functioning entity by proposing a battery of nine ways to reach the objective—the sharing of problems, producing for recognition, planning and preparation, diversity of interests, climbing with care, accepting rest and reward, tactful self-assertion, reassessment of values, and emotional control.[9]

The family is truly the center of great influence. Nowhere in modern civilization do individuals have as deep, as satisfying, and as enduring relationships. Blood is thicker than water; familial bonds are more ultimate than personal ties. Just as some observers miss the forest because of the trees, so also some church leaders overlook the family because of the persons who comprise it. This is a grave and oft-repeated blunder. So fundamental to American society is the family as an entity that many laws have been enacted to insure the responsible participation of persons in this fundamental institution.

Does Protestantism really recognize and understand the significance of this primary grouping of individuals? When the church sees a husband, wife, and children domiciled in a suburban house does she perceive anything besides several individuals who happen to reside at a single address? Is the family as a distinctive social entity noted? Whether Protestantism is aware of the fact or not, *as goes the home, so goes religion in suburbia.* Gordon stresses this point respecting suburban Jews. Greeley does the same with regard to suburban Roman Catholics. Both writers fear that the suburban family will become "too American," meaning over-secularized! What is Protestantism's viewpoint? Recognizing the dilemma of family life in suburbia, Protestantism can shape a ministry to cover the needs. If the household is not brought under the rule of Christianity how can the church keep the pressure of Christ's life upon individuals?

3. *Marks of marital success.* Upon what grounds does Protestantism in suburbia sanctify marriage? Does the church bless any kind of coalition which develops between male and female? Currently Protestantism needs

[9] See Chapters 11-19.

to articulate its views on married love and to indicate clearly the church's stake in family life. In Protestantism what are the criteria for marital success? Do the "climber's" criteria differ from those of the church? What do material success and business promotions do to family life? Does it really matter if the breadwinner overreaches his income and experience in order to get ahead? Many people are doing it. Indeed, the authors of *The Split-Level Trap* estimate that there are probably millions of American suburbanites who are striving hard for "quick status, quick recognition." [10]

How does Protestantism define success? What constitutes failure? What does material success or failure do to a suburban family? To what extent is this a concern of the Protestant churches at all? In the perspectives of Christianity, what must the mobile family in suburbia do in order to find happiness, wholesome homelife? By what criteria can one adjudge the suburban household as Christian? Whether it is possible to consider the husband's business success plus the wife's effectiveness in community activities plus the stability of the household taken together as evidence of an adequate home poses a difficult question. This kind of arithmetic hardly illuminates the focus of real concern.

Protestantism needs to discover a pattern of homelife which can withstand the stresses of mobile suburbia and yet function as a strong center of applied Christianity. An emphasis upon husband and wife teams in Christianity, such as Aquila and Priscilla (Acts 18), is a workable idea here. This blue-collar household shows the way. The suburban family that really prays together stays together. Research supports the truth of this aphorism. *As a devotional unit,* the suburban family can reproduce the quality of life which is found in the church. Possibly the greatest danger to Christian family life is the deleterious ideology of material success.

4. *Protestantism's word on child rearing.* The Protestant church can say something of spiritual significance about the rearing of children. What is this word? Most families move to the edge of the city in order to bring up their children in a wholesome atmosphere. The church can make sure that the rising generation is exposed to Christianity. Paul remarked appreciatively over the high quality of family religion which communicated faith successfully to children across three generations—from Lois to Eunice

[10] Pp. 98, 102, 108-9.

to Timothy (II Tim. 1:1-9). He concludes by urging the youth to stir up the gift of God which is within him.

An important contribution of the suburban home to the growing child is the twin heritage of "roots and wings." Youth should receive from family life a primary anchorage in the values of Protestantism. These are his roots. Moreover, his imagination and aspirations should be kindled by the possibilities of transcending man's past achievements in any sphere. All new things are possible to the person who believes. These are his wings. The heritage of roots and wings is a precious one. Another way of designating this feature is cited in the aphorism. The little house says stay; the open road says go. The pull in both directions can be felt in sound family life. The anchorage in Protestantism and the aspiration to take up the world's unfinished tasks are essential ingredients of family life.

Young people need both a working knowledge of the faith and a discipline to sustain the measure of faith which they appropriate. Often parents need considerable help by way of reinforcement and sanction of the Protestant church for standards of behavior. How does one articulate behavior norms in home situations? How much firmness can be used in enforcing parental rules? Various authors urge that Protestantism can aid suburban family life where parents need help in selecting, administering, and enforcing minimum standards of behavior for children. It is well known that boys and girls require a certain parental firmness; a set of values, rewards, and punishments; and devices for encouragement. In so vital a process Protestantism can and must have an unambiguous word for concerned parents.

In some advantaged suburbs the public school attempts to guide the total life of the child. Since the task of child rearing is so complex, some people urge that it should be turned over to "experts" out in the community. This is not the Christian way of meeting the situation. Protestantism urges parents to take primary responsibility for child rearing. Then Protestantism urges parents to make use of qualified agencies such as the school, church, recreation, et cetera. Parents still need to create the kind of home environment which is enthusiastic about religion, education, citizenship, and other aspects of living. The church is the family's best friend in the important task of child rearing.

5. *Dealing with religious skepticism.* Despite the popular impression of a revival of interest in religion, serious students of modern life generally

call attention to the opposite development. Following World War II there has accumulated a reservoir of skepticism respecting the power and relevance of Christianity. In *Crestwood Heights* religion is politely relegated to an inconspicuous place in suburban life. Although the authors claimed concern over the matter, they failed to provide adequately in the research design for a responsible study. Despite the methodological oversight and the inadequate character of the data assembled, the authors are willing to articulate the opinion that religion no longer occupies a place of central significance. These scholars urge that the school and the family now exercise a determinative influence upon the church. In *Working-Class Suburb* Berger equivocates respecting religion's importance in an auto workers' community. He reports that only 7 per cent of the sample (100 families) took their marital problems to the clergyman. He concludes the general analysis by pointing out that suburban residence has no marked effect on church attendance either for better or for worse. A survey of the literature purporting to deal with the subject leaves one greatly disappointed. Opinions are numerous; data are few.

There is a skepticism abroad also, especially among intellectuals. Some educated people rely upon cleverness rather than faith. Protestantism can confront this debilitating outlook which seeks to undercut the work of the churches. The problem is noted by Andrew Greeley, Albert Gordon, Joseph McCabe, and others. When families become preoccupied with the suburban trinity of success, health, and happiness they are likely to be rather indifferent to Christianity. Pessimism arises out of a scandalous ignorance of the claims and values of Protestantism. This ignorance continues as long as indifference keeps the family from an adequate knowledge of the church. Pessimism, ignorance, and indifference go hand in hand.

6. *New values for old.* The suburban family needs considerable help in finding its way respecting values, thinking, and ethics. Mobility has drawn together peoples of a wide range of cultural and religious backgrounds. These families have brought with them into suburbia their previous ideas, customs, and ways of living. Now as neighbors each family is thrown into challenging contact with others. The situation explodes into quarrels and misunderstandings. Thus many suburban communities seem like towers of Babel judged from the viewpoint of family patterns, values, and personal conduct. In these spheres the neighbors are hard to understand.

In the confusion of this pluralism parents who have high expectations for their children are constantly reminded of a lack of religious standards of behavior round about them. The suburban family which espouses the Christian way of life needs a lot of encouragement from the church. It needs help in withstanding the criticism of neighboring parents and in exercising firmness in discipline toward children. In all this Protestantism has an obligation. The mobile suburban family is especially exposed to a head-on collision with brash secular perspectives. In this encounter a reevaluation of standards of behavior has to take place. During this period of transition the church can teach its families Protestantism's norms of behavior. Why are not these standards known to every church family?

A closer connection with Protestantism can be expected to underlie the new pattern of family life. Actually there is abroad in suburbia a great interest and wistfulness to procure true religion from the church. That this expectation is genuine cannot be gainsaid. A deep religious relationship can open up a channel by which spiritual values can flow into the suburban home and intermingle with its life. Both external (e.g., grace at meals, prayer, family devotions, Bible reading, etc.) and internal (e.g., acquisition of faith, renewal of life in God, spiritual nurture, et cetera) manifestations of religion become evident. This deeper tie to Protestantism can undergird the development of Christian standards of behavior for both youth and adults. Eventually the suburban home can become an outpost for spiritual renewal and spiritual guidance; i.e., "a little church," serving truly as an extension of the Protestant local church. The closer Protestantism works with the family the more fully will the faith serve the suburbs—like family, like church, like community. Thus, it seems apparent that a new pattern of family life really can develop in suburbia, reaching out in several directions, gaining in strength, in depth, and in spirituality. Even the present suburban turbulence cannot hinder the emergence of a tough, sensitive, sophisticated, and spiritual pattern of family living. Let, then, the strong Protestant family appear.

VII

Tension in the
Suburbs

That some tension and strain normally characterize the fabric of
human life everywhere in society is a widely accepted fact. However, interperson and intergroup friction tends to be aggravated under suburban circumstances. Conditions of life here are more dynamic, more
explosive and more fiercely competitive. There are reasons for this turbulence. Disparate strands of life are thrown together in confluence in suburbia
yielding the basic ingredients for the ever-present possibility of covert or open
conflict.

Tension and struggle in many suburban places are covert and subtle.
This avoids embarrassment and public acknowledgment of its existence.
It keeps people guessing about which real issues are in contest. Yet, elsewhere in other suburbs local or out-of-town leadership drags controversial
issues out into the open, making shrewd use of newspapers, magazines,
and other mass media. Here the local community becomes the battleground
for various national social issues—racial integration, religious liberty, inter-
class tolerance, and rural-urban understanding. In view of this complicated
situation the reader is likely to welcome an examination of pertinent facts,
a delineation of the spheres of tension, a brief analysis of the issues, and
several proposed lines of constructive action. Regardless of prescriptive
measures undertaken, however, tension and conflict are likely to continue
as a prominent part of suburban life for years to come. Suburbia is
America's latest melting pot of colliding customs, preferences, goals, and
values. It is the center of a new turbulence which disturbs Protestantism
profoundly.

141

While paucity of space renders impossible an exhaustive analysis of the situation, at least five areas of tension and conflict can be underscored in the brief discussion which follows. The list includes (1) newcomer versus old-timer, (2) white-collar versus blue-collar, (3) Jew versus Christian, (4) Roman Catholicism versus Protestantism, and (5) Negro versus white. Evidently Protestantism has a deep involvement in such tension areas. Because Protestantism alone among the faiths is endemic to suburbia its churches cannot escape these disturbing issues. Indeed, escape is not sought, but rather the struggle, since out of the crucible of conflict can emerge a revitalized Protestantism. The denominations must find a new life.

NEWCOMER VERSUS OLD-TIMER

In the writings of Beatty, Spectorsky, Keats, Dobriner, Owen, and others the not-always-congenial relationship between newcomer and old-timer is explored. Beatty's pro-commuter discussion, crowded with facts and delicious humor, reveals the disdain which is directed toward the resident who earns his livelihood within the suburb where he lives. He is looked down upon because his life lacks the magic dimension of commutation. More exciting employment is supposed to exist in the nearby major city. Hence the newcomer, especially if he is a commuter, comes to believe that he is really someone rather special in the community where he resides. To him status at the office means status in the suburbs. The old-timer does not impress very easily, however. Rather he regards the newcomer as a kind of necessary evil.

John Keats describes life in the huge new development communities where old-timers are completely outnumbered. Indeed, here old-timers are invested with scroogelike characteristics and are reported to take advantage of the gullible newcomers in real estate, building materials, local ordinances, and various business transactions. The old-timer is preoccupied with the local situation. Residential mobility is underscored also by Keats as one of the distressing features of the new suburbanite. The newcomer refuses to stay put. He is here today and gone tomorrow. As soon as another salary raise comes he buys a bigger house elsewhere and moves on. Thus the old-timer is provided an additional reason for looking down upon the newcomer family. He recalls the ancient adage, "a rolling stone gathers no moss." Genuine friendship is difficult to achieve. Suspicion persists as a feature of the relationship between those who have roots in the community and those who do not. Each misunderstands the other. The atmosphere is one of uneasy hostility.

Moreover, this sphere of tension also is explored in remarkable detail by Havighurst and Morgan in *The Social History of a War-Boom Community.* Attention is directed to "the generally cool relations between old-timers and newcomers."[1] Here many of the old-timers consider themselves to be socially above the newcomers. Indeed, the wide disparities in economic, social, and moral behavior are a constant threat to the creation of community spirit and life. In summary, the authors assign six characteristics to the newcomer's pattern of life: (1) Temporary residence; (2) no local attachments; (3) unideal housing conditions; (4) freedom from the mores which obtain locally; (5) a minimal participation in local institutions; and (6) minimal social interaction with oldtimers.[2] This interesting technical biography of a small Illinois community embraces the time period before, during, and after World War II. Its perceptive discussion of newcomers and old-timers has a wider application, being pertinent to many current suburban situations. The treatment of individual and institutional aspects reveals insight in many dimensions of human life. Here the conflict between old-timer and newcomer is heroically dramatized. Mistakes and misunderstanding are on both sides.

How does the old-timer-newcomer conflict get started? Many suburban communities show the vestigial remains of former villages and rural communities. Since World War II the old towns were inundated by new residents. William Dobriner in *The Suburban Community* utilizes the terms "locals" and "cosmopolitans" to describe old-timers and newcomers, respectively. The "local" person lives in a world bounded by the suburb; the "cosmopolitan" individual combines knowledge of the outside world with local participation. Dobriner's illustrative material, drawn from Huntington Village, Long Island, New York, affords a striking example of old-timer-newcomer relations. Here the old-timer occupies a position of high status in the community which few newcomers are likely to attain. Usually the newcomer has brought along with him a divergent set of values, including new ways of looking at the schools, the church, politics, and other facets of community life. He is not satisfied with old

[1] See Chapter 4.
[2] *Ibid.,* p. 108.

ways of doing things. Hence, he is forever suggesting changes in local business, local government, local community services, local education, and local religion. Because the old-timer is often satisfied with the status quo a conflict soon emerges. The newcomer presses for changes; the longtime resident resists them.

Hence a collision of values and personal preferences emerges, yielding sharp conflict and hostility. While one resident commutes to an out-of-town place of business his next door neighbor, an old-timer, looks after his affairs or profession locally. The commuter's locus of business interest is far away in the big city. The old-timer's locus is local. The latter spends a twenty-four-hour day in the suburb, whereas the former merely spends nights and weekends there. The one is thoroughly domesticated to local community problems, values, and customs, whereas the other discovers the local issues with considerable difficulty and often with impatience.

Literature on the topic draws a clear-cut line between the newcomer and the old-timer. The latter is more familiar with the revered local pattern of life along with customs and values. Moreover, even more importantly, his memory encompasses the slow, arduous steps of progress which actually have been made across the years. He usually already knows the price that has been paid in money, feelings, and human values for changes thus far. But what the old-timer often does not know is how much more progress is still needed in order to catch up to the attainment of other more progressive communities. Children need to learn to live in the world of today and tomorrow. Community programs and institutional services need to be relevant to modern conditions. Today's standards of health, safety, and education are higher than older norms. By way of contrast with the old-timer, the newcomer with short roots in the community seeks to modernize the town, the school, the subdivision, the politics, the church, et cetera. Efficiency and self-interest appear to dominate here. The views, attitudes, policies, and practices of old-timer and newcomer clash in the P.T.A., in the board of education, in politics, in fire protection, in the church, and in many other places. This collision of viewpoints yields conflict and tension. Indeed, the road into the future is a troubled way.

To sum up the matter, wherever newcomers and old-timers reside together in the same suburb, there exists a potential situation of tension and hostility. A collision between honestly held but divergent values takes place. This serious friction is inevitable. Commutation is really a subsidiary issue to the main problem of old-timer-newcomer relations. This point is strongly stressed in *The Split-Level Trap* and *But Not Next Door*.[3] In the latter "side taking" by groups is evident on the part of church families, particularly with reference to positions taken by old-timers, who set the pace for others. Many residents hold back until it is seen what old residents do. Protestant leaders should become aware of the fundamental source of conflict here. Moreover, the faith can conceive its own participation in terms of both long-range goals and short-range objectives.

WHITE-COLLAR VERSUS BLUE-COLLAR

Recent investigations disclose to what extent suburban population composition is predominantly white-collar or blue-collar. Mention has already been made of Whyte's book *The Organization Man,* from which emerged the generalized concept now widely known. Gibson Winter expanded this concept into "the organization church"[4] and Robert Presthus extended the idea into "the organizational society."[5] Whyte's prototype of the white-collar suburban resident is not as broad as C. Wright Mills's,[6] but rather delineates the individual as being middle class, upwardly mobile, vocationally ambitious, and sensitive to public relations. The reader is reminded of an earlier discussion of this point and that the viewpoint can cause one trouble.

Bennett Berger, on the other hand, directs attention to the host of blue-collar employees residing in a working-class suburb. Here the breadwinner is an auto factory operative who is unlikely to go higher in terms of income or status. The blue-collar family is quite satisfied with the present level of new life in suburbia. Residents are happy to possess a modern kitchen, a rumpus room, yard furniture, and other fine facilities which make the home physically attractive and convenient. The garage contains an automobile or two. The family dresses well and today has adequate medical and dental care, plus increased insurance protection. The television set and radio solve the problem of leisure-time activities for many blue-collar suburbanites. Taking in the life situaton as a whole, upon their own say-so, they never had it so good.

[3] Harry M. and David H. Rosen (New York: Ivan Obolensky, Inc., 1962).
[4] *The Suburban Captivity of the Churches,* Chapters 3, 4, and 5.
[5] *The Organizational Society* (New York: Alfred A. Knopf, Inc., 1962).
[6] *White Collar* (New York: Oxford University Press, 1951).

145

In the foregoing discussion attention was drawn to two types of residents which are numerically strong in suburbia—white-collar and blue-collar. Indeed, a study which I directed in 1963 of 2,138 suburban communities disclosed that in many American suburbs the white-collar dweller is clearly outnumbered by the blue-collar resident. This pattern of dominance holds true regionally, whether East Coast, West Coast, Gulf Coast, Middle states, or Canadian border. Even in midwestern and prairie states blue-collar workers strongly outnumber white-collar in numerous suburban communities. An examination of several metropolitan areas suffices to illustrate the point. Of ninety-six suburban places studied in the Pittsburgh metropolitan area sixty communities had more blue-collar than white-collar workers residing in them. In the Detroit metropolitan territory twenty-eight of the fifty suburbs reported more blue-collar than white-collar residents. From these statements it is evident that blue-collar workers comprise a surprisingly large proportion of suburban residents. This fact hurls serious challenge at the uncritical acceptance of the Whyte hypothesis. Blue-collar workers constitute no minor group of suburban residents. Protestantism needs to weigh the significance of this fact and to reconsider the bent of its ministry.

Further, it is well to recognize that the two worlds of white-collar and blue-collar are radically different. Although both groups reside prominently in suburbia, there should be no mistaking the divergent milieux of their respective neighborhoods. Differences arise from contrasting vocational pursuits—working with one's hands versus working with one's personality or wits. All day long the blue-collar worker manipulates *objects*—tools, material, products, et cetera. On the other hand, the white-collar worker manipulates *people and ideas* all day long. The former becomes expert in handling material things; the latter achieves expertness in handling people. Endemic differences extend to include contrasts in earning power, working conditions, paid vacations, sick leaves, levels of cultural attainment, and leisure activities. Conflict is endemic to the situation where a mixture of residents is found, but it is especially acute where white-collar and blue-collar approximately balance each other in numerical strength. Friction arises not only from the collision between contrasting cultural preferences, but also between different value systems. The contrast in sophistication and methods of solving problems is also very great. Altogether the differences are both real and distressing at the level of community life.

146

Many white-collar persons are anxious to get ahead. Through espousal of salesmanship tactics and public relations methods these individuals have learned how to capitalize on any situation. It is simply a matter of selling oneself or one's product or both. Hence it is considered normal and desirable to push one's way into leadership positions of organizations in suburbia—P.T.A., politics, church life, et cetera. Inasmuch as leaders are needed, the white-collar person promotes himself into office, often through activity behind the scenes. He does not foolishly wait for true talent to be recognized or for democracy to take its plodding course. Rather, since he knows how things get done in the business world, he applies appropriate techniques in suburban life, making especially sure that he benefits from the process. Does not the situation afford him an opportunity to practice his skills in handling people? Practice makes for perfect competence.

Alas! Alongside such worldly shrewdness the blue-collar man appears naïve and slightly incompetent. His idealized notion of democratic processes is outmoded in the face of modern techniques for taking charge and manipulating people. His guard is down since he does not expect to be exploited in suburban school, suburban church, and other spheres of suburban life. Moreover, what is important in child rearing, in teenage discipline and values, and in adult notions of good and evil, right and wrong, usually contrast sharply with views held by many white-collar families. As a result of conflict here ideas about sincerity, honesty, sex, responsibility, and marriage are challenged and often ridiculed. Often the smooth-talking, well-groomed white-collar person can put over a cheapening of home and community life, not because the cause is right but because the man is clever. This manipulation of people and ideas creates serious conflict.

Protestantism needs to become aware of the suburban conflict between white-collar and blue-collar ways of life. The church needs to interpret the issue dispassionately, yet fully in the context of the Christian faith. In some ways *the blue-collar worker needs protection* from the aggressions of the white-collar citizen, who is perfectly willing to run the local church on the same ethical plane as he runs the town. The white-collar resident knows what he wants and works for his own objectives. Often he cares little about the democratic process and even less for values falling outside the range of his experience. Danger to the gospel lurks where this person takes charge. The mentality and rationale which go with this outlook *justifies the use of some deception and some personality pressure to accomplish parochial goals.*

For Protestantism this conflict produces special problems. There can be no doubt respecting the white-collar bias in church leadership selection. Blue-collar suburbanites are passed over in order to name to office the sales-trained, well-groomed white-collar candidate. Struggles in church life over values espoused by blue-collar residents have a strange way of resolving themselves in favor of white-collar preferences. As illustration, note the strong trend of evangelical Protestantism in suburbia toward a more formal worship service, comprising especially cultural elements preferred by white-collar residents. The drift emphasizes better music from a secular viewpoint, better literary style, neater format, less preaching, more careful ushering, more kneeling and rising—all of which would be recommended readily by a white-collar public-relations expert. There is little if any mark of blue-collar preference in this worship trend. Thus, Protestantism must achieve a new degree of cultural alertness and a recovery of a fresh knowledge of Christian faith in order to bring an adequate ministry to all kinds of suburbanites. The temptation is very strong to specialize in serving only the organization man. Today this means a ministry to less than one half of the suburban residents.

JEW VERSUS CHRISTIAN

According to Leo Pfeffer, Lipman and Vorspan, Benjamin Kaplan, Kramer and Leventman, Albert Gordon, and other writers, the American Jew recently has attained a new status.[7] He has moved out into the suburbs and thence up in the world. Some pertinent details of this important development are presented in Chapter II. Therefore, it suffices here to recapitulate briefly the significant outmovement of Jewish city residents to suburbia—a shift which has occurred on a grand scale in the United States.

In Metropolitan Cleveland, for example, 85 per cent of the Jews now reside in the suburbs. Only two of the twenty-five existing synagogues are still located within the city limits of Cleveland. In June 1961 an estimated one thousand Jewish youth graduated from high schools throughout metropolitan Cuyahoga County. Only a half dozen of these young people received their diplomas from high schools within the city of Cleveland.

[7] See works listed in the bibliography.

Soon there will be none, according to the authors of *A Tale of Ten Cities*.

Nationally, the half million suburban Jews is expected to double by 1980. Thus, the nationwide mass movement of Jewish residents to the suburbs signifies in a variety of ways the new status of the American Jew. Financially, educationally, and residentially he has attained to a new level. He has improved his lot. As a result he has grown self-confident and much bolder in articulating his cultural preferences and religious convictions. The more aggressive Jewish pacemakers are attempting to reshape the suburban community after their own interests. Not content with shops purveying kosher products, they now demand a milieu fully conducive to Judaism.

Pfeffer's provocative book *Creeds in Competition* presents the Jewish arguments against the religious celebration of Christmas, Easter, Good Friday, and other days which accountably hold Christian significance for many American people.[8] Toward any day or activity which emphasizes the christological Pfeffer has fixed a noisy antipathy. Apparently the attitude of some Jews toward Christians in the United States has drastically changed in recent years. Protestants and Catholics are acceptable now as fellow Americans only if they relegate Christian faith and Christian symbols to a private sphere. Hence the demand for the removal of all traces of Christianity from public life in suburbia.

These few pacesetting Jews stress a new pattern of *competition with other faiths,* replacing the alleged outmoded posture of co-operation. Pfeffer and Lipman and Vorspan, among others, boldly urge that Christians really welcome competition in a new context of coexistence. Will Herberg and other Jewish scholars insist that Protestant, Catholic, and Jew are now equal and independent. According to the new laws of coexistence faiths compete vigorously with one another in many spheres and in every way short of violence. To pit faith against faith is a good thing. Interest in mere co-operation, one is advised, has greatly diminished, and as a principle of intergroup relations such is declared to be outmoded. Undoubtedly this development comes as shocking news to a great many Protestants (possibly to many Jews also) who, old fashionedly continue to regard co-operation as a healthy activity among the faiths. Indeed, Pfeffer's harsh new pattern catches many Protestants napping.

[8] New York: Harper & Row, Publishers, 1958.

Thus surprised and chastened, Protestants are currently re-examining suburban interfaith relations. The turn of events is an interesting outcome of past amicable relationships. Prior to World War II Jews avoided provoking animosity. Today, especially since 1945, a few articulate Jews deliberately create intergroup tension by criticizing appearances of Christianity in public life. Interfaith tension and strife are expected concomitants of progress toward the desired Jewish goal of reshaping suburbia. Protestants now ask, Should the old amicable image be scrapped? Has suburban Christianity been too naïve toward other religions? Is it old fashioned to manifest interest in co-operation? It is unlikely that many Protestants are going to accept Pfeffer's belittling attitude toward holidays invested with Christian meanings. Pfeffer's personal inability to find spiritual significance therein does not mean that other Americans cannot find authentic religious expression there. Hence the crucial question: To what extent does Pfeffer speak for all suburban Jews?

An illustration of the tension which is emerging in suburbia between Jew and Christian can be noted from the incident at Ossining, New York.[9] This rural community became a suburban village early in the twentieth century. Following World War II a troublesome controversy broke out between Jews and Christians residing in Ossining. It started in a modest way. Some citizens, several of them Jews, joined forces in an effort to abolish the singing of Christian carols in the local school system. After a hard struggle, the effort failed to attain its objective. It did accomplish one thing however; it established an important precedent for attack upon the public display of Christian symbols. When, in 1956, a local committee of citizens discussed plans to place a Christmas crèche scene on the lawn of the Ossining Junior-Senior High School property a mild protest was registered by several Jewish residents. Conciliatory efforts were made at once to reassure these disturbed citizens. Eventually tensions were eased, and it appeared that peace had returned to the community.

Then somehow or other a Jewish organization plus several other bodies from outside the community became interested in the Ossining situation. Although the local committee made many efforts to reduce tension and animosity, outside groups kept the pressure on, forcing the matter

[9] Data from personal interviews, unpublished materials, and two articles: D. M. Kelly, "Merry Christmas: A Case Study in Community Conflict"; A. Gilbert, "Tensions Arising From Christmas Observances."

eventually into a showdown lawsuit against the school board. The National Conference of Christians and Jews offered to act as mediators, seeking to restore unity in the community. Moreover, a financial grant from the Fund for the Republic made possible a research study of Ossining's interfaith conflict. The state board of education in Albany sought to counsel in the situation also. However, continued interference by outside interests aggravated faith competition. Many heretofore friendly Jews and Christians now found personal relations shrouded in misunderstanding and sullied by antagonism. By 1959 the matter had smoothed itself out again, following a favorable legal decision in behalf of the community. Nevertheless, some years must elapse before the local wounds will heal and the higher courts settle the remaining disputed legal issues. Pfeffer's idea of faith competition can truly produce tensions.

In the Ossining incident a few Jews (not the rank-and-file residents) exhibited a remarkable eagerness to test the faith's growing power in American suburban life. This willingness to pit faith against faith indicates how some Jews regard their new status. Each faith assigns to itself the right to compete with another faith on matters of importance. Christological symbols is a basis for the Jewish quarrel with Roman Catholics and Protestants. Pfeffer's pejorative evaluation of the so-called Christian holidays is an illustration of the new policy line taken by a few pacesetting Jews. Where tension and misunderstanding arose among the faiths a few Jewish parents had lodged complaints. They have a right to do so.

Thus far mention has been made of the Jewish-Christian conflict with respect to Christmas holidays, Christmas carols, nativity drama in the schools, and the erection of Christian symbols on public property. Jews also are girded for battle against other faith groups on the separation of church and state, fair housing practices, open memberships in country clubs, and kindred issues. Albert Gordon expects the suburban Jew to take the lead in the fight against what he calls social inequities and in behalf of civil rights.[10] Already the suburban Jew belongs to P.T.A., League of Women Voters, Chamber of Commerce, Red Cross, and service clubs (Rotary, Kiwanis, and Lions). Yet some Jews want even more power in the community. Under such circumstances it appears wiser to emphasize competition rather than co-operation among the faiths.

Deliberate attacks upon what another faith cherishes invite retaliatory

[10] *Jews in Suburbia,* chapter 9.

measures however. Even the new suburban Jew should realize this. Tension between Jew and Gentile is apparently a *tactic* used by some pace-setting leaders to reach Jewish goals. Jews, while a pariah people, as Max Weber asserts, are likely to irritate Christians needlessly by seeking to impose minority preferences upon the majority. In a democracy a minority shares the obligation to act responsibly. Eventually Christians will tire of pushy self-assertiveness. Eventually a new basis for faith relationships will emerge. Unfortunately minor and parochial issues are likely to reduce the possibilities of co-operation across faith lines and increase the reasons for conflict. This strategy postpones indefinitely attention to the main issues of justice, freedom, and equality of opportunity. Religious tolerance is a principle which works best when it works both ways.

ROMAN CATHOLICISM VERSUS PROTESTANTISM

At the outset it is essential to recall that many thousands of Roman Catholics have taken up residence in suburbia since World War II. According to the relevant discussion which appears in Chapter II, the number of suburban Catholics residents will rise from approximately 3,000,000 currently to between 5, and 8,000,000 by 1980. Hence there can be no doubt now about the presence of Roman Catholicism in suburbia nor about its dynamic positive trends. Clearly the ratio of Roman Catholics to Protestants has been rising rapidly during the past twenty-five years. Suburbia, which used to be almost exclusively a mighty Protestant stronghold, now furnishes residence for many Jews, Roman Catholics, and sects. The one-faith monopoly is broken and gone, replaced in many communities by a three-faith melting pot. Indeed, suburbia has become a place of religious excitement and tension.

What is the meaning of this change? *Suburbia has a new look, faith wise.* The development reveals that Roman Catholics and Protestants now sit together on school boards, P.T.A., service clubs, and the League of Women Voters in hundreds of suburban communities across America. Prior to World War II Protestants and Catholics resided across town from one another. Now many live along the same suburban street and sit across the same suburban discussion table confronting one another. Thus, inevitably, the normal differences in political, educational, and religious values come promptly to each other's attention. Now it is a neighbor rather than a stranger who holds a dissenting viewpoint and with whom head-on collisions occur over community issues. A conflict of interests, goals, and values characterizes new life in suburbia. Gerhard Lenski has underscored the inevitability of interfaith tension in such situations.[11]

Recently in a New Jersey suburban community the Catholic priest mobilized his parish in order to procure the defeat of a worthy proposal to expand existing public elementary school facilities. This direct action and outcome came as a shock to many Protestants who had handled matters in their own way for years. They either had not noticed the in-movement of numerous Catholics or had failed to grasp the differences in voting behavior which might be expected to appear on such issues. Within twelve months after the defeat was achieved this same Catholic parish broke ground for an additional building to double the capacity of its own parochial school facilities. Once again Protestants were shocked. The impossible had happened. Another faith group had sought its own goals and achieved them under their very noses. This is another clue to the revolution which is occurring in suburbia. Comparable incidents can be reported for scores of other suburban places across the United States. The situation reveals that the Roman Catholics in suburbia knowingly exercise their democratic right to work for their own interests and to unite for the defeat of other proposals.

This new suburban force is slowly being recognized by denominational leaders. Moreover, with the prospect of Catholic population in suburbia doubling in strength by 1980, Protestantism will need to employ new strategies in order to attain its suburban goals. Catholics can be expected to continue to pursue their own interests and to strive for the achievement of parochial values. Protestantism, though indigenous, has entered now *a new phase of its suburban ministry*. The road ahead is one of certain conflict and struggle for power if Protestantism intends to survive and to exercise any noteworthy influence upon society. With the single-faith monopoly broken, Protestants need to take a sobering look at their church life under altered circumstances.

Similarly, other issues in public education, government, sex education, liberty, and so on, become the spheres of conflict between Roman Catholic and Protestant in suburbia. The two faiths disagree on such crucial matters as planned parenthood, state aid for education, relaxation of divorce laws,

---

[11] *The Religious Factor* (New York: Doubleday & Company, 1961), especially chapters 2, 7, and 8.

participation in politics, and so on. The disagreements are theological, sociological, political, and ethical. Many of these troublesome issues are delineated by Greeley, Underwood, Lipman and Vorspan, and Clark. The growing articulateness of Roman Catholicism has coincided with her recent arrival in suburbia. Pfeffer has coined a descriptive phrase designating conflict among the faiths. With a deep bow to the public relations experts, he proposed the term "culture competition." With surprising naïveté he insists that Protestants really welcome this struggle. One wonders how such a statement possibly can be documented. Pfeffer's phrase is more the expression of Jewish hope than the description of an interfaith reality. "Culture competition," however, properly modified can open up many new areas for dialogue, debate, and criticism across faith lines. In Pfeffer's hands it remains merely a device to put pressure upon suburban Protestantism. Neither Judaism nor Catholicism accept Protestantism's leadership in suburbia any longer.

NEGRO VERSUS WHITE

What is reality here? Are Negroes currently residing in suburbia in significant numerical strength? "Yes" is the resounding answer which comes back from many sides. This affirmative reply is reiterated in the writings of Albert Gordon, Frank Lee, Harry and David Rosen, James Wilson, and others.[12] Moreover, a recent study of 2,138 suburban communities in the United States reveals that *Negroes already reside in approximately 1,700 suburban communities.* Journalists, novelists, and even suburban residents themselves leave no doubt in the public mind respecting the concrete whereabouts of the new physical setting for Negro-white relations. Many American suburbs are already racially mixed. Here is the new setting. Here resides the "new" Negro.

Why do tension and hostility exist? Adequate answers are not easy to find. Some people fear the unknown. They have to get used to seeing new population groups around. Some distress arises from the disparity of socioeconomic circumstances. Some residents fear possible negative consequences of social intermingling. To this list of reasons can be added a nonrational element which at any time can reject both facts and common sense. A survey of the manifold explanations leads to the conclusion that there is really no sufficient reason for tension. Nevertheless, in particular

[12] See works listed in the bibliography.

communities anger flames, tension mounts, and misunderstandings appear. Sheer physical proximity of Negro and white Americans, particularly in suburbia, suffices to trigger off some unpleasant chain reactions. The people have had no opportunity to learn how to live together as neighbors.

This distressing phenomenon is dramatically described in *Peaceable Lane,* a novel by Keith Wheeler.[13] Here is an account of eleven upper middle-class families who reside along a single street in a Westchester suburb of New York City. A Negro artist and his attractive family sought to purchase a home in the all-white neighborhood. Reactions came quickly. Some of the neighbors became upset; one planned to sell at once and get out. Before long the action of the artist was followed by the activities of Negro "block busters," leaving a shocking trail of deception, intimidation, violence, and fear among the white residents. Tragedy came to Peaceable Lane when the Negro artist was killed in swerving his automobile away from two boys—one his son—fighting in the street over the race issue. Moreover, all the families up and down this quiet suburban lane became deeply involved in the situation and tasted a measure of tragedy in human relations. More than real estate was affected by the in-movement of Negroes. Outside interference forced people to line up on one side or the other of the issue. Neighbor was set against neighbor. Local residents were drawn into the affair which ended in a Pyrrhic victory. Oddly enough, true to the stereotype of suburban novels, *religion remained offstage,* although the shrewdly drawn characters unmistakably represent Judaism, Catholicism, and Protestantism. Truly this harsh novel leaves the reader with a sobering uncertainty of precisely where the solution properly lies. There seems to be no doubt about the tension and conflict engendered.

When one examines closely the nature of the Negro-white conflict there seem to be as many sides as there are persons involved. The central theme of the book-length report *But Not Next Door* is an exposition of the viewpoint of white residents who reserve the right to choose neighbors. Both clergy and church laymen participated openly in this complicated struggle. In this Deerfield, Illinois, situation a housewife made it clear that she had no objections to a racially integrated public school in the community. She did not, however, want a Negro neighbor—hence the title

[13] New York: Simon and Schuster, Inc., 1960.

of the book. Against this viewpoint, the Negro urges his right and his desire to live in whatever neighborhood he can afford to buy a house. Because he has attained to a higher level of socioeconomic competence, the Negro now presses with a new boldness and aggressiveness to procure what he feels belongs to him as an American. He insists upon having his rights. On the other side, the white resident meets this boldness with legal action and all other necessary resourcefulness to retain the white ghetto. The white man wants a white ghetto. The Negro wants an integrated community. It is this difference of opinion and outlook which makes for tension in the suburban community. The very presence of Negroes in approximately 1,700 suburbs leads to some tension and hostility. Not knowing what to expect in the racial change within suburbia, the residents expect trouble.

What are the prospects for the future? We have already noted the shift away from the time when Negro residence in suburbia was largely symbiotic in character. Today the Negro resides in suburbia as a free person who pays his own way and who is prospering in the business and professional world. As a citizen in a democracy he makes his home where he will. Today the new Negro cherishes a new suburban residence for the same reasons that other people do. Lewis E. Lomax and Pfeffer emphasize the necessity and the desirability of "culture competition," insisting that tension will continue until an equilibrium is found. Accordingly equilibrium coincides with the attainment of the goals of the minority group. But do not these achievements lead to new situations of tension? Unless negotiations and mutual compromise are involved the outcome is likely to be either a one-sided or Pyrrhic victory. It is not unrealistic then to expect that Negro-white relations will be marked by struggle into the foreseeable future. From the viewpoint of the suburban Negro the pattern of tension is a realistic one.

It is precisely because of the new status of the Negro in suburbia that tension occurs. While the Negro remained in the lowly vocational roles of chauffeur, maid, handyman, cook, and the like, he did not constitute a threat to the suburbanite. When he began to enter the professions, the business world, and the highly skilled trades, however, and thus began to earn and live on a high level of independence, income, and status and could afford to reside in better residential areas, he became a new Negro. No longer does he need to bow down to anybody or to ask favors. He wants for himself and his family the same things that white men in his salary bracket want.

Tension between Negro and white centers in several issues—access to jobs, schools, housing, politics, public facilities (theaters, parks, beaches, et cetera), and social and religious activities. It is unlikely that all such issues appear as crises in a single suburb; yet they are matters of grave concern throughout suburban life. Each issue has acquired an extensive literature and merits a detailed exploration which certainly would carry the reader beyond the modest scope of the present book. For many Negroes the critical issues are open housing, integrated schools, anti-discriminatory employment laws, and so on. Unfortunately there has emerged an abnormal emphasis upon "rights" and only a slight concern over "responsibilities." The new Negro is an aggressive, capable person who endures many insults and slights in order to realize part of the American dream—a home in suburbia. Undoubtedly the reaching after this goal, no matter how legitimate, will continue to yield many tensions.

PROTESTANTISM AND SUBURBAN TENSIONS

The foregoing account of conflicts is suggestive rather than exhaustive. Other issues probably can be cited. For our purposes, however, the present inventory suffices to reveal that tension is a reality and that it is no respecter of suburbs or faiths. These hostilities and tensions penetrate all religious groups and ultimately draw Protestantism into the struggle. The very turbulence of suburban life complicates Protestatism's witness giving and harasses its ongoing church program. Hence, whether or not the denominations are concerned, the brash power struggles intrude upon the life of the churches. What then is Protestantism's role in the suburban revolution? Many of the old guideposts have been swept away by the waves of change. At least six principles can be noted here:

1. *Recognize that the new suburban situation engenders tension.* This means that the combined local residence of Jew, Roman Catholic, Protestant, Negro, blue-collar worker, and sects provides the incendiary ingredients for debate, disagreement, misunderstanding, and conflict. Tension is endemic due to the vast population revolution which has occurred and is occurring in suburbia since World War II. Cultural differences and opposing religious commitments make suburbia one of the most

exciting places of residence in the metropolitan area today. Every institution and individual must expect to be under challenge and perhaps critical attack. The population pluralism and the colliding value systems engender tension. It is inevitable and therefore should be included in a basic understanding of the situation. The tension is neither evil nor good per se; it depends upon how the involved groups react to pressure and challenge. Crisis can be a fructifying experience. A recovery of alertness and deeper commitment may be the outcome.

2. *Establish an interfaith fact-finding process.* In the face of rapid and drastic changes it is absolutely necessary to find out what exactly is happening in terms of a factual nonpartisan viewpoint. Just how many persons of other faiths, race, and cultural orientation have moved into a particular suburb? What are the socioeconomic circumstances of the new residents? To what extent is one faith group seeking to dominate or harass another? Is any legal right being violated? What fact-finding process is needed in the face of crisis and drastic change in community life? An ascertainment of and reliance upon significant objective information can prevent suburban conflict from doing permanent damage to the community. People will need to acquire a respect for relevant facts and for a reliable fact-gathering process. This is the foundation of intergroup co-operation and dialogue.

3. *Call religious people to work toward constructive solutions.* The mobilizing of persons of good will and religious intentions to make common cause is necessary and desirable. These church people can be called upon to transmit among community acquaintances a reliable interpretation and an accurate account of the facts respecting an issue confronting the community. Religious adherents of all faiths will find it advantageous to take an interest and an active part in promoting constructive solutions. It is essential to keep channels of intercommunication open. Here, then, is a way in which church members demonstrate that they are not part of the problem but rather are part of the solution. The invitation to participate on a joint basis is a necessary early step in resolving crises about which Protestantism should be concerned. Facts plus concerned people affords a commendable beginning.

4. *Seek solutions beyond the present crisis or conflict.* When a crisis in human relations flames in suburbia residents need to look for a solution which lies beyond the present emotionally charged situation. This ap-

proach can set in motion an adequate effort whose purpose is to separate the primary issues from the secondary ones. When prejudice rears its ugly head or entrenched privilege marshals its parochial arguments wisdom suggests, not a showdown debate or fight, but rather a renewed search for a just solution beyond the existing context of hatred, misunderstanding, hostility, and conflict. The possibility of justice for all concerned parties is the desired goal. When a local suburban crisis marches in the front door, often religious affection and good will fly out the window. Usually the prevailing crisis furnishes the worst possible milieu for resolving the difficulty. Under the continual surveillance of an interfaith council or committee, the pursuit of solutions is carried on—even over a period of months or years. Eventually the passage of time may yield a worthwhile outcome. Truly the people are learning how to handle their crises and how to live in a community where differences are a normal occurrence.

5. *Let suburbia be a proving ground for pluralistic goals.* Contemporary life is charged with the responsibility of progress in religious and cultural understandings. Suburbia affords a unique and new opportunity for an interesting experiment. Can such an outlook find an adequate welcome in pluralistic suburbia? Will it become a principle of cohesion and of spiritual insight here? If available opportunity qualifies as a criterion, then Jews, Roman Catholics, Protestants, Negroes, sect groups and blue-collar workers, afford a ringing challenge. Such a striking diversity of people demands a serious experiment in pluralistic living. Whether the suburban slice of humanity can transcend differences in faith, ethnicity, and economics in the search for a workable pattern of living together remains to be discovered. There can be no doubt about the existence of important differences among Protestant, Catholic, and Jew; between Negro and white; between white-collar and blue-collar persons. The ultimate question is: To what extent do such differences hinder or contribute to the achievement of religious and cultural understanding? Because the suburban revolution is largely a post World War II development it would seem appropriate to experiment seriously with patterns of community life which are suitable for the future. *Suburbia should become a venture in interfaith, intercultural, and interracial living.* Its success can tell the world that the suburban revolution leads also to a revolutionary new way of life for all.

6. *Develop a new Protestant strategy for suburbia.* More than any other faith Protestantism has been challenged and harassed since World War II. It has been ridden over roughshod. So-called "friends" and enemies have attacked from all sides, charging the denominations with apostasy and treason against humanity. As a result, Protestantism is blamed for every unpleasant incident which occurs in suburbia and receives no recognition for displays of patience, tolerance, goodwill, and acts of helpfulness. Protestantism more than any other religious group is being put on the spot. It has more at stake in most issues. Protestantism must learn anew how to stand firmly by her own spiritual convictions, remaining fearless in the face of abuse and outside interference. The frequent diatribes should be met with patience and as little anger as possible. For the first time Protestants must reside in suburbia among people (Roman Catholics, Jews, and sect groups) with whom agreement in religious matters is not possible. Here religious pluralism is difficult to tolerate—from both sides. Further, Protestantism now is compelled to take an active part in political, educational, and other community affairs. Jews and Roman Catholics are surely doing so. These new suburban groups endeavor to dominate and control secular activities in order to procure advantages for their faiths. Whether Protestantism enjoys the turn of events or not it must exercise *influence or be influenced*. In suburbia there no longer exists a middle position. The new conflict and tension should stab the denominations awake, compelling them to act upon a new level of responsibility with respect to community life. The very crucible of struggle can become the occasion for finding a new relevance. The contents of this book are intended to be a useful contribution toward Protestant planning and strategy in suburbia.

VIII
Religion's New Frontier

That there developed on the part of organized religion a quick
and extensive response to the suburban revolution can scarcely
be doubted. However, the awareness of new church opportunity dawned
slowly at first upon the consciousness of Protestant leaders. Somewhat
belatedly, councils of churches stimulated interest in the unexploited
ministry around major cities, while at the same time seeking to control
denominational expansion by comity arrangements, by church planning
conferences, and finally by strong appeals to the ecumenical spirit. Then
the dam of effort broke. The vast scramble for new congregations got
out of hand in numerous metropolitan areas. Eventually church funds
became so scarce that no Protestant leader could guarantee that his
denomination would start all of its share of the new congregations demanded
by the rapidly growing suburbs.

This major struggle to provide an adequate ministry to the residents
of mushrooming suburbia needs to be told. It is an account of fierce
competition, numerous misunderstandings, shrewd denominational planning, and remarkable patience in the face of confusion. The accent here
will be positive rather than negative in order to promote a wide circulation of the more constructive ideas and practices. The critics' attempt to
ignore or to negate suburban life has been unsuccessful. It has not kept
suburbia from thriving.

TWO DEFINITIONS OF CHURCH EXTENSION

In terms of church extension or outreach two definitions appear to
be widely used—internal and external. *Internal extension* obtains when

a noteworthy in-movement of new families occurs within the parish boundaries of an already established Protestant church. New housing in the territory is an important visible clue. This means that from scores to hundreds of new homes are erected rapidly nearby. Usually the incoming people precipitate some changes within the suburban community, introduce a faster tempo, or sometimes even seek to alter basic institutions. Old ways of doing things are brought under challenge. Because of this many observers regard the suburb as today's melting pot of diverse population groups. It is a seething society.

This complicated problem receives detailed treatment in Shirley E. Greene's *Ferment on the Fringe* through an analysis of selected Evangelical and Reformed Church congregations scattered across the eastern half of the United States. Detailed descriptions of suburban parishes in "ferment" located in Michigan, Missouri, Maryland, Pennsylvania, Texas, and elsewhere are provided. Founded many years ago, the churches are now surrounded by new residents. Both the empirical and theological dimensions receive serious attention. The latter is stressed, however, in order to encourage parish leaders to take full religious responsibility for the newcomer families.

The significant point with reference to internal extension is that *a church is already there*. New people have moved in around it, affording a greatly expanded and often changed opportunity. Sometimes the old church is not ready or willing to extend a cordial welcome to newcomers. These new residents seem to be different. Hence the church fears them and fears the new needs which they bring into the community. This problem is rigorously explored in Havighurst and Morgan's book *The Social History of a War-Boom Community*. Walter Kloetzli also comments upon the importance of internal extension in *The City Church: Death or Renewal*. When, however, an established church throws open its doors and welcomes people, along with necessary changes, then it has entered into internal extension. Greene's perceptive book discloses how the turbulent transition actually takes place, how the old church fights to retain old patterns, and how eventually by losing its own inadequate life it finds a new life of Christian service. Basically it is a problem of widening the ministry, of opening the doors of the church again. While special techniques are required during transition periods, actually the rediscovery of the church's fundamental task is of foremost importance.

The theme of Russell H. Conwell's world-famous lecture "Acres of Diamonds" can be applied to the current suburban situation. All around the local parish lie the undiscovered elements of a rich significant ministry. Yet the congregation often is willing to ignore these possibilities. The future belongs to those who prepare adequately for it. Part of the necessary preparation is to serve the new population groups as quickly as they move in. This can be achieved by blending the old and the new elements into a fine congregation. This mutuality can enrich the church's life.

External extension points to a contrasting phenomenon. It signifies communities, usually all new, where numerous families reside beyond the reach of any established church. Who has not witnessed the present-day large-scale housing subdivisions which have spread out around the major cities of the nation? Where fruit orchards, meadows, and wood-lots used to be acres of new homes now abound. An astonishing blossoming of new housing has taken place. New communities call for new institutions.

Actually external extension simply means the establishment of new congregations, one by one, wherever new population groups settle in concentrations promising enough from a religious viewpoint. Detailed suggestions for surveying such new territories; for principles governing the selection of church sites; for the process of gathering people into the initial phase of the organization; for fund-raising programs which make possible the acquisition of a parsonage, pastor, and first unit building; and finally for the establishment of a permanent congregation can prove useful here. Several works can be cited. Dwight H. Shelhart's *A Church Is Born* provides a detailed account of the process utilized in establishing eleven new congregations in Wisconsin and Minnesota.[1] John Wilkins' pamphlet *Let's Build* explains how to start new Methodist churches.[2] What needs to be held in mind is that a profound evangelistic motivation underlies the impulse to establish new congregations. It animates the survey process and motivates the ministry in new fields. This is why many established churches are willing to contribute members,

[1] Philadelphia: Muhlenburg Press, 1947.
[2] Nashville: Abingdon Press, 1961. Consult also Shippey, *Church Work in the City*, Chapters VII and VIII.

leadership, and funds to aid this important outreach program. Nearly all new congregations get started by this means.

Because of the special importance of external extension for suburbia further amplification in succeeding sections of the chapter is necessary. The topic raises issues which require both thorough analysis and constructive prescription. To achieve these twin objectives the ensuing treatment subdivides church extension problems under several rubrics: (1) *Within a small denomination,* (2) *within a large denomination,* (3) *within suburban Protestantism,* and (4) *within a metropolitan territory.* Although church extension itself has other dimensions, it is our intention to focus upon the *suburban* aspect. Eventually it will be seen that external extension really means the planned establishment of new congregations. It is the launching of new local churches. This is a complicated, costly, significant, but necessary venture. A denomination which does not start new congregations soon loses its evangelical momentum. The issue becomes a matter of spiritual life or spiritual death.

WITHIN A SMALL DENOMINATION

Church extension activity occurs within denominations regardless of their size. Perhaps an illustration of such activity in a small denomination can dramatize the situation here. Among viable alternatives the Evangelical United Brethren was chosen because of the availability of adequate data which satisfy our purposes. Lewis W. Bloede has completed an interesting analysis of church extension in the United States and Canada, focusing upon the time period since the merger of the two antecedent groups—The Evangelical Church and The Church of the United Brethren in Christ.[3]

Among other objectives the investigator sought the number of new congregations established since 1946. When these data were in hand they were compared with kindred activity among other denominations. Bloede also investigated the success factors which obtained within the Evangelical United Brethren Church respecting these specific new congregations. During the eleven-year period selected for study, 136 new "missions" or congregations were established in 27 states and provinces. Bloede's doctoral dissertation provides an intensive study of these churches.

[3] "Development of New Congregations in the United States and Canada by the Evangelical United Brethren Church" (Th.D. thesis, Boston University, 1960).

He gathered data to test principles enunciated in the general literature.

An elaborate questionnaire was utilized, touching such traits as geographical location, size and cost of proposed site, its proximity to an elementary school or to shopping and transportation facilities, type of edifice, demographic characteristics (age, sex, occupation, income, size of family, et cetera) of the congregation, characteristics of the minister, methods of launching the "mission," and so on. Data collected on 108 new congregations were tabulated. Special case studies were made of three churches—two located in the United States and one in Canada.

Findings from Bloede's doctoral study include: (1) *Two new congregations out of three are located in suburbia,* plus an additional 20.4 per cent in other urban territory, (2) territories showing greatest growth did not all receive adequate church extension attention, especially lower income suburbs, (3) new congregations were launched dominantly in communities of moderately (under 20,000 dollars) priced homes, (4) one new congregation out of six was established under comity, (5) a house-to-house survey was utilized by 35.3 per cent of the new churches, (6) among important success factors involved in establishing new churches are comity clearance, field surveys, strategic site, experienced pastor, adequate funds, an attractive building, and a relevant program. Throughout the dissertation certain practical concepts were frequently referred to with approval—"one mile radius," "comity co-operation," and so on.

Since the completion of Bloede's study an intensive program has been in progress. Indeed, he reports that the denomination's objective for the period 1957-62 is to open 119 additional "missions." By means of a personal letter to headquarters in Dayton, Ohio, it was discovered that 111 new congregations have been added since Bloede's study. The cost of the anticipated future extension program was estimated at 6,203,000 dollars, based upon an estimated per unit average of 52,000 dollars, plus certain unspecified expenses. For a smaller denomination this is a very ambitious program. To sum up the matter for the Evangelical United Brethren, this outreach has yielded both institutional and religious growth. The boundaries of their ministry have been extended.

WITHIN A LARGE DENOMINATION

Let consideration now be given to church extension activity in a major denomination—The Methodist Church. Availability of data plus wide national distribution have dictated the present choice. Materials drawn from Bonneau P. Murphy's *The Call for New Churches* provide the reader with a remarkable account of developments occurring across the past decade.[4] Moreover, projected plans embrace the ensuing decade. Reading this book along with other denominational church extension materials one encounters a range in quality of factual data which would be of interest to the social scientist. Published reports disclose a major denomination's response to the latest population explosion, to population mobility, and to the sensational rise of suburban communities.

Little doubt can remain respecting The Methodist Church's awareness of important population changes. The church lives in the midst of change, and even finds herself in transition. The denomination knows that 25,000,000 American people move each year, one half shifting to new neighborhoods. It also knows that since 1949, one million new nonfarm households have been started each year. Specific knowledge of the rise of many new towns and cities is pertinent also. It underlies sound patterns of action.

Looking backward, one observes that The Methodist Church has organized 1,053 new congregations in an eight-and-a-half-year period ending 1958. This yielded an average pace of 132 new churches per year. Another way of breaking down the data is to show extension activity by quadrennia: 1952-56, 569 new congregations were organized; 1956-60, 680 new churches were established. Glowing reports from across the United States document the church extension alertness and action at the local community level. For example, a North Carolina city has established twenty-two new congregations over the past 16 years; a Texas city launched thirty-one new churches in ten years; the east coast of Florida started twenty-two new churches in five years; a California conference reported seventy-three new churches in ten years; and so on. The past record of church extension activity within a major denomination is a glowing account, whether viewed upon the national or local level.

Looking toward the future one takes cognizance of the current quadrennium goal of 1,600 new congregations, or 400 each year for the period 1960-64. Indeed, the Southeastern Jurisdiction alone has set up a regional goal of 831 new churches to be organized during the period 1960-69.

[4] New York: The Board of Missions of The Methodist Church, 1961.

Ohio Methodism expects to establish at least seventy-five new suburban churches by June, 1967. The full report of church extension goals would easily overflow the space available in these pages. An exhaustive list drawn up for the entire nation truly would be impressive. Expectancy runs high at the present time, but efforts will need to be redoubled in order to keep pace with the unfolding population opportunity.

These are not "castles in the air" nor idle plans for church extension activity. The very expectation has a real history. Out of the tested experience of launching new congregations during the 1940's and 1950's twelve effective methods for raising funds have emerged. These financial plans are described fully by Murphy. The list includes club arrangements, a tithing proposal, a "mother" church plan, special campaigns or crusades, and self-assessment programs. Monies are raised for ministerial leadership, for parsonage, for site, and for first unit building. It is estimated that the financial cost of a typical new congregation approximates 100,000 dollars or approximately *double* the estimated amount set by the small denomination mentioned in the preceding section. The anticipated four-year Methodist program will probably cost more than 70,000,000 dollars.

In summary and recapitulation, the highlights of the church extension activities within a major denomination, The Methodist Church, are as follows: (1) Successful experience since World War II in organizing hundreds of new congregations, (2) due to population explosion the need for church expansion continues unslackened, (3) a momentum for this extension activity has been achieved, (4) adequate funds still can be raised for this worthwhile objective, (5) research and survey methods have reduced the number of common mistakes in choosing territories and sites, (6) the denomination must expand even more rapidly in order to retain its ratio to the total population, and (7) to launch new congregations is consistent with the major denomination's spiritual goals.

WITHIN SUBURBAN PROTESTANTISM

While it must be acknowledged at the outset that one cannot present the complete Protestant situation with respect to church extension in the United States, nevertheless, important fragments of the whole will be read with interest. Some relevant information is better than none at all.

According to B. P. Murphy certain data are available from the National

Council of Churches sources.[5] He draws attention to a report of thirteen denominations covering church extension activity year by year, 1950-55. The number in parenthesis following each name indicates the average number of new churches established per year. These bodies are American Baptist (37), Brethren (4), Congregational Christian (11), Disciples of Christ (44), Evangelical and Reformed (10), Augustana Lutheran (14), Evangelical Lutheran (20), United Lutheran (50), Methodist (117), Presbyterian U. S. (58), Presbyterian U. S. A. (59), United Presbyterian (6), and Reformed (9). It is interesting to note that taken together these thirteen denominations established a total of 2,625 new congregations over the six-year period. The total number organized per year beginning with 1950 is 306, 339, 394, 499, 494, and 593.

From Bloede's material it is possible to inspect data from twenty-two denominations. This second list omits Presbyterian U. S. but adds Assemblies of God (214), Southern Baptist (435), Church of God (52), Church of the Nazarene (162), American Lutheran (22), Wisconsin Synod Lutheran (10), Missouri Synod Lutheran (101), Protestant Episcopal (84), and Christian Reformed (17). (The United Church of Canada established 361 new congregations during the period 1947-58.) The bracketed number following the name indicates the *annual average number of new congregations established*. It should be noted that the basic time period was not uniform but rather ranges from seven to thirteen years in length. Hence the yearly average might change slightly, were data from a uniform period available.

Protestant Denomination	Murphy 1950-1955	Bloede 1946-1958	NCC Study* 1958-1960
American Baptist	37	31	50
Brethren	4	10	12
Congregational Christian	11	13	26
Disciples of Christ	44	44	34
Evangelical & Reformed	10	10	17
Augustana Lutheran	14	14	14
Evangelical Lutheran	20	23	1
United Lutheran	50	58	66
Methodist	117	139	166

[5] *Ibid.,* p. 105.

Protestant Denomination	Murphy 1950-1955	Bloede 1946-1958	NCC Study* 1958-1960
Presbyterian U. S.	58	**	41
United Presbyterian	33	73	73
Reformed	9	3	12
AVERAGE ANNUAL TOTALS 438		418	514

* 1962 Report of the National Council of Churches.
** Data unavailable.

A third source of church extension information comes from the National Council of Churches under the title "New Churches Organized 1958-1960." [6] This report updates the material from Murphy and Bloede and also extends the list of denominations. For our purposes, however, a three-way comparison among Murphy, Bloede, and the National Council report suffices. This tabulation embraces twelve denominations and is self-explanatory. According to the Bloede study 17,924 new congregations (including Canada) were established for the period 1946-58. This yields a yearly average of 1,553. Moreover, the National Council study reports 1,544 new churches, with a per annum average of 514. All three reports are incomplete, since important denominations are omitted from the list; e.g., Southern Baptist, National Baptist, Mormons, Protestant Episcopal, and others.

The future goals for church extension within Protestantism furnishes an interesting subject for exploration. Unfortunately data for an exhaustive report probably would be impossible to procure. Since the total field cannot be delienated it is desirable to report such data as are available. Denominations named below have projected plans extending from four to fourteen years ahead, many beyond 1970. Therefore, to achieve a basis for comparison the materials have been computed as the number of new congregations to be established per annum: Wisconsin Synod Lutheran—5; Augustana Lutheran—20; Disciples—20; Evangelical United Brethren—20; Evangelical and Reformed—30; Church of God—50; United Lutheran—67; United Presbyterian—100; Protestant Episcopal—120; Missouri Synod Lutheran—135; Christian Churches—150; Methodist—400; Southern Baptist—3,000. Even this handful of denominations intends to

[6] Report prepared by the Bureau of Research and Survey (New York: National Council of Churches, October, 1962).

establish 4,117 new congregations per year. A projection to include all of American Protestantism would yield an amazingly large number, possibly 7,000 new churches annually. This church extension potential for all denominations is a staggering one to contemplate.

CHURCH EXTENSION IN CHATHAM

In a recent study William Rodda describes Protestantism expressing itself in the life of Chatham, New Jersey, a community of 9,500 residents.[7] The investigation seeks to discover the response of organized Protestantism within an expanding commuter suburb twenty miles west of New York City. This monograph assumes that growing population produces significant changes in the community which eventually will affect the church and other local institutions. For Chatham Protestantism is defined in terms of the four indigenous churches—Congregational, Methodist, Presbyterian, and Protestant Episcopal—which were selected by Rodda for intense study with respect to trends in church membership, Sunday-school enrollment, church finances, and parish organizations. The four congregations properly represent local Protestantism. No other denomination is established here.

Concerning trends since 1920 in the Chatham community, the criteria utilized included population characteristics, public-school statistics, municipal status, and socioeducational organizations. When these materials were analyzed it was discovered that the town is no longer a small village but rather has developed into a dynamic growing suburb with school population, municipal operations, and socioeducational organizational life scaled up to a higher level. The community has grown considerably population wise, making necessary an extension of commercial activity and many new ways of doing things. Reluctantly the town fathers have accepted the unprecedented changes and have adjusted to them.

More reluctantly, however, organized religion has adjusted to change. Trends within local Protestantism were differential. Some congregations thrived during the period since 1920, while others remained relatively static. Generally speaking, the response of Protestantism to Chatham's growth pattern has been "irregular." A definite lag appeared during the middle portion of the trend period. Indeed, Protestantism appears to be off the pace of growth. Rodda wonders why one denomination reported gains in

[7] "An Exploration of the Response of Organized Protestantism in an Expanding Commuter Suburb" (Ed.D. dissertation, New York University, 1953).

institutional strength while another did not. Both churches are situated in the same expanding commuter suburb. The American Legion and the P.T.A. registered greater numerical growth than did Protestantism in Chatham.

Because of population changes which came to Chatham an Inter-Church Council was organized in recent years. This representative body of local Protestantism functions through three main co-operative activities—a Good Friday Service, the summer exchange of pulpits, and a Thanksgiving Day Service. Moreover, there exists a modest United Church Women's program. Welcome Wagon service to Chatham's newcomers further cements amicable relations between local business and the Inter-Church Council. Protestantism, under the pressure induced by population changes, found itself changing in at least two directions—the promotion of community-wide youth programs (e.g., Scouts, YMCA, et cetera) and the cultivation of united congregational efforts to promote common religious goals. Both developments have far-reaching significance for religion.

Before turning to an account of practical program considerations, let attention be turned to a basic issue. Despite the customary optimism about unitive Protestantism, it remains too easy for individual congregations to go separate ways. Throughout the discussion Rodda stresses the point that United Protestantism is always the result of *adequate effort expended* to achieve the desired goal. The goal is never automatically assured. Hence the practical program at the community level relates to this basic objective.

Therefore the Chatham study closes with heavy stress upon Protestantism's obligation to rise to the suburban situation in a multipronged attack. Public relations and publicity no longer should continue on a unilateral basis but should originate in the local Inter-Church Council. Every two or three years there should be another community-wide door-to-door religious census in order to locate the unchurched suburban residents. This kind of co-operative project has been conducted successfully in the recent past. An Inter-Church Council sponsored, united, young adult club should be set in motion to reach "the forgotten person" (the young adult) in Chatham. Moreover, a stewardship week should be instituted during which all Protestant churches carry forward simultaneously financial campaigns for annual budgets. Guidance should be sought from the appropriate department of the National Council of Churches. With reference to local church life, leadership training schools should be set up locally, drawing upon available indigenous talent. Public lecture programs treating religious themes should be sponsored by the Inter-Church Council. Special programs for retired people and their spouses should be provided through local Protestantism. Protestantism needs to enter into social action programs touching such problems as juvenile delinquency, interracial friction, public-school needs, and kindred concerns, in order to bring the conscience of the churches to bear upon matters of public issue.

Since the research study was completed the following important developments with respect to buildings, program and Protestant co-operation have occurred.[8] The Methodist Church has relocated to a new site and has built a new church edifice at a cost of 950,000 dollars. Local Presbyterians and Episcopalians have erected new religious education facilities. The Congregational Church has remodeled its nave. Associate ministers have been added to the staffs of the Congregational, Methodist, and Episcopalian churches. A Senior Citizens Club has been organized jointly.

The direction of united Protestant effort has shifted since Rodda completed the study. Now two of the Protestant churches have set up individual summer worship services, thus withdrawing from the united program. Deep concern for community problems—racial integration policies, public school programs, and youth's leisure activities—has yielded a closer co-operation here, however. The new phase of co-operation is developing a deeper sense of unity, according to Rodda. The clergy hold monthly meetings with doctors, educators, realtors, and so on. Finally, although no new congregations have been launched in Chatham proper, the Lutherans and Presbyterians have each started a new church in the adjacent township territory. The updating of this research study discloses both internal and external church extension activity.

Thus one can observe that Rodda's study provides a dual analysis: A scrutiny of the institutional fortunes of Protestantism in a suburb, plus congregational concerns toward some of the current social issues in contemporary life. Not only does the community afford its own special set of problems but it also inherits the usual complicating aspects of human nature and society. This stimulating study of Chatham calls attention to many of the customary headaches of suburban church life and provides some possible

[8] The materials in Rodda's dissertation were brought up to date through interviews with the author and personal visits to the community.

solutions. It reveals that church extension and co-operative Protestantism are dynamic processes rather than static goals.

CHURCH EXTENSION IN A METROPOLITAN AREA

A scrutiny of the pattern and process of church planning and extension among Protestant denominations in a single metropolitan territory can provide a demonstration of principles involved at this significant co-operative level. Possibly Greater Indianapolis can serve as a model of what may appear in many American urban territories.[9] This is a reasonable expectation. Indianapolis was chosen because: (1) The suburban developments are impressive and continue to grow, (2) an explicit church-extension planning program has been in operation since 1959, (3) it has elicited the support of the leading denominations, (4) it features a working relationship with the city (metropolitan) planning offices, and (5) the leaders are realistic about the plan's merits. A detailed account follows.

Population Change. Certain features of the suburban setting affect Protestantism in Greater Indianapolis. While it is assumed that most suburban communities are growing population wise, what is often missed is the changing character of the religious opportunity around the edge of the city. Truly Protestantism has always been strong in Marion County. This numerical strength persists today. Since World War II, however, several important alterations have occurred and are continuing. Already these features have caught the attention of alert Protestant leaders.

Jews began taking up residence in Marion County following World War II, especially in the high-income areas. As a result Jewish congregations are being relocated from deep within the city. These relocated synagogues are newly built in elite suburbs or on the edge of the city close-by. Though not new congregations, technically speaking, the buildings have followed the people out from the heart of the city in a striking post World War II shift. More and more Jews are expected to succumb to the attractiveness of suburban living.

Around Indianapolis one may see also a number of new Roman Catholic churches and parochial schools. These structures bear witness to the shift of many Roman Catholic families out into Marion County. The old per-

---

[9] The materials utilized in this section were examined and evaluated by the late Fred Michel of the Federation of Churches, Indianapolis, Indiana. I spent several days in Indianapolis in order to examine the suburbs and to discuss church extension planning. This section summarizes the findings.

centage of 13 per cent Roman Catholic for the county as a whole is being revised upwards in the suburbs. The new population thrust is conspicuous in this Midwestern metropolitan territory and it coincides with the advances in socioeconomic status accomplished by urban Catholics. Other types of Roman Catholic institutions are finding the Indiana city's suburbs attractive too. Marion County reports an increasing Roman Catholic population. This change parallels nationwide developments.

Around the periphery of Indianapolis the sect groups are springing up like dragon's teeth. They are positively warlike in their aggressiveness. By definition, reference is made here to Jehovah's Witnesses, Seventh-day Adventists, Christian and Missionary Alliance, and kindred religious bodies. There can be no doubt about their appearance currently in suburbia and the emergent character of the trend. The antidote, however, according to old line denominational leaders locally is found in the observation, "sect groups are a threat to Protestantism only when they are *alone* in a territory!" Hence the co-operating denominations need to follow up as soon as possible upon their own new church development plans. In attractive indigenous church work can be found an effective answer to thriving sect activity. It is another goad to sound and continuous church life.

The Negro also is moving out of Indianapolis into the adjacent suburbs. Already he has settled in strength there. It marks a new development in this metropolitan territory. Indeed, since World War II the Negro population has increased 90 per cent. In 1950 approximately 1,200 Negroes were residing in the suburbs of Indianapolis. By 1960 the figure had jumped to 2,000 persons. Indianapolis presents an interesting situation. The Negroes have not yet started a suburban church of their own. These suburbanites of color continue to be the leadership and financial strength of many churches within Indianapolis. At the present time they show no enthusiasm for launching a new church. Indeed, the city Negro ministers would fight against such a project. Further, the Caucasian churches in the suburban territory show little enthusiasm over the presence of Negroes. Indeed, at least one white congregation has relocated its edifice from one suburb to another in order to avoid the racial situation. Possibly this strengthening trend of Negro suburban residence locally reflects the general direction of the national development. In some metropolitan areas this outward movement is more dynamic and in a more advanced stage than one witnesses in Marion County.

Another expanding newcomer group in suburbia is the blue-collar worker.

An examination was made of suburban changes for the period 1940-60 in Marion County. The number of blue-collar workers here has more than doubled since World War II. In 1960 the county population outside the city of Indianapolis showed 45 per cent of the employed in the blue-collar categories. Data from such towns as Speedway, Beach Grove, and Southport are included. Why is this so? Several reasons can be cited. Consider the ease with which the worker can procure mortgage money to purchase a new home, whether he is an ex-G. I. or not. Federal government policy has encouraged sweeping changes in this sphere. Hence the blue-collar worker, instead of residing perpetually in an old house in the inner city (property upon which he probably is unable to procure a sufficient mortgage), moves out to suburbia, procures an ample mortgage loan on a new house, and pays off the indebtedness in modest monthly amounts approximating house rent. Is it any wonder that great numbers of better-paid blue-collar workers are shifting to suburbia?

Thus, it is necessary to note how the alterations in suburbia since World War II complicate the task of church planning and development for Protestantism. Jews, Roman Catholics, sects, Negroes, and blue-collar workers have now taken up residence with growing strength in Marion County. Among other considerations, this multipronged population out-movement calls for more intelligence, more Protestant co-operation and more enthusiastic planning in the future. This understanding supports the formation of the Federation of Churches' plan in Greater Indianapolis.

Planning for Church Extension. An adequate description of the situation includes the following details. At the beginning the thirteen co-operating denominations (four others joined later) were invited to present a current list of the places in which they hoped to start new congregations. Then the local interdenominational planner personally went over the metropolitan territory by auto and subsequently by corroborative studies of new housing projects, finding all the additional spots which currently or within the foreseeable future—the ensuing fifteen years—should receive church extension consideration by some denomination. Next, all the spots were located on a master map of Marion County. Moreover, this proposed list was checked by the metropolitan planner's office for omissions and for suggested changes. Other knowledgeable community leaders were consulted also.

The next planning step involved a time schedule, an explicit chronology for extension development. Three units of time were utilized: (1) *Immedi-*

ate attention, (2) *within five years,* and (3) *within fifteen years.* Code symbols were assigned to the proposed church extension locations on the master map as follows: A *triangle* where new churches were needed immediately, a solid *circle* where new churches were needed by 1965, and a *square* where new churches would be needed by 1975. For facile reference each spot was assigned a number. Once again this arrangement of church extension spots was examined by the metropolitan planner, as well as by denominational leaders and other local experts, in order to insure the placement of each territory in the proper time category. Various leaders were consulted to make corrections and necessary adjustments. Although time consuming, this necessary step proved to be a second major hurdle to get over.

Thus, eventually an adequate master map showing church extension places arranged in a time schedule was completed and approved by an inter-denominational committee. Evidently this outcome emerged normally from a three-way co-operative process involving the church federation's research office, the denominational leaders, and the secular community's planning officials.

Possibly it will now be of interest to the reader to learn how the actual suggestion of church extension territories to denominations was achieved. The existing congregations of each denomination were mapped so that the areal distribution of each denomination could be analyzed. Starting with this reality, an attempt was made to design *an ideal church extension plan for each denomination,* holding in mind the number of churches each denomination should be able to start within a fifteen-year period. The denominational plans were then correlated, each being studied in the light of the others. Adjustments were made so that the denominational plans, when combined, became a valid, comprehensive Protestant plan. When this process was completed each co-operating denomination was provided with a map showing the location of its projects.

An Overall Church Plan. The following denominations are involved in the church-planning process: American Baptist, Church of the Brethren, Congregational Christian, Disciples of Christ, Protestant Episcopal, Evangelical and Reformed, Evangelical United Brethren, Friends, American Lutheran, Missouri Synod Lutheran, United Lutheran, Christian Methodist Episcopal, Free Methodist, The Methodist Church, Wesleyan Methodist, Moravian, Cumberland Presbyterian, and United Presbyterian. Each of these religious bodies participates in planning, in decision making long before any crisis which might appear. The denominational representative feels free to drop in at the federation research office whenever a problem arises. He receives direct and practical benefits from the co-operative relationship. This includes a map upon which is shown all the church extension spots for which the denomination has taken responsibility. Moreover, he receives free counsel on principles of site selection and is aided in the negotiations for land from the developer. Altogether this range of professional services gratis makes a strong appeal to the co-operating denominations. It is a good deal no matter how one looks at it.

According to the adopted plan 114 church extension possibilities were listed for metropolitan Indianapolis. In terms of the time chronology these were distributed as follows: For immediate attention, twenty-five situations; by 1965, fifty-one places; and by 1975, thirty-eight places. It will be remembered that some of the denominations had previously committed themselves to certain continuing projects. In addition each denomination was encouraged to study the master map and to select places for which it desired to accept further responsibility. One remarkable outcome of this interdenominational discussion can be cited here was that by 1962 ninety-eight territories had been accepted, leaving only sixteen "not taken." The detailed situation is summarized by the accompanying table. Already sites have been purchased in twenty-six cases. Ecclesiastical edifices are newly erected in seven locations. Some interest and/or activity is evident respecting sixty-five specific situations. This last category covers a wide variety of negotiations and activity. Here is the current situation.

Category	Total places	Not taken 1962	Site purchased	Building erected	Other
Immediate	25	4	8	4	9
Before 1965	51	7	12	3	29
By 1975	38	5	6	—	27
TOTALS	114	16	26	7	65

In twenty-seven cases sponsoring denominations with money in hand are looking for property to buy. A few denominations cannot act due to lack of funds. Moreover, suitable vacant land is not available in some of the promising neighborhoods.

In summary, there exists an undoubted commitment to utilize the church extension plan, to help make it work, to express church extension or development expectations within this concrete interdenominational frame of reference. Every effort has been made to accommodate the aspirations and needs of the co-operating bodies. At the time of this writing not only have the member denominations participated fully and enthusiastically in the master plan, but also other denominations have been attracted to the planner's research office for consultations and even have made application for admission to the co-operative group. This built-in appeal which gets results should not be overlooked. Clearly the master plan here has proved to be a powerful witness to unitive Christianity.

Reactions to Church Planning. To what extent does this church planning approach really work? Are the denominational leaders satisfied with it? Is it really wise planning according to the acknowledged criteria of the religious researcher and the criteria of the metropolitan planning commission? In short, to what extent is it good for Marion County and good for local Protestantism?

Whether or not the denominational executives really are satisfied can be discovered in part by weighing their response to a letter inquiring about the situation. Here are the results drawn from six selected Protestant leaders. Reaction from these administrators serving large and small denominations can be summarized under three rubrics—new congregations, useful information, and climate of co-operation. Among them, the six responding denominations already have established twenty-five new congregations under the plan. Moreover, in decision making they have benefitted from such shared information as data on suburban growth, methods of survey work, shared Protestant leadership, knowledge of other denominations' plans, community information, and technical counsel on suburban problems. Finally, the very process itself has yielded a new climate for co-operation; order has been brought out of confusion; mutual confidence has replaced suspicion; and church vision has replaced competition and debilitating conflict. The personality and patience of the planner himself contributed greatly. In summing up the personal reactions, it appears that there is a general acceptance of this pattern of church planning. Undoubtedly it meets the church extension interests and needs of the denominations.

From the viewpoint of sound planning which features the long-range development of the total metropolitan community, the findings are also favorable. The pattern keeps pace with the differential growth of Marion

County around Indianapolis. It satisfies the principle that wherever people reside there should be a church regardless of the level of socioeconomic conditions and/or color of residents. It meets the tested principle of geographical spacing between denominational units and of clustering across denominational lines, the latter invoked where population density justifies an accumulation of Protestant churches. It matches responsibly the unfolding development of other community institutions such as schools, commercial establishments, municipal government, and the like. It contacts the developer while the subdivision is still on the drawing board, placing the need for church sites in the mind of the developer early in his unfolding plans. Through the alertness and enterprise of the research department of the federation of churches, it is possible to have land set aside early for an adequate number of Protestant church sites of an appropriate size and at suitable locations. To date, it has been possible to get fourteen church sites planned into the subdivisions; i.e., in original plan and original zoning. These sites are not given to denominational groups but rather are sold to them at a reasonable price—generally at the actual cost to the developer, plus his normal expenses of surveying and improvements.

Probably what makes the *Indianapolis Suburban Church Plan* work so well is the combination of long-range values with short-range practical considerations in a blend which satisfies the Protestant leaders. It is neither pure "blue sky" nor totally pragmatic. It looks toward a more orderly and beautiful metropolitan area. It anticipates the situations of potential tension. It does not wait for trouble to start brewing, but rather takes the initiative and endeavors to ameliorate the situation before there is occasion to become angry or to develop antagonisms. Indeed, it endeavors to remove the cause for mistrust and suspicion, replacing such with objective planning, dispassionate analysis, and mutual confidence. It is a shift from comity to planning.

Fortunately, Marion County has continued to grow at an estimated pace of 5,000 new homes per year, furnishing numerous opportunities for church extension far beyond what the denominations have been able to handle currently. Financial limitations hinder somewhat the speedy purchase of sites and the prompt erection of buildings. There still remains a backlog of unassigned allocations. All the denominations are too involved, financially and otherwise, with existing allocations to scramble for any additional development projects. Hence the combination of wise co-operative planning, plus a dynamic growing county, supports the impression that Indianapolis qualifies as a microcosm of the national problem. It demonstrates what can be done where Protestant leaders and secular agencies are willing to work together in finding a solution to church extension in the suburbs.

IMPLICATIONS FOR PROTESTANTISM

Evidently suburbia rapidly is becoming a changed and changing world. This is religion's newest and largest American frontier. It is a place of sensational growth. No longer can Protestantism remain nonchalant respecting the leafy outskirts. No longer can the church be indifferent or negative or leisurely in its approach to suburban life. A new, exciting frontier has opened up for all religious groups. Protestantism's understanding and efforts need to be updated and upgraded in order to match the new conditions.

Several observations emerge from the present analysis. First, the church extension "fever" swiftly spread among the denominations following World War II. Indeed, the struggle to get ahead institutionally shifted into high gear. As church executives witnessed the acres of new homes being erected around American cities they wisely anticipated the establishment of numerous new congregations. Subsequent success justified this expectation. Despite the fact that the suburban housing boom still continues, some denominations are decelerating church extension activity. By now all denominations have learned that it takes more than "fever" to start new churches; indeed, it requires planning, co-operation, experience, religious commitment, pastoral leadership, and money. Since church extension activity now has settled down to a long hard pull, only those denominations which accurately diagnose the potential, correctly estimate the future shape of American Protestantism (i.e., allow for future suburban dominance), and invest adequate resources can stay in the race. Others will drop out of contention. While the religious potential of suburbia cannot be equated with the pearl of great price alluded to in the Bible (Matt. 13: 45-46), nevertheless, the idea encourages the perceptive church, deeply concerned over tomorrow's fortunes, to invest heavily in this land of promise. No denomination will be strong in tomorrow's world without strength in the suburbs. Spiritual power begins with new churches. This is the greatest outlet for evangelistic activity.

Second, deferred maintenance and an enormous need for better physical facilities on the part of established congregations has emerged from the suburban population explosion. Thus, along with the external extension program noted above, there developed a race for more adequate religious buildings in suburbia. All denominations were caught up in the contest. Improvement of facilities had been postponed for years. The telltale marks of deferred maintenance were apparent in thousands of local communities. Inertia, burdensome mortgages, lack of vision, and absence of pressing need characterized many situations. Then came the population explosion. Suddenly there broke out in suburbia a rash of construction projects—new education plants, drastically remodeled church edifices, and new auxiliary buildings. According to a recent survey comprising a sample of 117 suburban congregations, 114 or 97.4 per cent had remodeled, rebuilt, or added new buildings since World War II at a total cost of 15,000,000 dollars.[10] Since 1945 expenditures for new construction or drastically remodeled facilities yielded an average of 130,000 dollars per congregation. Who knows how many additional millions of dollars have been spent by the remaining thousands of suburban congregations scattered across the United Stataes. Literally millions of dollars have been spent, are being spent, to bring church facilities up to date; i.e., to improve appearance and utility, and, of course, to expand to serve the flood of suburban newcomers. Stimulation for remodeling and expansion arises from at least three sources—denominational competition, expanded religious opportunity, and secular comparison. Respecting the last, one has merely to observe the new public-school buildings, new shopping malls and centers, and the drastically remodeled old business houses to become aware of embarrassing comparison. Ample off-street parking facilities are but one of the prominent features of remodeled suburbia. The general rash of construction indicates that the church has sought, and is still seeking, by means of renovation and rebuilding to meet the drastically altered conditions in suburbia. Who is to say that this is an unworthy objective?

Third, rapid population growth around the edges of American cities yields a phenomenon which sociologists call *culture clash*. One aspect becomes the focus of our attention here. Persons who espouse rural values often collide with individuals who have adopted an urban way of life. This encounter between newcomers and old-timers in the suburb is often a turbulent experience. Sometimes just being a longtime resident creates a tension and suspicion toward newcomers. This is a vestigial hangover from the old notion that there is something wrong with the mobile person. Why did

---

[10] Shippey, "Trends in Suburban Church Life" (unpublished manuscript, 1960).

he have to leave the previous community? Why does he have to settle here where no one knows him. He seems nice enough, but what is lurking behind the pleasant exterior? At any rate the population explosion has thrown together disparate population elements. People representing diverse value systems are cast together in the same suburban communities. As a result there is engendered a struggle for leadership and a struggle for diverse goals in parent-teacher groups, in politics, in grange, in business, in real estate, in fraternal orders, and finally in the church. Indeed, culture clash is endemic and inevitable within thousands of suburban communities across the United States. It is part of the "growing pains" of frontier life. At church meetings, as elsewhere, there occurs a collision of opinions and of values with respect to such matters as remodeling the old church edifice, erecting a new religious education unit, improving off-street parking facilities, and even in the selection of program elements and study materials. Usually the frictions in church life are carried over from the frictions in secular life, and vice versa. Unless the religious leader is alert, perceptive and patient, he is likely to interpret erroneously the frictions as personal challenges to his leadership or unjustified criticisms of his work. Neither conclusion is necessary.

Finally, an adequate list of significant implications should include reference to at least four additional points: The church-school bonanza, the task of membership assimilation, the opportunity for interdenominational vision and planning, and the possibility of deepening the religious life of the congregation. It is not our purpose here to lengthen the list of possible implications, but rather to underscore the importance of this central concern of outreach. As American Protestantism seizes its suburban opportunity on religion's newest frontier, and as it rides the crest of this great wave of new residential development, there is needed a corresponding intensification of interest and effort expended in deepening its own spiritual life. New congregations must be launched. Old congregations need adequate facilities. Both can benefit from a deepening of commitment and an enrichment of spiritual life. This is the hidden demand of the gospel. It is the unfinished task of every generation.

IX

Suburbia: Zion or Calvary?

In this concluding chapter let attention be turned to a general recapitulation of the materials and to a responsible delineation of
some of the relevant implications. After an opening comment upon the three
faiths in suburbia, the new shape of suburban Protestantism will be described in terms of how its exciting ministry becomes accessible to suburbanites.

JEW, CATHOLIC, AND PROTESTANT

Jewish students of suburbia have examined the pros and cons of Hebrew faith situated on the edge of the city. When an evaluation was completed the scholars applauded the large-scale suburban settlement. Evidently
the migration is a beneficial one for the Jews. Elsewhere attention has been
drawn to the fact that 500,000 Jews are currently residing under suburban
circumstances in America. The figure is expected to double by 1975. There
can be no doubting that this amounts to a large-scale relocation of Jewish
people. While the territory does not qualify fully for the appellation "promised land" or Zion, nevertheless, the Jews find suburbia no more spiritually
hazardous than other parts of the American urban environment. Indeed
the pace of the out-movement reveals a suburban enthusiasm. Residence
here is regarded as very desirable. The synagogues have followed the people
outward.

It is known that Roman Catholic scholars have scrutinized suburban life
and have reported favorably. The demands of the church truly can be ful-

filled here. Indeed the writings of Andrew Greeley and others describe suburbia as a kind of "promised land" for Roman Catholics who have been ghettoized for generations in the poorer sections of the American city. To move out now is to move up into first-class citizenship. Nevertheless, Greeley calls attention to the challenges which suburbia hurls at Catholicism, insisting that some reforms have been instituted in suburban parishes. Yet Greeley does not feel that the true church is endangered by such modifications. Therefore he concludes that the great new out-movement of Roman Catholics to suburbia since the 1940's is bound to continue and should do so. By 1980 the figure is expected to reach approximately 8,000,000. Roman Catholicism has girded its loins for this splendid new religious opportunity. For this faith group suburbia is a boon. Indeed it is Zion.

What about Protestantism? For many decades Protestantism has maintained an established ministry in numerous suburban communities across the nation. What denominational leader or pastor or high-placed ecumenical executive does not know this? Moreover, that suburban Protestantism exists in strength is witnessed to by thousands upon thousands of indigenous churches. Many denominations report that their leading (e.g., the largest, wealthiest, or most influential) congregations are suburban. Some of the greatest American preaching originates in suburban pulpits. The Christian witness here in music, art, architecture, religious education, and so on, is something to see. Suburbia has been good for Protestantism across many years, but the time has come for the denominations to wake up and really see the shape of the new situation. Therefore let a closer look be taken at the structure, function, and prospects of the faith.

STEEPLES AMONG COUNTRY CLUBS AND SMOKESTACKS

It would be unfortunate if Protestantism possessed no adequate understanding of the diverse socioeconomic status of residents in contemporary suburban developments. Suburbia ranges from "tin can colonies" to "mink and cadillac communities" or to put the matter another way, it includes both country clubs and smokestacks. Protestant leaders have been compelled to extend their vision beyond the well-known white-collar stereotype to discover numerous blue-collar workers who live in suburbia. Within some suburbs blue-collar actually exceed white-collar in a ratio as high as two to one. Oddly enough, books which purport to discuss who resides in suburbia either have overlooked or grossly underestimated the proportion of persons who are employed in the manual occupations. It is a serious error.

Hence a correction in understanding is demanded if Protestantism is to be realistic about the suburban task. Protestantism's work is complicated by two kinds of pluralism in suburbia—socioeconomic and religious. The first comprises the range of economic fortunes; the second clutters suburbia with manifold administrative practices, attitudes, and ecclesiastical relationships. The outcome is a perplexing set of variables which calls for a more sophisticated brand of church work. A much broader ministry is required than has been supposed before. It is now apparent that church work is needed among the rich and the poor, the educated and the uneducated, the white-collar and the blue-collar workers. Protestantism must transcend the white-collar stereotype in thinking about suburbia.

To serve a territory comprising country clubs and smokestacks involves a broad range of ministry. Hence Protestantism can make use of a wide range of ministerial talents and abilities mobilized to procure new levels of church effectiveness. It is now necessary to provide a ministry which penetrates the upper, the middle, and the lower classes in suburbia. Yet local Christianity must possess qualities which are timeless and universal. Considerable flexibility in pastoral strategy is called for lest a single pattern of church work should be applied erroneously to all the suburbs. An adequate ministry embraces the full breadth of this Protestant opportunity. At the level of the local congregation a total ministry requires outreach to whomever lives nearby. A pluralistic strategy is demanded. Only thus can Protestantism truly render accessible to suburban residents an adequate knowledge of God through Jesus Christ.

SUBURBAN CLERGYMAN: FOP OR PROPHET?

An adequate understanding of the Protestant situation around the edges of American cities calls for a determination of whether the suburban clergyman is a fop or a prophet. Is he a foolish person who is overimpressed with his own importance? Or is he a reliable spokesman for God? Several diverse explorations are needed to discover an answer.

Novelists of the suburban milieu provide one kind of answer. One recalls Peter De Vries' novel *The Mackerel Plaza*[1] which attempts to suburbanize Sinclair Lewis' *Elmer Gantry*.[2] Here the Protestant suburban clergyman is

[1] Boston: Little, Brown and Company, 1958.
[2] New York: Harcourt, Brace & Company, 1931.

seen through the eyes of a person who evidently knows little about Christianity and even less about the pastor. The stance of the novel is strictly pejorative. Church life within the congregation is reduced to the level of continuous power struggles and personality conflicts. The minister is portrayed as a neurotic esthete devoid of Christian commitment. A razor-sharp wit and cleverness in riposte and epigram comprise the equipment which the minister in *The Mackerel Plaza* brings to his profession. At no point in the novel does De Vries attempt to interpret the suburban Protestant clergyman as other than a sophisticated fop. Only the cheapest human dimension of the ministry is presented, omitting the deep meaningfulness and sacrificial commitment found in thousands of suburban clergymen. The clever human half is depicted here.

A group of nonfiction writers have provided a similar image of the Protestant clergy. It emerges from between the lines of *The Organization Man, The Suburban Captivity of the Churches, The Noise of Solemn Assemblies,* and kindred volumes. Here the suburban pastor is unveiled as smooth, sophisticated, intelligent, well-cared for, and capable of being brought over to the organization man's outlook. What reader does not know of suburban clergymen who hint around for free new automobiles and prepaid trips to the Holy Land or to Europe donated by wealthy laymen or well-heeled congregations? Sometimes the pastor becomes a tool of a captive church and hence furnishes the disconcerting image of a fop. So impressed is he by his own importance and selfish interests that he loses sight of the discipline of the Protestant ministry.

Fortunately there is another side of the situation. From the crucible of suburban life itself one discovers instances of intelligent, well-disciplined, tough-minded, dedicated men of God who function in a spiritually prophetic role. Nearly every reader can contribute names of outstanding Protestant pastors and younger suburban clergy who belong in this classification. It is erroneous to assert that there are no prophetic voices and no creative leadership in suburbia.

This other side of the situation is suggested by the materials summarized in the monumental mid-century study of theological education in American and Canadian Protestantism under the direction of H. Richard Niebuhr.[3]

---

[3] Niebuhr, *et al., The Purpose of the Church and Its Ministry* (New York: Harper & Row, Publishers, 1956).

Here is disclosed a vastly different conception of the clergyman than that which emerged from the novelist and the "experts" on the suburban milieu. According to the Niebuhr studies the Protestant clergyman, suburban or otherwise, has always been required to be a Christian personally and to have a personal sense of vocation which arose out of the deepest level of commitment. Moreover, he was required to attain an acceptable level of formal education.

There is no evidence to indicate that these praiseworthy requirements were waived respecting suburban Protestant clergymen. The contrary is more likely, especially since World War II. The academic and spiritual standards have been pushed upwards in recent years. Yet *Christian truth through Christian personality* continues to be the twentieth-century norm. No matter if the continuing suburban church is larger, more complex, and more highly organized than in the past, it remains mandatory that the clergyman function as witness of the Word, the shepherd of the flock, the symbol of its unity in fellowship and purpose and above all the leader of its ministry. In his own life is embedded the tension between gospel and world, but personal commitment yields the gospel the dominating place. As a prophet and reformer the pastor remains sensitive to man's needs and problems. Here is the Protestant ministry.

What then is the suburban clergyman? Certainly he is not the wicked and useless individual depicted by the novelist, nor does he measure up to the ideal model espoused by the profession. Realistically he finds himself somewhere along the continuum between the two designated poles. He is ambivalent; although he has foppish days, he also rises up in prophetic hours. As a Protestant leader he seriously seeks to fulfill his ministry in a particular suburban community. Whether one approves or not, this dedicated, capable minister whose efforts are so frequently abused is the chief carrier of Protestantism to residents of suburbia. Without him the faith would fail to have a witness on the edge of the city. His task is uniquely important.

FUNCTION OF SUBURBAN PROTESTANTISM

What is the overall role of Protestantism under suburban circumstances? This can be seen in an interesting way. It is possible to bring suburban denominations together into a functional entity which can be identified as Protestantism. Peter Berger speaks of this possibility in *The*

Noise of Solemn Assemblies. Indeed this local entity of the faith has been there all the time. Only in the scholar's mind has the unity been shattered for purposes of analysis. A recognition of the actual Protestant entity needs to be recovered. It is essential for an understanding of the faith's suburban fortunes.

Readers will argue with some justification that it is rather difficult to behold any such unity. Is not American Protestantism broken into more than 250 sects and denominations? Has not this very splintered condition taken root and flourished in suburbia? Certainly the manifold forms of American Protestantism must be acknowledged. There is another side of the picture, however. The very existence currently of more than a thousand metropolitan, county, state, and national councils of Protestant churches indicates that a sense of unity exists among the manifold denominations and sects. This yields a kind of functioning entity which is not contradicted by the reality of community life. Indeed, one really can think of Protestantism in suburbia as a distinct faith group, as distinguished from Judaism and Roman Catholicism. In such terms a discussion can be pursued fruitfully.

If such a unity can be acknowledged what, then, is the role of Protestantism in American suburban life? From an appraisal of the situation, at least three basic functions of Protestantism can be delineated. It is: (1) An outlet for salvation, (2) a nurturing agency of spirituality, and (3) the Christian conscience of the community. When held in an indissoluble unity these several elements facilitate definition of Protestantism's constructive role in suburbia. At this juncture a brief exposition of these points can prove useful.

First, wherever people reside, in that place religion has a mission. The resident is the object of interest. This is the basis for the work of suburban Protestantism. Every noteworthy community study discloses a significant Protestant potential residing in suburbia. Just as the rabbi is concerned over the needs of local Jews, and as the parish priest seeks out Roman Catholics, so Protestantism takes responsibility for its own people. This is a viable principle of religious work. Clearly there can be no doubt about the unique and essential function of the indigenous church as the outlet for the mercies of God, for religious salvation. Each year an uncounted number of persons come to God through Jesus Christ via suburban Protestantism. For many this is the first major religious decision. For others it is either the conscious renewal of religious vows or the continuation of an institutional relationship begun with Protestantism elsewhere. In any case, local Protestant churches in suburbia carry out a significant obligation to residents of this religious persuasion.

Second, the Protestant church is afforded an educational and nurturing opportunity in suburbia. Literature is replete with instances of acknowledged needs of people for a more adequate faith, for more knowledge of religion, for guidance in practice, and for inspiration and courage. Thus a primary function of suburban Protestantism is to render accessible the resources of spiritual development. This is a primary goal of church extension activity. The church is challenged to function as a center for the Christian renewal of life. To the church comes the spiritually battered and defeated suburbanite. Here is a nurturing station where people limping with an inadequate faith find maturity and where the faltering adherent finds assurance. Like a Good Samaritan the suburban church stands at the confluence of need and nurture. Thus Protestantism can provide enrichment not only in the skills of prayer, worship, Bible reading, devotions, and so on, but also in the unstaged deepening of personal religious life in God. The existence of the church signifies the availability of spiritual nurture at any hour, day or night. In the hour of need Protestantism is there.

Third, the Protestant church can function as the conscience of the suburban community. The residents should look to the faith for moral guidance, ethical insight, and spiritual courage. They learn what is right and wrong, true and false, high and low. What is called for is the persistent articulation of the norms of human behavior and human relationships drawn from New Testament Christianity. This witness discloses the embarrassing gap which exists between the religious ideal and the local suburban practice. The suburbanite is prodded to take Christianity seriously. When the Protestant church functions at its best the conscience of the community is revealed. Worthy objectives for the community are exhibited. This obligation of the church to point out the unfinished character of suburban life and of human relationships is more than a gadfly role. Protestants learn to live under a spiritual discipline worthy to become universal. Thus a transcendence over the suburban culture is achieved by means of Protestant resources. But attainment cannot be left to chance or caprice. All aspects of suburban life are under Protestantism's critical sur-

189

veillance as the faith confronts, weighs, judges, and challenges the evil of suburbia. Thus Christianity comes into a dynamic focus within the life of today's suburbanite.

THE NEW SHAPE OF SUBURBAN PROTESTANTISM

In the light of the revolutionary population developments following World War II let us consider what form the contemporary suburban Protestant church should take. A recapitulation of the foregoing chapters can focus attention upon the emerging new shape of suburban Protestantism being designed as it is to match the surprising new suburban patterns. Many old suburban ways went out with the horse and buggy. A fresh way of looking at things is demanded now. Surely the features cited below should *not* be regarded as pleasing alternatives but rather should be seen as minimal obligatory elements which together comprise an adequate expression of Christianity. They should not be isolated from each other. They belong in a discrete entity. The suburban Protestant church should acquire and exhibit at least eight evangelical characteristics. It should see itself and suburbia as a Christian symbol, a surviving community, a human fellowship, a spiritual neighbor, a redemptive society, a keeper of families, a master of tensions, and an outreaching congregation. The shape of suburban Protestantism emerges from the hidden entity which focuses Christ's ministry here.

1. *A Christian Symbol.* Protestantism was the first religion to appear in the American suburb and it continues as the dominant faith there. It is indigenous. Suburbia surely symbolizes the unfinished religious task in the modern world; i.e., the necessary but oft-postponed encounter between God and man. Suburbia should be seen as a Jabbok, a place where the protracted struggle for the human soul occurs. Despite the power of secular forces as seen in the domination of material values, the apotheosis of the family, and the preoccupations of "grass roots" democracy, man cannot escape the obligation to respond to God's imperious call. Regardless of how much status the world accords to the suburbanite, God ultimately determines man's standing. Until the resident recognizes the need for the divine-human encounter, he really has no name, and no earth is sacred beneath his feet. Materialism cannot speak to man's deepest nature nor disclose his true destiny. Hence Christian faith dares to transcend the cultural context, seeking a remarkable renewal of faith and an adequate

stewardship of life's possessions. The spiritual potential here leads Protestantism to expect great things from suburbia. The church should sponsor vigorously a pacesetting life and action. It should help man to meet God through Jesus Christ. Suburbia is a Jabbokian symbol of the beginning and the continuing of a vital personal relationship with God. If it does not occur in suburbia where will it take place? To Protestants this is a basic meaning.

2. *A Surviving Community.* Suburbia is in the throes of a vast and continuing upheaval. Remarkable growth and disrupting change is everywhere. New suburban patterns emerge from the vanishing old suburbs. Indeed, the in-migration since World War II of a half million Jews, several million Roman Catholics, a half hundred diverse sect groups, several million Negroes and several million blue-collar residents could not happen without a far-reaching impact upon Protestantism. This faith should be among the first to recognize drastic change. Thus, the question of a surviving spiritual community arises out of the vast population and religious alterations. Protestantism should confront and survive these new challenges to its existence and worth. Once again the faith is compelled to reach down into its own life for resources adequate to the contemporary suburban situation. Tested values and relevant services should undergird the continuing work of Protestantism and commend it for adequate local acceptance. No matter how many Jews, Roman Catholics, or other religious and ethnic groups crowd into suburbia, Protestantism must continue to renew her own life at the deepest spiritual springs and to exercise her ministry. The faith should elicit appropriate recognition of its own valid ministry, however, and should ever reiterate the legitimacy of its own persistent and vigorous life. Out of the maelstrom Protestantism should emerge chastened, purified, vigorous, and eager to undertake new tasks. It can survive the revolution in suburbia.

3. *A Human Fellowship.* The 60,000,000 residents of suburbia represent roughly a cross section of America. While some minority population elements are missing, yet the melting pot aspect of suburbia has become a fact of increasing importance. A preliminary understanding of suburbanites is aided by a relevant classification of people. The scheme embraces six types which should concern suburban religious leaders—the marginal Protestant, the pioneer, the stranger, the organization man, the wistful pagan, and the regular churchgoer. These categories suggest relationships

which suburban residents have with institutions, with other people, with the community, with the larger society, and with God. Some relations stress secular influence; others underscore the religious impact. Personal posture ranges from thoroughgoing materialism to deep church commitment. Moreover, the types reveal action patterns in which suburbanites find themselves partly captive. These considerations are not remote from the task of the church. Rather suburban Protestantism is obligated to provide a suitable fellowship opportunity on the human level which will draw people together and which can yield additional adherents to the faith. Functioning to find people where they are, Protestantism takes advantage of natural subgroupings. The church seeks to reach suburbanites through their manifold centers of need, interest, and concern. Protestantism should not ignore the human fellowship dimension in pursuing its significant suburban ministry. People need to be found where they are.

4. *A Spiritual Neighbor.* Due to population mobility more people than ever before have thrust upon them willy-nilly the role of stranger. The reverse side of the coin is this: Neighborliness has become an urgent demand! Thus, the suburbanite affiliates with many organizations but actually belongs to only one community where he is neighbor. Times and communities have greatly changed. Being a neighbor today has become both a complicated and difficult affair. The in-movement of new religious and ethnic groups has made it so. What is the duration of this role of stranger? Some people shed the role within a week after arrival in a new community; others require a year or longer before achieving the status of neighbor. For some matriculation from nigh dweller to neighbor is an arduous journey. Therefore Protestantism should specify acceptable standards of person-to-person relations. Evidently the New Testament affirms a process of neighboring which is invested with Christian love, understanding, and service. Standards of affection and mutual helpfulness are given. Protestantism should emphasize Christlike relations among neighbors. Moreover, a spiritual neighbor expresses concern and action with respect to areas of the inner city, denominational growth, and ecumenical relations upon all levels. The 1963 Montreal Faith and Order Conference of the World Council of Churches stressed the meaning of Christianity at the community level. This "across-the-street" or neighborhood ecumenical emphasis underscores the strong obligations of neighborliness. Can the Protestant churches handle the responsibility of being a neighbor in sub-

urbia today? Neighborliness should replace nigh dwelling. The suburban church is challenged to become a pacesetter in religious life both within and beyond the boundaries of its own community.

5. *A Redemptive Society.* Because sin, delinquency, and crime are indigenous to suburbia, Protestantism should never relinquish its redemptive activity. Beneath the surface of suburbia there exists a seamy side. Material goods alone fail to make a man happy. Something diabolical fouls up man's search for meaning and happiness. Indeed, suburban living surrounds people with the considerable temptations of materialism, encourages the rejection of traditional values, turns over church and parental responsibilities to public education, breaks up homes, sends children on wayward paths, and spreads the contagion of delinquency. Suburbia brings out the weaknesses of some men. Satan in the suburbs generates much mischief and many problems. Some suburbanites fail in personal and social life. Indeed, Satan seeks to corrupt the whole man. Despite externally pleasant circumstances, manifold hidden problems harass the hardworking suburbanite. An erosion of values and moral standards occurs here. People who may reside under conditions of privilege or quasi-privilege have difficulty avoiding temptation, tension, and trouble. The most experienced pastors describe suburbia as a sea of troubles. While suburbia is not a crime center of civilization, its unsavory behavior surely needs the crucible of the church society. Protestantism is obligated to work among people whose lives are failing for whatever reasons. The local church should increase its capacity as a redemptive society, bringing the deepest resources of religion to bear upon trouble. Since the church is the only source of adequate concern and adequate resources, its role as a redemptive society should be greatly magnified today.

6. *A Keeper of Families.* The most neglected ministry of Protestantism is the preservation of the family as an auxiliary spiritual outlet for members of the household. During days of harsh persecution in France the Huguenots let the churches be closed but charged the families to preserve and practice Protestantism within their homes. This high responsibility of the "house church" as a spiritual ally needs to be revived in suburbia. Too many church activities are focused solely in the church edifice. The home as a unit should aid in the work of Christianity. In microcosm, the home is the "little church." Thus, suburban Protestantism must change its strategy. Instead of every activity's being focused in the church building,

193

some decentralization of spiritual effort should be carried out. Instead of working solely with individuals at church, Protestantism should nourish families at home in a strong new way by being a keeper, a guard, a guide, and a guest. In the secular world a new importance has been assigned to the suburban parent, especially to the mother. This development suggests a new pattern of ministry. The family needs to be recognized as a fundamental social institution which should receive help, guidance, and inspiration from the church. In the past Protestantism has been reluctant to divide its ministry or even to recognize seriously the spiritual possibilities of the home. Thus, the role as keeper of families is a new and very important shape of the Protestant church. As a keeper of families Protestantism must nourish the suburban home in a new focus.

7. *A Master of Tensions.* Since World War II suburbia has become more and more heterogeneous, ethnically and religiously. This increasing heterogeneity has had at least one powerful effect—an increase of tensions in suburbia. The mixing of diverse population elements has yielded collisions among values, attitudes, and interests. Many newcomers are "pushy," promoting self-interest and parochial concerns even to the denial of the rights of others. Such people are perfectly willing to ride roughshod over the concerns of other residents. They expect to get away with it. A new boldness and some evidence of anti-Protestantism is abroad in suburbia. How many new residents care about what happens to Protestantism? Because of the changes which have come Protestantism no longer finds itself in a favorable or neutral environment. Rather it must learn to face opposition, criticism, fault finding, and jealousy. The time has come to leave behind its naïveté. In the setting of unfriendly heterogeneity Protestantism now must learn how to accomplish its legitimate objectives within a context of tensions. This condition is not likely to improve; it can get worse. Hence the faith must confront the situation with strong purposes, a friendly aggressiveness, and an unswerving concern for its ongoing important ministry. The tension engendered can be utilized to muster adherents to a higher level of spiritual achievement. Christianity must rise above the frictions and differences to a mastery of suburban tensions. Protestantism will not exploit other faiths nor will it tolerate such exploitation of itself. This is a new situation.

8. *An Outreaching Congregation.* The astonishing population growth of suburbia has provided a great rush for church extension activity. Some

congregations have expanded their own ministry remarkably; others have launched new congregations. Suburban change dramatizes the need for Protestantism to consider her role as part of a denominational movement rather than an isolated self-sufficient parish. Suburbia dramatizes the need for a team approach in metropolitan church work. No single congregation functioning alone could match the vast extension needs of the city's periphery. Several dimensions of this co-operative pattern are important— within a small denomination, within a large denomination, within a suburb, and within a metropolitan area. Taken all together these instances of church extension consultation, co-operation, and action disclose manifold concrete possibilities of an outreaching congregation. This spiritual obligation is lifted up in manageable terms. How frequently the local church fails to catch this vision of its possible ministry! Nearly all suburban churches can reach out and participate in the larger ministry of the denomination and faith. An adequate suburban church undertakes work among the unserved people of its own and nearby communities. It is an outreaching congregation.

The aforementioned eight evangelical characteristics of suburban Protestantism may not yield at first glance an aspect of newness. Yet it is there. Hence the reader is encouraged to scrutinize the materials more closely. Protestantism is asked to take adequate notice of the enormous population revolution which has occurred in suburbia, yielding numerous newcomers of manifold economic, ethnic, and religious backgrounds. Much of this information comes as new knowledge to the church leader. It provides a new basis for understanding suburbia. Protestantism is asked to observe that some people, residing among pleasant surroundings and possessing an adequate income which permits luxuries, fall into sin, crime, and delinquency. In the midst of an abundance of material blessings some suburbanites become unhappy, frustrated, and evil. The new milieu does not keep some people out of trouble. Protestantism is urged to weigh all these changes judiciously and then to determine what new responsibility is laid currently upon the suburban church. Protestantism is urged to utilize all its new knowledge to develop a more adequate ministry to suburbanites.

In view of these serious deliberations it is probably no exaggeration to assert that *Protestantism is taking on a new shape* as it renders a ministry in contemporary suburbia. The radical newness is not on the level of novelty, however, but rather upon the deeper level of radical Christian concern. The new shape rests upon new knowledge of facts and processes, an awareness of a new milieu and mood and the newly acknowledged failure of material possessions as a source of happiness and well-being. Because of important community changes Protestantism emerges wiser, more dynamic, and more relevant in its ministry. It has a new shape.

THE CHURCH: COMFORT STATION OR PACESETTER?

A confusion exists in suburbia as to whether the church should function as a spiritual pacesetter or serve as a comfort station. It is the primary issue of Calvary versus Zion. Protagonists who favor a spiritual pacesetter's role insist that the ecclesiastical enterprise lead the way in all aspects of church work, including an adequate faith and an adequate social concern for underprivileged mankind everywhere. On the other hand, those who regard the church as a kind of comfort station are eager to settle down into a benevolent inertia and to keep peace with everybody at any price. Here church leaders and/or laymen dare not "rock the boat" with proposals for significant change or new duties in the contemporary world. Whichever type of church prevails determines whether suburbia is Zion or Calvary. With this complex problem in mind, let us examine the suburban church in two dimensions—as people and as an institution.

1. *Suburban Church as People.* Many of the fault-finding comments of Winter, Berger, and Whyte actually criticize suburban laymen. A challenge is hurled at the adequacy of personal religion in suburbia. These people are accused of being "asleep in Zion." The impatient critics place suburban faith as held by laymen at a very low level of spiritual effectiveness. "Asleep in Zion" refers to suburban men and women who, possessing previous church experience and leadership ability, refuse to take responsibilities in the suburban church. Such people have a noteworthy contribution to make, but they refuse to bestir themselves. Pastors report that only a small percentage of the ablest suburbanites will accept major tasks in the local church. This unfortunate attitude has produced congregations which are satisfied with half-hearted action. It suggests that a spiritual lethargy has settled over suburbia. Church attendance is less than the national average. Financial church support falls far below ability. Ethical leadership loses its sharp edge in a milieu of complacency. Religious mission sees religion as a comfortable cloak rather than as a living flame.

The sterner demands of the gospel fall upon too many unheeding ears.

Has the suburbanite outgrown Christianity? Some people place themselves outside the church and hence do not feel under obligation to live by its spiritual ideals. Rightly or wrongly some people really feel that they have outgrown religion. Many such individuals reside in suburbia. People of exceptional economic and cultural achievement often wonder if they really need religion any more. College-educated persons often feel that they have "graduated" from the church. The individual who develops a lively interest in avocational pursuits (music, art, the theater, and so on) wonders sometimes whether he really needs a personal faith. Respecting such questions the suburbanite often gives himself a negative answer. The heavy hand of material success often disrupts a person's proper sense of values. Culture's challenges of Christianity are usually intensified under suburban circumstances. Competition with other value systems is sharper, making it necessary for the individual to lay hold upon a more adequate faith. Without help from the church the suburbanite is likely to give the wrong answer.

Possibly the question noted above should be asked the *opposite* way: Has Christianity kept abreast with the achievements of modern man? Confronted by education, talent, leadership, financial competence, and worldly experience, what does suburban Protestantism have to say? Is the world too sophisticated? Can the church speak to the condition of the successful? Or must one conclude that faith, prayer, and salvation are only for the uneducated, the mediocre, the uncultured, and the indigent? Suburban Protestantism cannot evade such questions, nor can it escape responsibility for frank and disturbing answers. Historically Protestantism has related itself constructively to advancing human knowledge, to altered technological conditions, and to many types of cultural challenge. Protestantism is not afraid of suburban change. The church should confront any major alteration with an appropriate set of practical suggestions telling how to be a Christian under changed conditions. This type of concrete guidance is called for now in the American suburbs. Most residents do not desire to repudiate Protestantism, but rather seek wistfully to discover what its central tenets are.

Today laymen are called upon to surrender their talents and skills to the local suburban church. Protestantism should keep the pressure of Christ's life upon suburbanites. Protestantism should sponsor that kind of fellowship in which Christ is revealed as a living reality and as a spiritual force in the life of the community. To be custodian of this valuable treasure places the demand of genuineness upon the local suburban congregation. Eventually the Protestant church should expose all phases of suburban life to thoroughgoing criticism. This is a worthy goal. Every private and social aspect should come under spiritual surveillance. Each should be searched out and placed in the crucible of Christian evaluation. As a result either the ugly elements of private and social life will be changed or a repudiation of religious ideals will ensue. From the crucible can emerge many people who will assume the role of pacesetters.

2. *Suburban Church as Institution.* Here one hears again the disturbing question: Is the church *institutionally* a pacesetter or a comfort station? In view of its enviable potential does the suburban church set the spiritual pace for sister congregations or does it merely sink down into the oblivion of comfort and irresponsibility? A scrutiny of the church's shortcomings can focus attention upon the organizational flaws, the inertia of the group, the backward pull of tradition and the tendency of the structure to swallow up the puny efforts of individuals. Properly so, the institution itself becomes a center of concern in an appraisal of the suburban church.

What needs to be understood at once is that Protestantism possesses a relationship of embeddedness to suburban society: *The Protestant church is only part of this society.* The denominations are set solidly into the larger culture along with other religious groups and the secular organizations. This very suburban embeddedness places the church in close proximity to the secular forces and in a position of constant danger. Secular values creep into the church. The religious group is always on the verge of being swallowed up into the larger society. This frightens some people. Protestantism is exactly where it wants to be, however; i.e., in close proximity to the people and institutions over which it seeks to exercise spiritual influence. Dangers of institutional success arise, therefore, from the fact that the church is exposed constantly to powerful secular influences. In the contest for transcendent influence Protestantism's equipment seems puny and inadequate. In appraising the dilemma H. Paul Douglass has urged that institutionalization is "dangerous, inevitable, yet manageable." [4] Muelder, Ballard, and other scholars concur.

[4] *The Protestant Church as a Social Institution* (New York: Harper & Brothers, 1935), p. 13.

Moreover, institutionalization is always in danger of getting out of control. This is patent. The possibilities of gaining cultural success rather than spiritual effectiveness yield hazards to the proper work of suburban Protestantism. Music, art, drama, and recreation can become more important than the suburban church's spiritual goals. When this unfortunate development occurs secular standards dictate choices of music, art, and drama as well as answers to other program or policy questions. Thus, the goals of church life become subordinated to increasing cultural sophistication. Worldly influence may extend from the format of the church bulletin to church architecture, dictating even the organization of subsidiary groups within the congregation. Institutional efficiency may supersede all other objectives. As Protestantism's spiritual goals cease to be normative secularism takes over the local church. Such tragedy has already struck in some suburban communities.

What precisely does the institutional success of a suburban church mean? Are the conventional criteria of number of members, material prosperity, and size of organizational structure applicable here? Are there not other criteria which merit consideration? The suburban church should acquire a clearer idea of what mere institutional success means. To prosper or not to prosper, that is the question. At what point does institutional success yield diminishing returns? Walter Muelder recommends "limited institutionalization," thereby indicating that *some ongoing structure is necessary and desirable* in the proper function of significant church work.[5] Without some adequate social structure such accomplishments as visibleness, continuity, nurture, and the transmission of the gospel would be impossible in the suburban church, or elsewhere.

Possibly one should raise the disturbing question in the opposite way. *Dare the church not be reasonably successful institutionally?* Why should not the church achieve a measure of institutional success? Can the most cherished values in Christianity be preserved and transmitted without some measure of institutional continuity? Some Protestant leaders accept "limited institutionalization" as a solution of the persistent problem. Possibly the dangers of visible success appear chiefly when the Protestant church loses

[5] "Institutionalism in Relation to Unity and Disunity," *The Nature of the Unity We Seek,* edited by Paul S. Minear (St. Louis: Bethany Press, 1958), pp. 90-102; and "Institution and Church in the North American Situation," Frederick A. Shippey in Ehrenstrom and Muelder, eds., *Institutionalism and Church Unity* (New York: The Association Press, 1963.), Chapter 3.

sight of its primary spiritual objectives. At what point in the process of visible achievement does this neglect take place? Certainly the suburban church should function upon its true level of capability, recalling its pioneering heritage and the ever-present need to stir up its evangelical fires. Dedicated laymen should mobilize in order to undergird the suburban church as a spiritual pacesetter in the contemporary world. This effort can launch the congregation upon the road to Calvary, a route which leads away from the quiet town of Zion.

SUBURBIA: BOON OR CROSS?

Finally one turns to a comment on the suburb itself. Is suburbia really a boon or a cross for Protestantism to bear? All the materials treated in the present volume are intended to aid the reader in developing an adequate answer. Suburbia certainly can be considered as a boon. The territory has yielded numerous benefits and blessings for many of the residents. Suburbanites are a highly favored people by virtue of the physical, psychological, and social benefits which derive from where they live. A dozen serious writers (Gordon, Greeley, Dobriner, Wood, *et al.*) have elaborated this point. Thus, upon what grounds can Protestantism say that there have been here no benefits for the faith? When suburbia is viewed as a cross, however, one confronts the reality of an affliction regarded as a test of Christian patience or virtue. For the genuinely Christian person suburbia constitutes a real test of faith. Material advantages and attractive secular dimensions make it not an easy place in which to live as a Christian.

Actually it is wiser to look at suburbia as a mixed situation—partly boon and partly cross. This confusion of boon and cross is a more realistic appraisal of the city's edge. For this reason the discussion can and should issue in an account of religious *community*. The demand for Christian community (fellowship) cries out from the far corners of suburbia. Possibly this is why H. Richard Niebuhr has commented so strongly upon the "community authority" of the Protestant ministry.[6]

What makes Christian community possible? Perhaps the combination of several elements can point in the direction of an answer. Religious community begins with a gathering of the *committed* Christians. Joint effort aimed at a deepening of personal religious understandings carries it beyond mere individual enrichment. Whenever Christian concern which

[6] *Op. cit.*, p. 86.

knows no frontiers is implemented in behalf of needy humanity the objective or religious community is advanced still further. Finally, as a Protestant congregation participates in religious mission tasks lying beyond the immediate boundaries of the suburban community the potential for Christian unity is developed. These four elements contribute measurably to a rationale for religious fellowship. Christian community does not just happen. Rather it is an end product which has been sought for patiently, intelligently, and assiduously. The sense of Christian community often has a secular counterpart. Both dimensions are needed; the one reinforces the other. The values around which coherence is achieved are quite dissimilar, however.

In discussing the demand for Christian fellowship or community it should be made clear that we do not have in mind Taizé's Great Community, which, as a Protestant monastic order, forges its witness after the rule of Saint Benedict.[7] This would not work in suburbia. Nor do we refer to Suzanne de Dietrich's "witnessing community," which sees the church as a new society emerging from biblical origins albeit with ethical and ecumenical dimensions.[8] Rather it is more like the church as a human community as envisaged by James Gustafson.[9] It is an institution of believers which possesses a particular vocation, purpose, and power. Adherents are held together not only by common belief, but also by an order which is of God. This discussion of the existence of the church's life as *both* a fellowship and an institution underscores the profound demand for Christian community. This is rooted in the deepest biblical and theological understanding of the church as well as in the social interpretation of the church. This conception of Christian community is needed in the suburbs. Here is where New Testament religion confronts and relates itself to general human achievement, but it is a struggle, a mighty contest for supremacy.

Apparently suburbia will never cease to harass the Protestant church in an attempt to lower its standard of life, to shift its point of emphasis, to compromise its teachings, to blunt its message, to swallow up its endeavors, and to win it with honest trifles to betray it in deepest consequence. Indeed, suburbia will not let the church alone until the latter changes, quits,

---

[7] Roger Schutz, *Living Today for God* (Baltimore: Helicon Press, 1962).

[8] *The Witnessing Community* (Philadelphia: The Westminster Press, 1958).

[9] *Treasure in Earthen Vessels* (New York: Harper & Row, Publishers, 1961).

or moves away. Thus, no matter how one looks at the situation there appears to be an endless wrestle between the church and the suburban world.

Yet Protestantism refuses to be intimidated. It has learned to turn suburbia's challenge and pressure into occasions for creative response. It has discovered that no suburban situation is intractable. Through a series of wise responses the milieu, however ugly and unpromising, has been changed. The church has proved a redemptive force in suburbia over and over again. Thus, Protestantism even now possesses the power to change the suburban world. Whether the environment is boon or cross, Calvary or Zion, the faith will continue to seek for "the city which has foundations, whose builder and maker is God." (Heb. 11:10). Certainly Protestantism will have no easy time impressing its spiritual ideals upon suburbanites or in securing genuine commitment to its way of life. Yet the time has come for Protestants to rise up and possess the territory in the name of the Lord. How laymen and ministers respond to this injunction will provide an answer to the haunting question: Is suburbia a boon to enjoy or a cross to bear?

Selected Bibliography

PRIMARY SOURCES

Abrams, Charles. *Forbidden Neighbors: A Study of Prejudice in Housing*. New York: Harper & Row, Publishers, 1955.

Barclay, Dorothy. *Understanding the City Child*. New York: Franklin Watts, Inc., 1959.

Berger, Bennett. *Working-Class Suburb*. Berkeley, Calif.: University of California Press, 1960.

Bloede, Lewis W. "Development of New Congregations in the United States and Canada by the Evangelical United Brethren Church." Unpublished Th.D. thesis, Boston University, 1960.

Christie, Richard, and Jahoda, Marie, editors. *Studies in the Scope and Method of the Authoritarian Personality*. New York: Free Press of Glencoe, 1954.

Conant, James Bryant. *Slums and Suburbs*. New York: McGraw-Hill Book Company, 1961.

Cox, Oliver C. *Caste, Class and Race*. New York: Monthly Review Press, 1959.

Dewey, Richard. "Peripheral Expansion of Population in Metropolitan Milwaukee." Unpublished Ph.D. dissertation, University of Wisconsin, 1946.

Dobriner, William M. *Class in Suburbia*. Englewood Cliffs, N. J.: Prentice-Hall, Inc., 1963.

——, editor. *The Suburban Community*. New York: G. P. Putnam's Sons, 1958.

Douglass, H. Paul. *The Suburban Trend*. New York: The Century Company, 1925.

Ehrenstrom, Nils, and Muelder, Walter G., editors. *Institutionalism and Church Unity*. New York: Association Press, 1963.

Fairchild, Roy W., and Wynn, John Charles. *Families in the Church: A Protestant Survey*. New York: Association Press, 1961.

Fava, Sylvia F. "Urban-Suburban Contrasts in Social Participation: A Study of Neighboring in New York City and Nassau County." Unpublished Ph.D. dissertation, Northwestern University, 1956.

Fichter, Joseph. *Social Relations in the Urban Parish*. Chicago: University of Chicago Press, 1954.

Form, William H. "Sociology of a White Collar Suburb: Greenbelt, Maryland." Unpublished Ph.D. dissertation, University of Maryland, 1944.

Futterman, Robert A. *The Future of Our Cities.* New York: Doubleday & Company, 1961.

Glazer, Nathan, and McEntire, Davis. *Studies in Housing and Minority Groups,* Berkeley, Calif.: University of California Press, 1960.

Gordon, Albert I. *Jews in Suburbia.* Boston: Beacon Press, 1959.

Gordon, Richard E., *et al. The Split-Level Trap.* New York: Bernard Geis Associates (Random House), 1961.

Gottmann, Jean. *Megalopolis.* New York: The Twentieth Century Fund, 1961.

Greeley, Andrew M. *The Church and the Suburbs.* New York: Sheed & Ward, Inc., 1959.

Greene, Shirley. *Ferment on the Fringe.* Philadelphia: Christian Education Press, 1960.

Grier, Eunice, and George. *Privately Developed Interracial Housing,* Berkeley, Calif.: University of California Press, 1960.

Gustafson, James M. *Treasure in Earthen Vessels.* New York: Harper & Row, Publishers, 1961.

Jaspan, Norman, and Black, Hillel. *The Thief in the White Collar.* Philadelphia: J. B. Lippincott Company, 1959.

Jones, Arthur H. "Cheltenham Township—An Ecological and Social Description of a Suburban Area." Unpublished Ph.D. dissertation, University of Pennsylvania, 1940.

Keats, John C. *The Crack in the Picture Window.* Boston: Houghton Mifflin Company, 1957.

Kramer, Judith R., and Leventman, Seymour. *Children of the Gilded Ghetto.* New Haven, Conn.: Yale University Press, 1961.

Laurenti, Luigi. *Property Values and Race.* Berkeley, Calif.: University of California Press, 1960.

Lee, Frank F. *Negro and White in Connecticut Town.* New York: Bookman Associates, Inc., 1961.

Lee, Robert. *The Social Sources of Church Unity.* Nashville: Abingdon Press, 1960.

Lenski, Gerhard. *The Religious Factor.* New York: Doubleday & Company, 1961.

Liell, John T. "Levittown: A Study of Community Planning and Development." Unpublished Ph.D. dissertation, Yale University, 1952.

Lipman, Eugene J., and Vorspan, Albert, editors. *A Tale of Ten Cities.* New York: Union of American Hebrew Congregations, 1962.

McCord, Joan, *et al. Origins of Crime.* New York: Columbia University Press, 1959.

McEntire, Davis. *Residence and Race.* Berkeley, Calif.: University of California Press, 1960.

Martin, Walter T. *The Rural-Urban Fringe.* Eugene, Ore.: University of Oregon, 1953.

Moberg, David O. *The Church as a Social Institution.* Englewood Cliffs, N. J.: Prentice-Hall, Inc., 1962.

Murphy, Bonneau P. *The Call for New Churches.* New York: Board of Missions of The Methodist Church, 1961.

Rapkin, Chester, and Grigsby, William G. *The Demand for Housing in Racially Mixed Areas.* Berkeley, Calif.: University of California Press, 1960.

Rodda, William F. B. "An Exploration of the Response of Organized Protestantism in an Expanding Commuter Suburb." Unpublished Ed.D. dissertation, New York University, 1953.

Rodehaver, Myles. "The Rural-Urban Fringe: An Interstitial Area." Unpublished Ph.D. dissertation, University of Wisconsin, 1946.

Schauffler, Mary. "The Suburbs of Cleveland." Unpublished Ph.D. dissertation, University of Chicago, 1945.

Seeley, John R., *et al. Crestwood Heights.* New York: Basic Books, Inc., 1956.

Shelhart, Dwight H. *A Church Is Born.* Philadelphia: Muhlenberg Press, 1947.

Shippey, Frederick A. *Church Work in the City.* Nashville: Abingdon Press, 1952.

Spectorsky, Auguste. *The Exurbanites.* Philadelphia: J. B. Lippincott Company, 1955.

Underwood, Kenneth W. *Protestant and Catholic.* Boston: Beacon Press, 1957.

Vidich, Arthur J., and Bensman, Joseph. *Small Town in Mass Society.* Princeton, N. J.: Princeton University Press, 1958.

Vogel, Ezra F. *Japan's New Middle Class.* Berkeley, Calif.: University of California Press, 1963.

Voss, J. Ellis. "Ocean City: An Ecological Analysis of a Satellite Community." Unpublished Ph.D. dissertation, University of Pennsylvania, 1941.

Warner, George A. *Greenbelt: The Cooperative Community.* New York: The Exposition Press, 1954.

Williams, Dorothy S. "Ecology of Negro Communities in Los Angeles County, 1940-1959." Unpublished Ph.D. dissertation, University of Southern California, 1961.

Willmott, Peter, and Young, Michael. *Family and Class in a London Suburb.* London: Routledge & Kegan Paul, Ltd., 1960.

Wolff, Kurt H., editor. *The Sociology of Georg Simmel.* New York: Free Press of Glencoe, 1950.

Wood, Robert C. *Suburbia: Its People and Their Politics.* Boston: Houghton Mifflin Company, 1959.

SECONDARY SOURCES

Archibald, Katherine. *Wartime Shipyard.* Berkeley, Calif.: University of California Press, 1947.

Bainton, Roland H. *Yale and the Ministry.* New York: Harper & Brothers, 1957.

Beatty, Jerome, Jr. *Show Me the Way to Go Home.* New York: Thomas Y. Crowell Company, 1959.

Berger, Peter. *The Noise of Solemn Assemblies.* New York: Doubleday & Company, 1961.

Blood, Robert O. *Marriage.* New York: Free Press of Glencoe, 1962.

Boyd, Malcolm. *Christ and Celebrity Gods.* Greenwich, Conn.: The Seabury Press, 1958.

Brownell, Baker. *The Human Community.* New York: Harper & Brothers, 1950.

Chinoy, Ely. *Automobile Workers and the American Dream.* New York: Random House, 1955.

Campbell, Ernest Q., and Pettigrew, Thomas F. *Christians in Racial Crisis.* Washington: Public Affairs Press, 1959.

Clark, Dennis. *Cities in Crisis.* New York: Sheed & Ward, 1960.

Clark, Elmer T. *The Small Sects in America.* Rev. ed.; Nashville: Abingdon Press, 1949.

Davies, Horton. *A Mirror of the Ministry in Modern Novels.* New York: Oxford University Press, 1959.

de Dietrich, Suzanne. *The Witnessing Community.* Philadelphia: The Westminster Press, 1958.

Dodson, Garner. *Making the Most of Every Move.* New York: G. P. Putnam's Sons, Inc., 1958.

Douglass, H. Paul, and Brunner, Edmund de S. *The Protestant Church as a Social Institution.* New York: Harper & Brothers, 1935.

Fortune, Editors of. *The Changing American Market.* New York: Garden City Books, 1955.

————. *The Exploding Metropolis.* New York: Doubleday & Company, 1958.

Gelfant, Blanche. *The American City Novel.* Norman, Okla.: University of Oklahoma Press, 1954.

Gibney, Frank. *The Operators.* New York: Harper & Row, Publishers, 1959.

Handlin, Oscar. *The Newcomers.* Cambridge, Mass.: Harvard University Press, 1959.

Havighurst, Robert J., and Morgan, H. Gerthon. *Social History of a War-Boom Community.* New York: Longmans, Green & Company, 1951.

Hechinger, Grace, and Fred. *Teen-Age Tyranny.* New York: William Morrow and Company, 1963.

Jackson, Edgar N. *How to Preach to People's Needs.* Nashville: Abingdon Press, 1956.

Kaplan, Benjamin. *The Eternal Stranger.* New York: Bookman Associates, Inc., 1957.

Kinneman, John. *The Community in American Society.* New York: Appleton-Century-Crofts, Inc., 1947.

Kloetzli, Walter. *The City Church: Death or Renewal.* Philadelphia: Fortress Press, 1961.

————, and Hillman, Arthur. *Urban Church Planning.* Philadelphia: Fortress Press, 1958.

Landis, B. Y., editor. *Yearbook of American Churches, 1964.* New York: National Council of Churches of Christ in the United States of America, 1964.

Lee, Robert, editor. *Cities and Churches.* Philadelphia: The Westminster Press, 1962.

Lundberg, George A., *et al. Leisure: A Suburban Study.* New York: Columbia University Press, 1934.

McCabe, Joseph E. *The Power of God in a Parish Program.* Philadelphia: The Westminster Press, 1959.

MacIver, Robert. *Community.* New York: The Macmillan Company, 1928.

Marty, Martin E. *Second Chance for American Protestants.* New York: Harper & Row, Publishers, 1963.

Mills, C. Wright. *White Collar.* New York: Oxford University Press, 1951.

Niebuhr, H. Richard, *et al. The Advancement of Theological Education.* New York: Harper & Brothers, 1957.

————, and Williams, Daniel D., editors. *The Ministry in Historical Perspective.* New York: Harper & Row, Publishers, 1956.

————, *et al. The Purpose of the Church and Its Ministry.* New York: Harper & Row, Publishers, 1956.

O'Dea, Thomas F., editor. *The Church in the Changing Community.* New York: Fordham University Press, 1957.

Owen, Wilfred. *Cities in the Motor Age.* New York: The Viking Press, 1959.

Packard, Vance. *The Status Seekers.* New York: David McKay Company, Inc., 1959.

Pfeffer, Leo. *Creeds in Competition.* New York: Harper & Row, Publishers, 1958.

Presthus, Robert. *The Organizational Society.* New York. Alfred A. Knopf, Inc., 1962.

Raines, Robert. *New Life in the Church*. New York: Harper & Row, Publishers, 1961.

Roberts, Guy L. *How the Church Can Help Where Delinquency Begins*. Richmond: John Knox Press, 1958.

Rosen, Harry M., and David H. *But Not Next Door*. New York: Ivan Obolensky, Inc., 1962.

Salisbury, Harrison E. *The Shook-Up Generation*. New York: Harper & Row, Publishers, 1958.

Schutz, Roger. *Living Today for God*. Baltimore: Helicon Press, 1962.

Sutherland, Edwin H. *White Collar Crime*. New York: Holt, Rinehart & Winston, Inc., 1961.

Tunnard, Christopher, and Reed, H. H. *American Skyline*. Boston: Houghton Mifflin Company, 1955.

Warner, Sam B., Jr. *Streetcar Suburbs*. Cambridge, Mass.: Harvard University Press, 1962.

Whyte, William H., Jr. *The Organization Man*. New York: Simon and Schuster, Inc., 1956.

Winter, Gibson. *The Suburban Captivity of the Churches*. New York: Doubleday & Company, 1961.

Wood, Arthur E. *Hamtramck—Then and Now*. New York: Bookman Associates, Inc., 1955.

SUBURBAN FICTION

Birren, Faber. *Make Mine Love*. New York: Frederick Fell, Inc., 1958.

Carney, Otis. *The Country Club Set*. Boston: Houghton Mifflin Company, 1957.

———. *When the Bough Breaks*. Boston: Houghton Mifflin Company, 1957.

Cheever, John. *The Housebreaker of Shady Hill and Other Stories*. New York: Harper & Row, Publishers, 1958.

Connell, Evan S. *Mrs. Bridge*. New York: The Viking Press, 1958.

Davis, Christopher. *First Family*. New York: Coward-McCann, Inc., 1961.

De Vries, Peter. *The Mackerel Plaza*. Boston: Little, Brown and Company, 1958.

———. *The Tents of Wickedness*. Boston: Little, Brown and Company, 1959.

———. *The Tunnel of Love*. Boston: Little, Brown and Company, 1954.

———. *Reuben, Reuben*. Boston: Little, Brown and Company, 1964.

Franken, Rose L. *Another Claudia*. Garden City, New York: Rinehart & Company, 1943.

Gilbert, Edwin. *The Hourglass*. Philadelphia: J. B. Lippincott Company, 1959.

Green, Gerald. *The Last Angry Man*. New York: Charles Scribner's Sons, 1957.

Hunter, Evan. *Strangers When We Meet*. New York: Simon and Schuster, Inc., 1958.

Huston, McCready. *The Clouded Fountain*. Philadelphia: J. B. Lippincott Company, 1959.

Karp, David. *Leave Me Alone*. New York: Alfred A. Knopf, Inc., 1957.

Kelly, James. *The Insider*. New York: Henry Holt & Company, 1958.

McPartland, John. *No Down Payment*. New York: Simon and Schuster, Inc., 1957.

Marquand, John P. *Life at Happy Knoll*. Boston: Little, Brown and Company, 1957.

———. *Point of No Return*. Boston: Little, Brown and Company, 1949.

Pawel, Ernst. *From the Dark Tower*. New York: The Macmillan Company, 1957.

Roth, Philip. *Goodbye, Columbus.* Boston: Houghton Mifflin Company, 1959.

Russell, Bertrand. *Satan in the Suburbs and Other Stories.* London: Allen & Unwin, Ltd., 1953.

Schiddel, Edmund. *The Devil in Bucks County.* New York: Simon and Schuster, Inc., 1959.

Shulman, Max. *Rally Round the Flag, Boys.* New York: Doubleday & Company, 1957.

Treadwell, Sophie. *One Fierce Hour and Sweet.* New York: Appleton-Century-Crofts, Inc., 1959.

Ward, Mary Jane. *It's Different for a Woman.* New York: Random House, 1952.

Wheeler, Keith. *Peaceable Lane.* New York: Simon and Schuster, Inc., 1960.

Wilson, Sloan. *The Man in the Gray Flannel Suit.* New York: Simon and Schuster, Inc., 1955.

———. *A Summer Place.* New York: Simon and Schuster, Inc., 1958.

ONE HUNDRED PERIODICAL ARTICLES

Allen, Frederick Lewis. "Big Change in Suburbia, Part I," *Harper's Magazine* (June, 1954), 21-28.

———. "Crisis in the Suburbs, Part II," *Harper's Magazine* (July, 1954), 47-53.

Anderson, T. R., and Collier, Jane. "Metropolitan Dominance and the Rural Hinterland," *Rural Sociology* (June, 1956), 152 ff.

Barclay, Dorothy. "Children Within Suburban Limits," *New York Times Magazine* (February 10, 1957), 42.

Bell, Wendell. "Familism and Suburbanization: One Test of the Social Choice Hypothesis," *Rural Sociology* (September-December, 1956), 276 ff.

Berger, B. M. "Myth of Suburbia," *Journal of Social Issues,* (No. 1, 1961), 38-49.

Berger, Peter J., and Nash, Dennison J. "Church Commitment in an American Suburb," *Archives de Sociologie des Religions* (Janvier-Juin, 1962), 105-20.

Blizzard, Samuel W. "Churching the Rural-Urban Fringe," *City Church* (May-June, 1953), 6-7, 12.

———. "Research on the Rural-Urban Fringe," *Sociology and Social Research* (January-February, 1954), 143-49.

———. "Role Conflicts of the Urban Minister," *City Church* (September-October, 1956), 13-15.

Bollens, C. "Urban Fringe Areas—A Persistent Problem," *Public Management* (October, 1960), 218-21.

Bollens, John C. "Trends in Fringe Areas," *The American City* (December, 1953), 122-24.

Carroll, J. D. "The Relation of Homes to Work Places and the Spatial Patterns of Cities," *Social Forces* (March, 1952), 271 ff.

Clark, Dennis. "Strategy in Suburbia," *City Church* (March-April, 1963), 13-16.

Dietrich, T. S. "Nature and Direction of Suburbanization in the South," *Social Forces* (December, 1960), 181-86.

Dobriner, William M. "Natural History of a Reluctant Suburb," *Yale Review* (March, 1960), 399-412.

Douglass, H. Paul. "Suburbs," *Encyclopedia of the Social Sciences,* edited by Edwin R. A. Seligman (New York: The Macmillan Company, 1934), 433-35.

Dwyer, William M. "Experiment in Housing: Concord Park, Pennsylvania," *Commonweal* (August 12, 1955), 465-66.

Dykeman, Wilma, and Stokely, James. "The South in the North," *New York Times Magazine* (April 17, 1960), 8 ff.

Dynes, R. R. "Rurality, Migration and Sectarianism," *Rural Sociology* (March, 1956), 25 ff.

Engelman, Gerson S. "A New Church for a New City," *City Church* (March-April, 1953), 2-5.

Fava, Sylvia F. "Suburbanism as a Way of Life," *American Sociological Review* (February, 1956), 34-37.

Firey, W. "Ecological Considerations in Planning for Rurban Fringes," *American Sociological Review* (August, 1946), 411-21.

Fortune, Editors of. "Suburbia Snubs the Recession." *Fortune* (May, 1958), 114-16.

Frank, Mary, and Lawrence. "City versus Country," *New York Times Magazine* (November 13, 1949), 44.

Freedgood, S. "Life in Bloomfield Hills," *Fortune* (July, 1961), 144-49.

———. "Life in Princeton," *Fortune* (December, 1961), 106-9.

Gans, H. J. "Sociology of New Towns: Opportunities for Research," *Sociology and Social Research* (March, 1956), 231-39.

Gersh, Harry. "New Suburbanites of the 50's." *Commentary* (March, 1954), 209-21.

Gist, N. P. "Developing Patterns of Urban Decentralization," *Social Forces* (March, 1952), 257 ff.

———. "Ecological Decentralization and Rural-Urban Relationships," *Rural Sociology* (December, 1952), 328 ff.

Goldstein, S. "Some Economic Consequences of Suburbanization in the Copenhagen Metropolitan Area," *American Journal of Sociology* (March, 1963), 551-64.

Graybeal, David M. "Churches in a Changing Culture," *Review of Religious Research* (Winter, 1961), 121-28.

Greeley, A. M. "Suburban Parish," *Commonweal* (September 25, 1959), 537-39.

Greene, Shirley E. "Rurbanization Faces the Church," *Christian Century* (May 7, 1958), 551-52.

Greer, S. "Social Structure and Political Process of Suburbia," *American Sociological Review* (August, 1960), 514-26.

Griffin, C. W., Jr. "Car Snobs, Commuters, and Chaos," *Harper's Magazine* (July, 1962), 53-58.

Gruenberg, Sidonie M. "Homogenized Children of New Suburbia," *New York Times Magazine* (September 19, 1954), 14.

Ham, Clifford C., Jr. "How Does the Planning Process Operate?" *City Church* (May-June, 1961), 2-6, 8.

Haverstick, John. "The Land of Exurbia," *Saturday Review* (October 29, 1955), 9-11.

Hein, C. J. "Metropolitan Government: Residents Outside the Central Urban Areas," *Western Political Quarterly* (September, 1961), 764-69.

Henderson, Harry. "The Mass Produced Suburbs, Part I." *Harper's Magazine* (November, 1953), 25-32.

Holbrook, W. "Larchcrest Code: Satire," *Atlantic Monthly* (November, 1951), 103-4.

Jack, Homer A. "Test at Trumbull Park," *Christian Century* (March 21, 1956), 366-68.

Jaco, E. G., and Belknap, I. "Is a New Family Form Emerging in the Urban Fringe?" *American Sociological Review* (October, 1953), 551-57.

Janosik, G. Edward. "The New Suburbia: Political Significance," *Current History* (August, 1956), 91-95.

Keats, J. "Anyone for Elegance," *Coronet* (March, 1959), 156-63.

———. "Compulsive Suburbia," *Atlantic Monthly* (April, 1960), 47-50.

Kelley, Anne. "Suburbia—Is It a Child's Utopia?" *New York Times Magazine* (February 2, 1958), 22.

Kernahan, Galal. "Racism in Suburbia: A Constructive Answer," *Christian Century* (April 10, 1957), 457-58.

Kurtz, R. A., Jr., and Eicker, J. B. "Fringe and Suburb: A Confusion of Concepts," *Social Forces* (October, 1958), 32-37.

Laas, W. "Suburbs Are Strangling the City," *New York Times Magazine* (June 18, 1950), 22.

Lazerwitz, B. "Metropolitan Community Residential Belts, 1950 and 1956," *American Sociological Review* (April, 1960), 245-52.

———. "Suburban Voting Trends: 1948 to 1956," *Social Forces* (October, 1960), 29-36.

Leevy, J. R. "Contrasts in Urban and Rural Family Life," *American Sociological Review* (December, 1940), 948-53.

Leinberger, Hugo. "The Church in the 'New Suburb'," *Religious Education* (January-February, 1955), 11-14.

Lerner, D. "Comfort and Fun: Morality in a Nice Society," *American Scholar* (Spring, 1958), 153-65.

Lieberson, S. "Suburbs and Ethnic Residential Patterns," *American Journal of Sociology* (May, 1962), 673-81.

Liebman, C. S. "Functional Differentiation and Political Characteristics of Suburbs," *American Journal of Sociology* (March, 1961), 485-90.

Loeks, C. D. "What to Do About Fringe Areas," *Public Management* (March, 1959), 63-66.

McGinley, Phyllis. "Suburbia: Of Thee I Sing," *Harper's Magazine* (December, 1949), 78-82.

McMillan, George. "Big Botch at Savannah River," *Harper's Magazine* (November, 1953), 39-44.

Maddox, R. W. "Urban Fringe—Its Problems and Prospects in Oregon," *Western Political Quarterly* (June, 1958), 364-66.

Manis, J. G. "Annexation: The Process of Reurbanization," *American Journal of Economics and Sociology* (July, 1959), 353-60.

———, and Stine, L. C. "Suburban Residence and Political Behavior," *Public Opinion Quarterly* (June, 1958), 364-66.

Martin, Harold H. "Can We Halt the Chaos?" *Saturday Evening Post* (January 16, 1960), 30 ff.

Martin, R. G. "Life in the New Suburbia: Long Island Development," *New York Times Magazine* (January 15, 1950), 16.

Martin, W. T. "Socio-Psychological Aspects of Adjustments to Residence Location in the Rural-Urban Fringe," *American Sociological Review* (June, 1953), 248-53.

———. "Structuring of Social Relationships Engendered by Suburban Residence," *American Sociological Review* (August, 1956), 446-53.

Marty, Martin E. "The Suburban Church: A Second Look," *City Church* (March-April, 1962), 5-8, 13.

Miller, K. D. "Our Growing Suburbs and Their Churches," *Religion in Life* (Fall, 1955), 516-23.

Morris, J. A. "Can the Commuter Survive?" *Saturday Evening Post* (May 6, 1961), 32-3.

Moses, Robert. "Build and Be Damned," *Atlantic Monthly* (December, 1950), 40-42.

Mowrer, E. R. "Sequential and Class Variables of the Family—The Suburban Area," *Social Forces* (December, 1961), 107-12.

Munson, B. E. "Attitudes Toward Urban and Suburban Residence in Indianapolis," *Social Forces* (October, 1956), 76-80.

Oberdorfer, D., and MacKaye, M. "Will Negroes Crack the Suburbs?" *Saturday Evening Post* (December 22, 1962), 71-73.

Perry, Everett L. "Selection of a Church Site," *City Church* (September, 1952), 5-7.

Reeder, L. G. "Social Differentials in Mode of Travel, Time and Cost in Journey to Work," *American Sociological Review* (February, 1956), 56-63.

Schaller, Lyle E. "Public Policy Affects Church Planning," *City Church* (September-October, 1961), 2-6.

Schnore, L. F. "City-Suburban Income Differentials in Metropolitan Areas," *American Sociological Review* (April, 1962), 252-55.

———. "Components of Population Change in Large Metropolitan Suburbs," *American Sociological Review* (October, 1958), 570-73.

———. "Functions of Metropolitan Suburbs," *American Journal of Sociology* (March, 1961), 453-58.

———. "Municipal Annexations and the Growth of Metropolitan Suburbs, 1950-1960," *American Journal of Sociology* (January, 1962), 406-17.

———. "The Separation of Home and Work: A Problem of Human Ecology," *Social Forces* (May, 1954), 336-43.

———. "Socio-Economic Status of Cities and Suburbs," *American Sociological Review* (February, 1963), 76-85.

Science Digest, Editors of. "A Look at Suburbanites," *Science Digest* (December, 1956), 20.

Shippey, Frederick A. "Profile of a Suburban Church," *City Church* (May-June, 1955), 2 ff.

Stuart, McKain, Hatt, *et al.* "The Sociological Significance of the Rural-Urban Fringe," *Rural Sociology* (June, 1953), 101 ff.

Westley, W. A., and Elkin, F. "Protective Environment and Adolescent Socialization (A Middle-Class Suburb of Montreal)," *Social Forces* (March, 1951), 243-49.

Whetten, N. L., and Mitchel, D. "Migration from a Connecticut Suburban Town," *American Sociological Review* (April, 1939), 173-79.

Whitney, V. H. "Rural-Urban People," *American Journal of Sociology* (July, 1948), 48-54.

Winsborough, H. H. "Ecological Approach to the Theory of Suburbanization," *American Journal of Sociology* (March, 1963), 565-70.

Wyden, P. "Suburbia's Coddled Kids," *Saturday Evening Post* (October 8, 1960), 34-35.

Whyte, William H., Jr. "Are Cities Un-American?" *Fortune* (September, 1957), 122-27.

Wood, R. C. "Impotent Suburban Vote," *Nation* (March 26, 1960), 271-74.

———. "Metropolitan Government 1975," *American Political Science Review* (March, 1958), 108-22.

Wood, Robert C. "Saving the Metropolis," *City Church* (November-December, 1962), 2-4, 15.

Zeckendorf, W. "Cities versus Suburbs: A Struggle for Survival," *Atlantic Monthly* (July, 1952), 24-28.

Zimmer, Basil G. "Farm Background and Urban Participation," *American Journal of Sociology* (March, 1956), 470-75.

———. and Hawley, A. H. "Suburbanization and Church Participation," *Social Forces* (May, 1959), 348-54.

Index